ONE THOUSAND AMERICANS

Books by George Seldes (1890-1995)

You Can't Print That!	1929
Can These Things Be!	1931
World Panorama	1933
The Vatican: Yesterday - Today – Tomorrow	1934
Iron, Blood, and Profits	1934
Sawdust Caesar	1935
Freedom of the Press	1935
Lords of the Press	1938
You Can't Do That	1938
The Catholic Crisis	1940
Witch Hunt	1940
The Facts Are...	1942
Facts and Fascism	1943
1000 Americans: The Real Rulers of the U.S.A.	1947
The People Don't Know	1949
Tell the Truth and Run	1953
The Great Quotations	1961
Never Tire of Protesting	1968
Even the Gods Can't Change History	1976
The Great Thoughts	1985
Witness to a Century	1987
The George Seldes Reader	1994

ONE THOUSAND AMERICANS

by

George Seldes

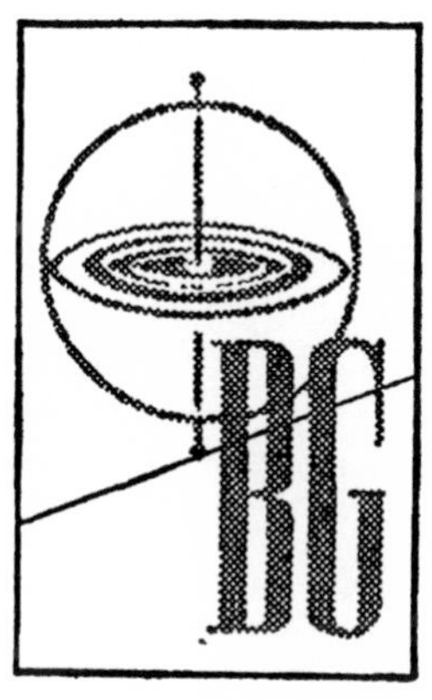

BONI & GAER · NEW YORK

1000 AMERICANS

The Real Rulers of the U.S.A.

by George Seldes

Facsimile of the Original 1947 Edition, Reprinted, with kind permission of the Seldes Family, by

ProgressivePress.com, PO Box 126,
Joshua Tree, Calif., 92252

Second reprint edition, July 4th, 2009. Printed in the USA
Length: 320 pages; 106,000 words
Cover photo © Constantin Jurcut

ISBN-10: 1-61577-900-0 EAN (ISBN-13) 978-1-61577-900-0

BISAC Classification codes:

POL042030	Political Science / Political Ideologies / Fascism & Totalitarianism
SOC052000	Social Science / Media Studies
HIS036060	History / United States / 20th Century
SOC050000	Social Science / Social Classes
POL043000	Political Science / Political Process / Political Advocacy

Library of Congress Catalog Information for the Original Edition:

LC Control No.: 48000432.
Main Title: One thousand Americans.
Author: Seldes, George, 1890-1995.
Published: New York, Boni & Gaer [1948, c1947]
Description: viii, 312 p. 21 cm.
Subjects: Fascism--United States. United States--Politics and government. Press--United States. United States--Economic conditions--1918-1945.
LC Classification: / Call. No. E743 .S43. OCLC 555287.

2009

To Helen Larkin Seldes

my wife and unrewarded assistant in the writing of twelve books

"MAN DEFENDS himself as much as he can against truth, as a child does against a medicine, as the man of the Platonic cave does against the light. He does not willingly follow his path, for he has to be dragged along backward.

"The natural liking for the false has several causes: the inheritance of prejudices, which produces an unconscious habit, a slavery; the predominance of the imagination over the reason, which affects the understanding; the predominance of the passions over the conscience, which depraves the heart; the predominance of the will over the intelligence, which vitiates the character.

"A lively, disinterested, persistent liking for truth is extraordinarily rare. Action and faith enslave thought, both of them in order not to be troubled or inconvenienced by reflection, criticism and doubt."

— *The Private Journal of Henri Frederic Amiel.*

CONTENTS

PART ONE

BIG POWERS

PART TWO

BIG MAGAZINES

PART THREE

BIG BUSINESS

PART FOUR

BIG REACTION

APPENDICES

PART ONE

BIG POWERS

CHAPTER 1

ENEMIES OF AMERICA

> "Whenever there is a conflict between human rights and property rights, human rights must prevail."
>
> —LINCOLN.

ONE THOUSAND Americans, testified liberal Republican Senator George D. Aiken of Vermont, stood in the way of a vast national undertaking which would benefit ten or twenty millions of their fellow citizens. These thousand Americans are interested in property rights, rather than the general welfare.

In the debate in the Senate which followed, the corporate interests which seem to be more powerful than the public itself, were named. But the American people never heard anything at all about this because our country is the only one which has a really free press, and the press exercised its freedom in this instance, as in most instances where the Lincolnian conflict is present, to suppress the news.

On another occasion, the Senate's Monopoly Investigation Committee reported that the 200 largest nonfinancial corporations control the economy of the United States, and in subsequent reports, from 1940 to 1947, the growth of monopoly—the enemy of free enterprise—was thoroughly exposed and its danger to the nation emphasized. But again the public heard little about this because perhaps 49,500,000 copies of the daily press issue of 50,000,000 did not contain the news.

Our Department of Justice, harassed by powerful interests, hamstrung by the Budget Bureau which reduces its funds to a minimum, was nevertheless able to bring indictments against the eight largest banking houses of the country, the men who monopolize the mortgage business, the men who control housing, and who, to insure profits, insist on the continuation of slums in big cities. The sacred name of J. P. Morgan & Company appeared in the government's case to the Federal Grand Jury, and that of other great rivals, but nothing was done to arouse public protest, nor was it noted that the same names which were prominent in the Aiken debate in the Senate, and which had already appeared in the various monopoly reports, again led all the rest in the finance and mortgage anti-trust cases.

It is common knowledge that there are powerful forces in Washington which influence the laws of the nation. They are known as lobbies. In 1946 the Congress, not for the first time, took action against this form of invisible government, and in 1947 hundreds of lobbyists registered and began filing quarterly reports on their moneys and their activities, all of which regularly appeared in the *Congressional Record.*

It is not common knowledge—because this happens to be one of the most flagrant cases of total press suppression—that the most important and incidentally the most sensational of the scores of reports and monographs of the Monopoly Investigation was one which stated that the really powerful lobby was that of the National Association of Manufacturers, which also happens to exercise considerable influence over the press of the nation. It claimed 16,000 members in 1947, but a previous investigation by the La Follette Committee had shown that it is actually controlled by 207 corporations, and that more powerful than even this small number is a group of 12 which meets secretly and directs its policies.

Of the 12, the majority would not be new names to those who had the lists of Senator Aiken's One Thousand Americans.

Nor would any one name be a new addition when the list was published of the few men—leaders of the National Association of Manufacturers and a newspaper publisher—who supplied almost all of the $53,700 fund which was used in South Dakota in 1942, and following elections, to send to the Senate and the House of Representatives four men who would support the measures which corporation heads, their associates and their lobbies, originated or sponsored. Fifteen million American members of labor unions were endangered in both their standards of living and in their rights as human beings by the Case Bill (which President Truman vetoed), originated by one of the men elected by this fund.

The few among the thousand Americans also control the cartel firms which through their dealings with the Nazis sabotaged to a substantial extent their own country's defense preparations, and later its war production program.

Former Assistant Attorney General Thurman Arnold, explaining how the patent monopolies robbed every citizen, also charged that a few small but dominant groups "plunged us into a depression with an irreducible minimum of 9,000,000 unemployed, want in the midst of plenty, idle capital and idle labor." Mr. Arnold named no "dominant" group names. But it is now obvious that the thinking of the people of the United States, their health and wealth, their work or lack of work, in short their general welfare, depend largely upon a dominant few whose actions are kept secret, whose names few have ever heard, whom they may suspect in a vague way, but of whose enmity, powers and activities they have no proof.

The same names, all of which will be disclosed in succeeding chapters, appear again and again in various Congressional reports, in the official exposés of the American Liberty League and its fascist, anti-Semitic and labor-hating affiliates, in the Washington lobbies, in the public utility scandals, in the Pecora banking investigation, in the cartel scandals of the Second World War, in the list of financial angels of the Committee for Constitutional Government, which was branded America's No. 1 fascist organization by several members of Congress, and the newest of the big business organizations fostering nationwide reaction under the glorious title of "free enterprise," the American Action Committee.

When all the evidence is in, the reader will be able to judge for himself whether there are just one thousand Americans, fewer or more, who block not only the development of the St. Lawrence Waterway but the progress of the United States of America and the inhabitants thereof.

The Euripidean stricture will be obeyed: the facts will speak for themselves, and a part of the vast documentation which is available will be presented. The first fact of all, however, is the fact that while the documentation is available it has not been presented to the public because the press and other avenues of communication are in the hands of the thousand Americans and nothing of such a nature is generally disclosed. The facts speak for themselves all right, but frequently in a vacuum, or in the *Congressional Record,* or via three or four liberal weeklies, or through the pages of books which have a sale of, say, 2,000 copies, so that altogether only a small minority of the people is aware of the monopolization of not only all the major industries, but of public thinking and public opinion, the forces which might create a better America if they were free of these controls.

As late as a decade ago, the Scripps-Howard papers, the most powerful chain in America (*New York World-Telegram, Cleveland Press, Rocky Mountain News, Pittsburgh Press, Washington News, Cincinnati Post,* etc.) still served the public welfare instead of the corporate interests. When the Federal Trade Commission published its findings these newspapers did likewise. The findings were simply that the light and power industry used a fund of between $25,000,000 and $30,000,000 a year to change the economic thinking of the people of America, that this was done by bribery and corruption, and that the recipients of this fund were largely the editors, owners and publishers of the newspapers of the nation.

There are 73 volumes, one of them an index, which document the foregoing statement. In view of such overwhelming evidence the newspapers, their owners and their spokesman, *Editor & Publisher,* today admit that in years gone by the press was corrupt. They will in fact admit that the press was corrupt at any time in the past, but they will never admit it is corrupt today. Nevertheless it is also a fact that during and after the Second World War the liberal administration of Franklin

Delano Roosevelt conducted several investigations which produced indisputable evidence of a more sensational and more important nature than did the utility trust investigation, and the American press, this time not openly bribed or corrupted by a $25,000,000 annual slush fund, again cut, buried and suppressed the news, and when possible spread in its columns a little whitewash for the corporations which had betrayed the best interests of the nation.

This time the Howard papers joined all the other press chains in the conspiracy of silence.

But the masthead of his nineteen papers still carried "Lusty" Scripps' noble inscription: "Give Light and the People Will Find Their Own Way."

The most important investigation ever undertaken by the United States Government was that into the concentration of economic power. Its findings have appeared in 37 volumes and 43 special monographs, all of them available to the press and to the public (from the Superintendent of Documents, Washington) and many of them containing that light which creates public opinion, which makes people act.

Between that light and the public, however, there is today a black wall (less penetrable than any "iron curtain" of a foreign nation), and it is composed almost entirely of the magazine and newspaper press. The reason that almost no news contained in these 80 volumes of enlightenment reached the public is obvious from the few disclosures of their contents which follow.

To begin with, President Roosevelt, in his message to Congress asking for the Monopoly Investigation, made an amazing statement which showed that he for one was aware of the ultimate danger of the concentration of wealth and economic power in the hands of the few—perhaps even less than one thousand Americans. Said Roosevelt:

"To the Congress of the United States:

"Unhappy events abroad have retaught us two simple truths about the liberty of a democratic people.

"The first truth is that the liberty of a democracy is not safe if the people tolerate the growth of private power to a point where it becomes stronger than their democratic state itself. That, in its essence, is fascism—ownership of government by an individual, by a group, or by any other controlling private power. . . .

"Among us today a concentration of private power without equal in history is growing.

"This concentration is seriously impairing the economic effectiveness of private enterprise as a way of providing employment for labor and capital and as a way of assuring a more equitable distribution of income and earnings among the people of the nation as a whole."

The President also stated that "government can deal and should deal with blindly selfish men" but he thought that the real menace to the country came from "men who are not selfish and who are good citizens, but who cannot see the social and economic consequences of their actions in a modern economically interdependent community." The investigation showed quite clearly that the blindly selfish men were not good citizens; but they knew what they were going after.

The President concluded that "once it is realized that business monopoly in America paralyzes the system of free enterprise on which it is grafted," action by the government would be welcomed by business as well as by workers. He was mistaken.

In 1942, in his introduction to the final report, Mr. Roosevelt again stated that "the power of the few to manage the economic life of the nation must be diffused among the many or be transferred to the public and its democratically responsible government," but in 1946 when David Lynch wrote an analysis of the investigation, "The Concentration of Economic Power," and economist Boris Shiskin reviewed it in *The Nation,* both agreed that this study was in the nature of an obituary of one of the greatest failures in modern history.

No other document ever published by the American Government has ever named the ruling families and the ruling forces of the country. The thousand Americans who block the nation's progress are not only included, they are for once shown up in all their ramifications and networks. There is no suppression of facts. The economists complain that the investigation "never attempted to find out what concentration was" and did not probe the question "whether concentration is inevitable, beneficial and desirable," and that "little attention was given to its effect upon economic, social and political life" of the nation, nevertheless the findings remain, in this writer's opinion, one of the most powerful indictments in our history, and it is only because of the suppression of the facts—so far as the newspaper and magazine reading and radio listening public is concerned—that no positive and heartening results have come from it. The people never saw the light. . . .

The Monopoly Investigation was conducted by Senator O'Mahoney. On his committee there also served numerous conservatives and reactionaries, including Congressmen Hatton W. Sumners and B. Carroll Reece, who in 1946 became head of the Republican Party. But neither Republican nor Democratic newspapers published anything but a few innocuous references and generalities. The most powerful lobbies which were named in Monograph 26 never became known to the public; the 13 ruling families analyzed in Monograph 29 (*See* Appendix 1) are still a mystery so far as the millions are concerned; and again it is evident that although the American press is the freest in the world, the American people are the worst informed among enlightened nations.

In this instance, suppression was doubly motivated: not only did the newspapers shield the sources which control them, the sacred cows, the golden calves, and the raging bulls of money and power, but they also suppressed the fact that for once an official document stated that the American press itself was nothing more than one of the instruments by which the hidden powers rule the nation.

Monograph 26, a study based on the documentation in other volumes, begins by stating the issues:

"The American people are confronted with the problem of who shall control the Government, by what means, and to what end.

"Since the founding of the Republic, the government process has been characterized by a struggle for control. . ."

The forces seeking control are named. There can be no doubt that if a public opinion poll asked millions of persons which of the pressure groups, the labor unions, the American Legion, or the National Association of Manufacturers, the farm lobby, the Methodists, the National Catholic Welfare Conference, and all the rest, was the most powerful in controlling the country, the popular vote would be the American Legion and the labor unions. But the monograph states:

> "From the beginning, business has been intent upon wielding economic power and, where necessary, political control for its own purpose. The purpose, moreover, is not solely profit, but includes the exercise of control per se, as an attribute of ownership.
>
> "Even today, when the purposeful use of government power for the general welfare is more widely accepted than at any time in our history, government does not begin to approach the fusion of power and will characteristic of business. . . ."

Business is the biggest and most powerful pressure group, business has political and economic power. The "peak organizations" of business are named and the men who control the peak organizations are known.

Although the American Legion is very powerful, perhaps more so than the GAR which for generations was said to control the government, although the farm bloc and the lobby of the organized unions, representing 15,000,000 voters or more, do exert great pressure, in the "struggle for dominance" between pressure groups, "the largest and most important . . . is to be found in 'business' . . . as dominated by the 200 largest non-financial and 50 largest financial corporations, and the employer and trade associations into which it and its satellites are organized."

After that come all other pressure groups, from the Daughters of the American Revolution to the Woman's Christian Temperance Union.

At this point in the monograph a footnote states that "in 1935 the 200 largest non-financial corporations controlled over $60,000,000,000 of physical assets." The National Association of Manufacturers, with some 16,000 members, is also said to represent just $60,000,000,000. Actually, the National Association of Manufacturers includes the 200, with the exception notably of Ford and only two or three other billionaire firms.

All hidden and open forces which are represented by lobbies and pressure groups not only visit members of Congress but they employ even more powerful means: they use the means of public communication "to mold public opinion to accomplish their aims." The controversy may be over public ownership of public utilities, or it may be "regulation and expansion of social services." In most instances profits are represented on one side, the public welfare on the other. But who wins?

"Through the press, public opinion, and pressure groups it is possible to influence the political process. While all three of these factors have played a part in the process since our beginnings as a nation, the extent and consciousness of their use has grown inordinately. They are employed by all contestants in the struggle for control, but reflect the viewpoint of business more accurately than that of others. . . . The revolution in communications, produced by American ingenuity and promoted by American business, makes the press, the radio, and other opinion-forming instruments far more important in the political process than ever before. Both press and radio are, after all, 'big business,' and even when they possess the highest integrity, they are the prisoners of their own beliefs. . . .

"The business orientation of the newspaper press is a valuable asset. In the nature of things, public opinion is usually well disposed toward business. . . . Even where editors and publishers are men of the highest integrity, they are owners and managers of big business enterprises, and their papers inevitably reflect, at least to some extent, their economic interest. When organized business deliberately propagandizes the country, using newspaper advertising as one medium, the press is a direct means of channeling business views into the public mind. . . .

"Chief among the organized groups representing business generally is the Chamber of Commerce of the United States. The outstanding group is the National Association of Manufacturers."

It is most important to note here the fact, disclosed by the La Follette Investigation but not publicized, that the United States Chamber of Commerce was actually one of the many subsidiaries organized by the National Association of Manufacturers.

The monograph lists other business pressure groups, peak organizations, almost all of them affiliated with or dominated by the rulers of the National Association of Manufacturers. It continues with one of its most significant disclosures:

> "Among industry's satellites, commercial banking presents a united front to government through the American Bankers Association, while the Investment Bankers Association of America functions in the same capacity for investment banking. Although it includes by no means all the country's lawyers, the American Bar Association is the part of the legal profession most closely allied in thought with American business. Through the American Newspaper Publishers Association the country's daily newspapers join their strength for business and against government. . . ."

Apparently it is the mention of the ANPA which resulted in the press, whose leading owners are its officers and members, suppressing this item. The press is here denounced in an official document as the agent of business and the press neglected to report the findings of the Monopoly Investigation.

The monograph then takes up in detail the history and policies of the Chamber of Commerce and the National Association of Manufacturers, noting first of all the fact that the latter founded the former.

> "Business exerts its influence on industrial relations policy through the NAM, its members and affiliates, and other sympathetic organizations. . . .
>
> "Through the National Industrial Council . . . instituted and dominated by the NAM, employer activity is mobilized and directed on the political front. . . .
>
> "The American Bar Association has, by framing and pushing legislative proposals designed to achieve this purpose (opposition to the Wagner Act), indicated its fundamental community of interest with business. The American Newspapers Publishers Association shares a similar community of interest."

In the First World War, as congressional inquiries immediately afterwards, and the Nye-Vandenberg and other investigations later revealed, the corporate interests held up and robbed the government and the American people of billions of dollars. The profits were beyond belief. No less than 23,000 persons became millionaires and multimillionaires out of that war. It was determined that this must never happen again. The American Legion went on record with an official resolution that the profits must be taken out of war, and that the nation must conscript business and wealth as well as men—a resolution it betrayed in 1941. Bernard M. Baruch issued the slogan "take the profits out of war" and drew up blueprints for the mobilization of industry.

However, all these things were forgotten in 1940 when the defense program went into effect. But from 1940 on, and to this very day, the standard newspaper press repeats and repeats, until a vast majority believes it, that labor went on strikes, labor did not do a patriotic job, and that business was not only patriotic but noble, and that free enterprise saved the country and the world.

The opposite of course is true.

After recounting the corruption of business in the First World War, the monograph adds:

> "In the 1940 national defense crisis business displayed much the same attitude that it had done 23 years earlier. Business would help the Government and the people, but the basis of payment therefor would have to be fixed before the wheels would begin to turn. Profits, taxes, loans, and so forth, appeared more important to business than getting guns, tanks, and airplane motors into production."

In fact and in truth, the great sit-down strikes of 1940 and 1941 and even later, was the strike of big business, of the members of the National Association of Manufacturers and Chamber of Commerce, against the American people and against the war effort. If any one group in America betrayed the rest, it was the big business group. The "treason" of big business in the Second World War, once publicly denounced by Truman, was never mentioned in the press, no investigations were ever made of business as a whole, and no books have yet been written documenting this un-American history.

The monograph concludes:

> "Speaking bluntly, the Government and the public are 'over a barrel' when it comes to dealing with business in time of war or other crisis. Business refuses to work, except on terms which it

dictates. It controls the natural resources, the liquid assets, the strategic position in the country's economic structure, and its technical equipment and knowledge of processes. The experience of the World War, now apparently being repeated, indicates that business will use this control only if it is 'paid properly.' In effect, this is blackmail. . . .

"Business apparently is not unwilling to threaten the very foundations of government in fixing the terms on which it will work. It is in such a situation that the question arises: What price patriotism? . . .

"Democracy in America is on the defensive. In the preceding pages, it has been shown that pressure groups as now operating usually fail to promote the general welfare."

The general welfare!

In this phrase, the TNEC explains many things. It is the general welfare of the nation which is endangered by the pressure groups of selfish interests, led by the National Association of Manufacturers and its affiliates (notably the Chamber of Commerce) and its satellites (including the newspaper and magazine publishers' associations and the bar associations). The Legion lobbyist speaks for at least three million, the labor lobbyist speaks for at least 15,000,000, but the National Association of Manufacturers lobbyist, while speaking for at most 16,000 members, actually speaks for the "Brass Hat" clique of the 207 who put up the money.

This situation could never exist if America had a really free press. But the press itself is forced by the financial power of the organized pressure groups to ally itself on the side of the enemies of the general welfare of the United States. As pointed out (in "Lords of the Press," page 19) in one year the American press made this great record:

1. Fought all issues where their profits were involved;
2. Led the attack against a real pure food and drug law;
3. Opposed the Wagner Act, the Magna Carta of labor;
4. Urged amendment of proposed social insurance legislation putting newspapers in a special class;
5. Proposed compulsory arbitration of labor disputes with the outlawing of strikes.
6. Favored child labor.

7. Frowned at the Securities Act.

(It was recalled by the *New York Post* in one of its house advertisements in 1946 that in the 1850's it alone among the New York newspapers supported the abolitionists. The rest of the press of the metropolis either was neutral or it supported human slavery.)

During the Roosevelt regime the nation enjoyed an era of liberal legislation, it made progress, it went forward. When Roosevelt died, reaction was re-born.

The result of the 1946 election was regarded by the majority Mr. Gallup polled as a "mandate" to destroy the New Deal, the Wagner Act, and almost all of the reforms of the past decade. Government controls were to end and an era of profiteering, robbery and free enterprise was heralded. "The economic liberty of all of us is being threatened by greed and profiteering of a few," said President Murray of the CIO in his Labor Day address.

The men of the status quo and reaction, Republican and Democrat, came back to power. But while the status quo men were content to remain stationary, the men of reaction were for going backward—and because reaction marches backward, it will arrive at that same feudalism to which Mussolini himself gave the name fascism.

The eras of marching forward are few and short. "The reactionaries are in possession of force, in not only the army and police, but in the press and schools," the noted philosopher John Dewey wrote years ago.

In the following chapters, the reactionaries will be named and the indictment will be documented, showing how detrimental to the general welfare of the people of the United States they are.

It will become apparent that in big business, in politics, in the big press and in the big reactionary movements of our time there are only a few men, perhaps only a thousand Americans, who with their organizations and their power to maintain the status quo system or to move backward, stand in the way of the coming of "the Century of the Common Man."

CHAPTER 2

POWER, PRESS AND POLITICS

IF IT SHOULD so happen in the 1950's that a crusading newspaper, or a magazine, free from the pressures of the power and light industry disclosed the fact that atomic energy for civilian use had been sabotaged for years by a powerful alliance of corporations, politicians and the press, all interested in a 6% profit, it would not surprise anyone who throughout the Twentieth Century watched the sabotage of the universal use of electric power.

Many years ago great leaders of the pre-atomic world saw the emancipation of mankind through the use of electric energy. Health, wealth and a more successful pursuit of happiness were made possible for not only the citizens of the United States, but for the two billions who inhabit the whole earth.

Today the scientists predict the end of drudgery by the harnessing of atomic power. Provided, of course, that free enterprise does not enslave it.

The economic emancipation of the people of the world has always been opposed by the few who could profit from the ownership or control of natural resources and the potentialities of nature. If atomic energy is delayed it will be because of investments, profits, monopoly, and the lust for power by those who control money, the press and public opinion, the political rulers of cities and nations.

In this and the next chapter the system of control will be illustrated in contrasting locales, in one of the least populated states, and in New York. There will be vast differences, but the system will be found to be the same; the results will be the same; the public will always suffer, and the press will always protect those who profit at the expense of public welfare.

* * *

The small state is Montana, third largest in size in the

Union, fortieth in population. The people of Montana are intelligent citizens, and every one in the state knows what is wrong. Everything that is wrong is summed up in the words "the Company." Every person talks about "the Company" if he talks at all about politics, farming, ranching, mining, electrification, water power, prosperity or unemployment, and the press. The State of Montana is dominated by the Anaconda Copper Mining Company, everyone knows it, a few want it so, the majority is opposed to this control, but little is ever done about it.

The reason the people of Montana cannot do much about it, the reason an aroused public will frequently fail at the polls, is that the Company controls substantially all of the press of the state, and when that instrument is in the control of private interests it is almost impossible for any program for the benefit of the majority to assert itself. The Company, the press and their politicians rule the state and retard its progress.

Whether or not the situation is more vicious than in several other states may be a matter of controversy, since investigations have shown that similar conditions prevail elsewhere, but there are two reasons for reporting on Montana: first, the press-money-politics-anti-general welfare alignment has a certain Western frankness about it; it is out in the open, crude, defiant and challenging; and, second, it has been challenged by no less a person than the senior Senator of the state, its foremost citizen, and one of the few statesmen in Washington.

However, the conspiracy of silence against the people is so complete in Montana that even Senator Murray was not able to break through it. Time and again he found that the press of his state was suppressing him, and so he had to address reprints of his political statements to the good citizens (notably the liberals, labor union and Farmers' Union people) with the following slip attached:

YOUR ATTENTION, PLEASE

The reprint herein of my statement before the Senate Banking and Currency Committee dealing with a free press in Montana contains incontrovertible facts that every citizen in Montana should be familiar with. Our State's future prosperity and growth depend upon an informed public. Please read the attached pamphlet and pass it on to other citizens to read.

Sincerely yours,
James E. Murray, U.S. Senator

The scandalous journalistic situation in Montana has been exposed time and again for several decades. Villard, Sinclair and others produced evidence of the control of newspapers of the state by the copper interests. It has been found that certain papers are owned outright, others have been bribed, others have mortgages in the copper company's banks, others have their annual deficits paid by the copper kings, and almost without exception all of them get the "good will" advertising of Anaconda Copper and Montana Power Company, and express an editorial good will towards these corporations.

The only Montana papers which have both defied the Company and supported Murray for Senator are a few free country weeklies. They also published the Senator's testimony, which is one of the most important documents in recent history exposing the newspaper situation that exists not only in Montana but in other states. Senator Murray testified in part:

". . . . Only in a few cities of our State have we an honest press furnishing news free from propaganda. It is a well known fact that the Anaconda Copper Mining Company owns a string of newspapers in Montana. These papers are published in Helena, Butte, Anaconda, Missoula, Livingston and Billings. They own and publish both Democratic and Republican papers, so-called, and their policy is directed from the headquarters of the Anaconda Copper Mining Company in New York City.

"In my home city of Butte, for example, the Anaconda Copper Company owns the morning paper, *Democratic,* and the evening paper, *Republican,* both printed on the same press, and the news is censored by the Anaconda Copper Co.

"The news they publish is colored and distorted in such a fashion as to deceive and confuse the public on important issues. These papers, because of their affiliation with the Anaconda Copper Mining Company are subsidized with federal funds—in other words, the Anaconda Copper Mining Co. is making huge profits from Government contracts and is able to maintain these papers at a loss because of the excessive profits they are able to make from the Government in wartime. . . .

"The company has been engaged in acts of wholesale fraud in the sale of wire and cable of such a defective nature as to endanger the lives of our boys on the war fronts. Anaconda itself carries expensive ads in its own papers which, of course, constitute deductible items in its income reports. Thus it finances its own papers with the taxpayers' money while it opposes Government ads in the country press.

"The large metropolitan press and magazines of the country are also subsidized through costly advertising contributed by the big industrial corporations engaged in war work. The cost of this advertising is deductible expense—in other words, the money expended by these corporations for advertising in their own newspapers and in the metropolitan press and magazines is furnished by the United States Government. In this way the large papers and magazines of the country are being subsidized by big business, but the small country papers have been left out in the cold and are having a difficult time to survive. . . .

"The papers in Butte are owned and controlled for no other purpose than to control politics in the State of Montana. It started years ago in the big fight between the copper kings of Montana, and they have ever since controlled and kept those newspapers which gave them the power to dominate the State Legislature and to dominate the Federal elections as well, through suppressing news of what is going on, and suppressing the issues in the campaign.

"That is acknowledged in Montana generally. It has been written up in the newspapers. It has been written up, I believe, in a number of books that have been issued in this country in recent times. For instance, George Seldes, in his book, "Freedom of the Press," has a whole chapter on it in which he discusses that situation. . . .

"They have carried on that conspiracy now for some years; and, had it not been for the country press keeping my name before the people of the State, I would have been defeated in the last election.

"They (Anaconda and the press it controls) are interested only in their own properties and the exploitation of the State. They are holding back the development of the State, and under their domination, the population of Montana, the third largest state in the Union, is dwindling. . . . They are compelling Montana to exist on the basis of a raw-material economy. They are blocking the development of our great water resources and preventing the creation of cheap power which would develop industry and vastly increase our population. . . .

"The death of the smaller publications would spell the doom of the free press in America. They have contributed in the past some of our most fearless and capable journalists and crusaders of worthy causes. They may be counted upon to make similar contributions in the future.

"I really am sorry that this situation exists. . . . It seems to me that the free press of America would be doing the country a great benefit if it would condemn such practices in any part of the United States, because we should have a press in America that the people will have confidence in, and they cannot have confidence in newspapers if they believe that they are widely owned by corporations and used for their own propaganda purposes."

Years ago, Oswald Garrison Villard wrote that the following Montana newspapers were owned by the copper interests: *Montana Standard of Butte, Butte Daily Post, Anaconda Standard, Helena Democrat, Helena Record-Herald, Missoulian, Missoula Sentinel, Billings Gazette* and *Livingston Enterprise.*

The Postal Laws require an annual statement of ownership, nevertheless there is evidence that a few publications conceal their real backers. The advertising of Anaconda and Montana Power, its colleague in controlling the state, are visible to the naked eye, but other controls are invisible to the inquiring mind.

Among the independent small weeklies, H. E. Bruce's *People's Voice* is indeed a voice crying in a copper-colored wilderness. In his issue of February 2, 1943, Mr. Bruce's headline was: "Value to Corporations of Kept Press Shown by Fiscal Condition." He declared that "the Anaconda Copper Mining Company is willing and finds it advantageous to pay tremendous sums to maintain its hold on most of the channels of public information in the State," and alleged that although its name does not appear in any of the reports of the corporations publishing newspapers "it has never been denied that the staggering 'debts' of these publishing houses represent the subsidies made by the copper company to control them and to dictate the policies of the daily papers published by them." Here follow the figures of the capital stock and debts of the majority of Montana's daily newspapers:

Montana Record Publishing Company: *Montana Record Herald,* Helena; Capital stock paid in, $38,945; Existing debts, $188,376.

Missoulian Publishing Company: *Missoulian*, Missoula; Capital stock paid in, $50,200; Existing debts, $47,066.
Independent Publishing Co.: *Helena Independent;* Capital paid in, $75,000; Debts, $210,616.
Standard Publishing: *Montana Standard*, Butte; Capital $100,-000; Debts, $383,017.
Post Publishing Company: *Butte Daily Post;* Capital paid in, $124,500; Debts, $116,251.

It will be noted that several of these papers now heavily in "debt" are the very ones listed years ago by Villard as being owned outright by the copper interests.

The venality of the Montana press was brilliantly illustrated when the Senate Committee investigating war frauds found that an Anaconda subsidiary was manufacturing defective wire which it was selling the War Department for immediate use by America's allies (in 1943) and probably for eventual use by our own troops. The accusation was made by Senator Truman and later sustained in the courts.

Brooks local of the National Farmers' Union, meeting at Gunnar Mickelsen's Spear T Ranch in Lewistown, had the news of the Anaconda scandal—but not from Montana papers. It passed the following resolution:

> "As farmers and ranchers of Montana we feel particularly indignant over the light punishment given the Anaconda Copper Company which was guilty of cheating the government on war materials and endangering the lives of American soldiers, including our own sons."

The copper-controlled press suppressed the news, just as it has suppressed all news the Company wants suppressed.

To an overwhelming extent the daily Montana press is anti-labor, anti-farmer, anti-rancher; in other words it is against the interests of the people of Montana. This was illustrated again when, following the success of TVA, it was proposed that the Missouri Valley Authority should be the next big step in the electrification of the nation. The Missouri, and the real West, begin in Montana.

The Montana Power Company is opposed to the MVA, but since Montana Power is linked to Anaconda and between them control the state's press and politics, 559,000 persons are kept from getting something which would benefit every one of them immeasurably.

As usual, the press is the instrument of the big money, and it is the press which appears openly as the enemy of the people.

The controlled Montana press lied about TVA, it lied about MVA, it repeated the lies of the politicians linked to Anaconda and Montana Power, and succeeded in confusing or prejudicing so many people that they actually voted against their own best interests.

The State Farmers' Union tried its best to supply an antidote for this steady flow of poison. It realized that little could be done with the daily newspapers, but it was especially angry that the Associated Press also should lend itself to corporation propaganda. At a statewide convention the Farmers' Union passed the following resolution:

"It is common knowledge in all informed quarters throughout the nation that the daily newspapers of Montana, with only two or three exceptions, consistently present a one-sided picture of the news that affects the welfare of their readers. The chief cause of this one-sided presentation of the news is the fact that most of the state's papers have large outstanding loans made to them by the corporation and that direct control of the editorial and news policies of those papers is under J. H. Dickey of the Anaconda Copper Mining Co. with offices on the sixth floor of the Hennessey Building in Butte.

"There are literally thousands of instances of abuse of the freedom of the press in Montana to prove the bias of the press in favor of Big Business and against working farmers, working men and women everywhere and their organizations. However, the treatment of one current and immensely important news event by the Montana press will serve. to vividly illustrate the charge. This is the reporting of news concerning the Missouri Valley Authority (MVA).

"The controlled newspapers of Montana have always protected the Montana Power Co., which advertises heavily, against unfavorable news When the company went into court against a group of Montana farmers and claimed ownership of all the water in the Missouri River, not a word appeared in the press. When the federal circuit court decided in favor of the farmers, not a word was printed. Yet this was one of the most important court decisions in Montana's entire history.

"Similarly now, when a great national movement is underfoot to develop the Missouri River Valley, give jobs to thousands, including returning veterans, stop floods, create millions of fertile farm acres and provide cheap electric power to business, farms and homes, the newspapers of Montana and the Associated Press in Montana are giving their readers an almost unbelievably false picture of the whole situation."

The rest of the resolution accused the Associated Press of sending out biased reports. The AP replied it was the newspapers which altered or suppressed the news it furnished them. If the AP is right, it makes the case against the press the stronger.

In politics as well as in the press, Anaconda is all-powerful. When Sam Ford was elected governor in 1944, first Republican in 20 years, even *Time* admitted (November 6) that "the big business twins that run Montana politics, Montana Power and Anaconda Copper, were behind . . . Ford."

The career of the once great liberal politician, ex-Senator Burton K. Wheeler, is an excellent illustration of Company politics. There was a time when Wheeler had as his enemies all the great money powers of Montana and most notably "the Company." There was also a later time when Mr. Wheeler went to the Senate with the blessings of the press and Anaconda. The turning point in Wheeler's career came in 1939 when the presidential bee got under his stetson.

From 1939 to 1946 Wheeler became one of the foremost orators of reaction in the nation. America First of isolationist days and the America First Party of Gerald L. K. Smith both approved of him, and one of his anti-Semitic speeches—a denunciation of the Rothschilds and Sassoons—was reprinted by the majority of the groups that were named in the Government's sedition indictments.

In 1946, Wheeler failed for nomination in the Democratic primary. If he had embraced the GOP at the time he embraced the NAM the result might have been otherwise. But even with the support of all the reactionaries, including the copper interests and the press, he could not turn the tide of liberalism which still flowed through the democratic fields of his state, and he was defeated by a trusted representative of the New Deal.

Leif Erickson's platform was openly anti-Company. "Cheap power, protected water rights, use of Montana water in Montana for irrigation and not downstream for navigation, full irrigation and resource development in Montana through valley authorities locally administered," stated the Democratic platform, and Montana Power and Anaconda didn't like it a bit.

The power company replied by placing advertisements in the Montana press attacking TVA, MVA and Erickson. The press scared little business men with threats of the proposed valley authorities putting them out of business. It alleged that TVA was engaged in "operating farms, directing operations in a large area of farmlands, lumbering, experimenting in socialized medicine, operating grocery stores and service stations, operating drug stores . . . tourist cabins . . . taking over certain police duties . . . readjusting families, instituting a super government superior to the state and local authorities." This left out almost no one. The ads scared the rancher, the farmer, the doctor, the grocer, with their falsehoods which a paid press disseminated.

Zales Ecton, a corporation farmer, was called by the Democrats "the darling of the Anaconda mining interests and the Montana Power Company." He had earned the friendship of business interests by introducing and supporting anti-labor laws in the state legislature, he had voted against a minimum wage scale for women, against prohibiting the sale of goods made by child labor, against a state little Wagner Act, and similar legislation, all of which indicated he was a friend of the corporations, an enemy of the welfare of the people. He was quite naturally endorsed for the Senate by no less an American than Gerald L. K. Smith!

With the aid of the Anaconda press Ecton resorted to the usual subterfuge of empty men: he waved the red flag, roared accusations against the opposition as being befriended by Moscow, "accused the Truman administration of every sin attributed to McKinley" and did his best to keep away from meeting the one real issue: The Missouri Valley Authority. When he could not meet it, he redbaited. In his Lewistown speech he said that "the MVA is as communistic as anything Joe Stalin has ever thought up." The small unbribed weekly papers pointed out that even the most reactionary among the GOP, as for example, B. Carroll Reece, had endorsed MVA.

When the vote was in so was Ecton. The GOP campaigners, Federated Press reported to the labor papers, got away with a tremendous hoax: they cooked up a fraudulent broadcast from Moscow, in which Erickson was endorsed, and they peddled a retouched or faked photograph showing Erickson supposedly buying a copy of the communist newspaper, *Daily Worker*. Altogether, the GOP is said to have spent $100,000, or many times the Democratic fund, in the 1946 election.

The GOP would have gotten nowhere with its fraudulent broadcast and fraudulent photographs if it had not had a willing, corrupt and venal press to publish them so that none of the voters among the 559,000 could possibly escape their effect. Denials were in vain. The headlines and the press fakery won out, swamping the solid liberal-labor vote which joined the Democrats, but was insufficient to withstand falsely created "public opinion."

The red-baiting campaign, which was also part of the national Republican strategy of 1946, continued in Montana after the election. On November 15 of that year, Carolina Brammer reported in *People's Voice* on her talks with many "good people," "God-fearing, church-going people, people who would not knowingly harm another person" and found them all inflamed for a war against Russia. The controlled Montana press, in its campaign of falsehood for the purpose of destroying MVA and electing Ecton, had created such a corrupt atmosphere that only the lightning of war would clear it—in the minds of these people.

Montana is an enlightened state. It is something like Vermont in character and natural beauty, although it is ruggedly liberal whereas Vermont is ruggedly (and honestly) conservative, although many of its fathers and grandfathers speak many foreign languages, while Vermont traces itself back to an older immigration.

Montanans know what is wrong with Montana, but since they have practically no free daily press with which to fight, they frequently lose to the corporate interests.

Both Anaconda and Montana Power are no longer owned by natives. The rulers are in Wall Street. Actually Montana Power is now part of the American Power & Light Corporation, which is now a part of the Morgan Empire (*Congressional Record,* November 22, 1944), and Anaconda's officials are in New York. Senator Murray years ago referred to Montana as being exploited as a colonial land, by private firms instead of armed governments.

The absentee owners also exercise control over the state's press through two types of good will advertising: Edison Electric Institute propaganda telling how cheap current is, how lucky the people are that private business and not TVAs and MVAs run this country; and general "free enterprise" propaganda. Here is a fine example (from the *Lewistown Democrat-News,* August 22, 1943):

"THE FOURTH ESTATE

"Because of an American press that is free and fearless, that brooks no Hitlerian control, no state subsidies, Americans are the best informed people in the world.

"We honor the men and women of the Fourth Estate who have contributed so much to the social and cultural progress of Montana communities."

This advertisement in the Lewistown daily and in other papers was paid for by the corporation which is known to every citizen of the state as ending its free and fearless press, subsidizing reaction, and blocking the social and cultural progress of Montana.

CHAPTER 3

J. P. MORGAN STOPS THE ST. LAWRENCE RIVER

A DEMOCRACY is dedicated to the greatest good for the greatest number. If the resources of a nation belonged to its people, economic security, a base for democracy, would be assured.

In the United States the private interests have seized most of the natural wealth of the country. Up to the time of the discovery of atomic power, only one source of wealth remained in public hands, water power.

"Before many years have passed," Newton D. Baker wrote to Ernest Greenwood during the Wilson administration (Utility Corporation Reports), "it will be necessary for us to use water power wherever possible and conserve coal.

"Our water powers are therefore our great unexhausted and inexhaustible national assets. Whoever owns them in a large sense may be said to own the United States, industrially and commercially. . . .

"If I were greedy for power over my fellowmen, I would rather control Muscle Shoals than to be continuously elected President of the United States."

Today a project which would supply the greatest good for the greatest number is the St. Lawrence development.

"I know of no single project of this nature more important to this country's future in peace or war," declared President Roosevelt in asking the Congress to approve the St. Lawrence Seaway. "Its authorization will demonstrate to the enemies of democracy that, however long the effort, we intend to outstrip them in the race of production. In the modern world, that race determines the rise and fall of nations.

"I hope that authorization will not be delayed." (Special Message to Congress, June 5, 1941.)

President Coolidge declared for it immediately after he succeeded Harding (and the Ohio gang).

President Hoover approved the project.

President Truman is on record as heir of the Roosevelt policy.

Republicans and Democrats, the governors Al Smith, Herbert Lehman and Tom Dewey are on the record for the St. Lawrence.

The secretaries of state Hughes, Kellogg, Stimson, Hull and Byrnes, the War and Navy Departments, the chiefs of staff, have approved the plan, and Canada has frequently asked the United States to start the work.

In fact, all six presidents who faced the issue, from Wilson to Truman, officially, and it is to be presumed sincerely, declared in favor of the St. Lawrence, and since the governors of New York and their alternate numbers in Canada did likewise, as did the leading citizens of both countries, Supreme Court Justices, Senators, Representatives, and others, it is pertinent to ask who Senator Aiken meant when he said one thousand persons were blocking the project.*

Whether or not the opposition numbers only 1,000, it is worth while looking into. Some of its members were named in the full-dress debates on the St. Lawrence in November and December, 1944, and the mere fact that at least 90% of the press (probably 99%) suppressed the names of the men and corporations openly or secretly fighting the St. Lawrence should have given anyone interested a glimpse into the power these few possess. All the following were named in this debate by Senators Aiken, La Follette, Langer and Murray:

1. The Mellon interests, Aluminum Company of America (Alcoa) and Canadian Aluminum, Ltd., and related firms.

2. The duPonts, the biggest industrial empire in America, owners of the controlling interest in General Motors.

* The statement was confirmed in a letter dated January 31, 1947, to the writer. Senator Aiken also sent along the UP report of his statement which says: "Washington April 21 [1945] (UP)—Sen. George D. Aiken, Republican, of Vermont, charged today that a group of 'not more than 1,000 people in the whole country' is blocking completion of the St. Lawrence Seaway.

"Senator Aiken, author of a bill to authorize completion of the $200,000,000 waterway and hydroelectric power development, said in an interview that the '1,000' are 'more interested in seeking profits for themselves than they are in helping the welfare of 136,000,000 people.'

"He identified the 1,000 as executives and stockholders of private utility companies which have fought the St. Lawrence project for many years."

3. The Duke interests: power and light corporations, tobacco, and Duke University.

4. General Electric Corporation.

5. The railroad lobby, the Association of American Railroads.

6. J. P. Morgan & Company.

Not named in this debate were the following interests:

1. The coal producers' lobby and (strangely enough) their great enemy, John L. Lewis.

2. Frontier Corporation. Senator Aiken charged that in 1921 "the Aluminum Company, the General Electric Company, and the duPont Company united under the name of the Frontier Corporation to acquire and develop the power of the St. Lawrence frontier." When they could not grab it for themselves, they fought government control.

3. Fifty-six Senators, a majority, who voted against the measure in 1944.

4. The self-styled "free" press.

5. The United States Chamber of Commerce and affiliates.

6. The Chamber of Commerce of New York State.

Here again we have one of the greatest combinations of money and power in the history of America. We have three of the powerful interests which had working agreements with the great Nazi cartel system (Alcoa, duPont, General Electric).

We have also a story of front-page sensation and importance. But the reader can search not only the front page but any page of his daily paper for the first fortnight in December, 1944, and not find any mention of the great forces which were blocking this necessary development. The best that can be found in all but one or two newspapers is a reference to "the public utility lobby" (*New York Post,* December 13, for example). Such generalities are meaningless. Unless the enemy is named every time, unless he is exposed, the public cannot identify him, cannot fight and defeat him.

The documentary evidence is to be found in the *Congressional Record,* not in the daily newspapers. There is no space here to repeat the 100 pages of evidence, but here are a few sample paragraphs:

"Senator La Follette: Ever since 1902, first the Aluminum Co. of America, then the General Electric Co., the duPont Co., and later the Niagara Hudson Power Corp., have all been successively interested in acquiring power sites . . . for the development of the water power of the St. Lawrence River."

Senator La Follette described in detail how Colonel Cooper, who built the Dnieper Dam for the Soviets, planned a $1,300,000,000 St. Lawrence project for Frontier Corporation, subsidiary of Niagara-Hudson. But Governor Smith opposed it.

"After Gov. Alfred Smith came Gov. Franklin Roosevelt. They believed that the good of the people requires the development of river resources of the country for the benefit of all the people, and they would not relinquish the public heritages for private profit.

"I shall shortly give proof as to the very devious ways in which the private power companies have opposed the St. Lawrence project. . . . They have conjured all through these years since 1932 [the New Deal] the most fantastic stratagems to deviate public opinion from the real issue." One of the ways was propaganda inserted as news items and editorials in hundreds of newspapers. It is put out by the *Industrial News Review,* "owned, edited and published by an outfit called E. Hofer & Son" of Salem, Oregon, which was also accused of going "so far as to sign the names of fictitious persons to fictitious articles" (CR p. 9167).

Senator La Follette named newspapers deceiving the public by spreading utilities propaganda in the following places: Ashland, Ky.; Woonsocket, R. I.; Davenport, Iowa; Johnstown, Pa.; Paterson, N. J.; Niagara Falls, N. Y.; Lynn, Mass.; Terre Haute, Ind.; Waterbury, Conn.; Ottumwa, Iowa; Wheeling, W. Va.; Lowell, Mass.; Washington, Iowa; Salt Lake City, Utah; Lima, Ohio; Port Arthur, Tex.; Clinton, Iowa, and Waterville, Maine.

"Senator La Follette: This indirect and devious method of influencing public opinion is, in my opinion, a violation of edi-

torial trust, and if carried on indiscriminately and unchecked, it would undermine the very foundations upon which democratic government must rest. . . . The Senate of the United States cannot afford to be fooled by these devices."

Senator La Follette inserted sample propaganda pieces from the Hofer press bureau, half of whose expenses are paid by utility corporations. The Hofer bureau boasted that its big business propaganda aimed:

"To help minimize regulation of industry. . . .

"To discourage radicalism in all its forms. . . .

"To fight for reasonable taxation. . . .

"Straight-from-the-shoulder arguments against socialistic propaganda, of whatever nature, because socialism does not square with our American industrial system and is contrary to the very foundation principle of our constitutional form of government." [By this is meant public ownership of public utilities —including TVA—one of the greatest American achievements of the generation.]

The Hofer bureau claimed that 14,000 newspapers accept its free propaganda—there are fewer papers than that in the country today—use it without disclosing it is propaganda, and that in one instance 600 papers used the same item. (*Congressional Record,* December 8, 1944, pp. 9164-9170.)

"*Senator Aiken:* Let us not deceive ourselves. We are dealing here with some of the most ruthless and powerful economic interests that have sought to intervene in the concerns of any government, and to influence its domestic and international policies.

"We are dealing here with international utility interests which have succeeded over the past 20 years in trebling waterpower development in Quebec, where they own and control it, and in absolutely blocking the development of the latent power in the International Rapids section of the St. Lawrence River, where the State of New York and the Province of Ontario have set up public agencies to develop that power for the public benefit.

"We are dealing here with an international aluminum

monopoly which has consistently fought the St. Lawrence project, while developing its private power sites in Quebec to engage in a world-wide cartel which supplied Japan with aluminum prior to Pearl Harbor and gave Germany the lead over the United States in aluminum capacity and production prior to our entrance into this war."

Senator Aiken had already mentioned Aluminum Corporation. He then told the story of the Shipshaw development.

"*Senator Aiken:* Grants were acquired in 1913-14 by the James L. Duke interests. . . . The Aluminum Corp. of America took over the Shipshaw power rights from the Duke-Price Company in 1926. In 1926 Alcoa also acquired the upper development, Isle Maligne, by purchase of 52⅔% of the stock of the Duke-Price Co., now known as the Saguenay Power Co. . . .

"Plans made by Alcoa in 1925 comprehended a scheme to get the Shipshaw project under its control, to speed its development, and to seize upon every device to delay the St. Lawrence project."

Finally, Senator Aiken read the report of the Power Authority of the State of New York, dated January 31, 1944, which makes the charge that the Aluminum Company, Ltd., and the Alcoa cartel agreement with the Nazis "had the effect of limiting the production of strategic light metals in the United States." Japan was also served. The Canadian works were exploited because wages "range as far as 50% below wages paid in New York, Washington, California and other producing areas." (*Congressional Record,* December 11, 1944, pp. 9271-9285.)

One of the chief controversies in the Senate concerned the role of the House of Morgan. Its spokesman, Thomas W. Lamont, had denied controlling the light and power industry and lobbying against the St. Lawrence. (*See* Appendix 3.) In rebuttal, Senator Langer, on November 30, 1944, introduced the following statement of the late Senator Norris:

"Through interlocking directorships between banks dominated by Morgan and through the control of the Morgan-founded, Morgan-operated United Corporation, this banking house within the past few years has come into a position of absolute dominance in the power business . . . the Niagara Hudson Power Corporation . . . dominates the upstate utility picture in New York . . . United Corporation also is buying into Electric Bond and Share, which in the past has been headed by Sidney Z. Mitchell who, with Insull, dominated the old-time National Electric Light Association (NELA).

"At the present rate of progress, Morgan will soon control the industry. That famous banking house is already well on the road in that direction. The record of the functioning of these various Morgan-controlled corporations in this new Edison Electric Institute will bear watching. . . . Of the 22 trustees of the new organization 18 are so closely linked to the Morgan-Carlisle-United Corporation interests that it would be impossible to have the slightest independence of action."

This statement was followed by the disclosure of Senator La Follette's reply to Mr. Lamont (*see* Appendix) in which he declared:

"The entire record supports the conclusion that organizations and agencies in which the influence of J. P. Morgan & Co. is notorious have been using every resource to block public development of St. Lawrence power in the interest of lower electric rates."

The claim that no member of the Morgan House opposed the project was answered by the fact that the chief agency by which St. Lawrence was being fought was the Chamber of Commerce of the State of New York. J. P. Morgan and 12 partners, including Lamont, were members of the Chamber at the time it initiated the campaign, and at the time it financed this campaign its treasurer was Junius S. Morgan, Jr.

La Follette further charged that the Morgan firm had an agent named Machold as its New York State lobbyist, and quoted Republican State Committeeman W. Kingsland Macy saying:

"It is intolerable that the invisible government set up by Mr. Machold in Albany during the legislative sessions, . . . should be permitted to continue."

Senator La Follette's reply to Lamont was devastating. It showed, for the first time, the means by which the Morgan Empire operated in New York State: its control of the Chamber of

Commerce. Yet not a line about this sensational disclosure appeared in most of the newspapers of New York, or the rest of the country. To this day it may be said that not one person in a hundred knows of this important activity of the Morgan firm.

The mention of the "invisible government" was a challenge to the press to break through the iron curtain of corporation power and get the news. It made no such effort.

Years earlier, as everyone now admits, the "invisible government" at Albany resorted to outright bribery and corruption to obtain special privileges in New York State. Solicitor General Henry Epstein wrote in 1943 that in "the Gay Nineties . . . the power gang greased through the legislature three grants to the predecessors of the present Niagara Falls Power Company giving the company in perpetuity the right to use all water available for diversion from the Niagara River."

What the invisible government is up to now no one can tell because neither political party is willing to investigate, but the work of the visible lobby, the press and politician lobby, is evident to all.

No one could possibly allege that the situation in New York in any way resembles the situation in Montana, where Anaconda and Montana Power either own 7 dailies or control them through loans or through advertising, but a large majority of the dailies of the Empire State are, through a community of interest with big business if not through loans and advertising, just as devoted to the power trust as their colleagues in the Treasure State.

Take the great *New York Times,* for example. In 1941, when the President proposed the St. Lawrence as the greatest single project to benefit the American people, the *Times* began its editorial sabotage. A student of journalism should make a scientific study of its columns for that year, measure the space given to the pros and cons, write a thesis for the benefit of all journalism schools. In the editorial columns he will find scores of references to policy, among them:

January 10: "The more the case for the St. Lawrence power

and navigation is studied as a defense measure the weaker it becomes. . . ."

March 20: "The plain facts are (1) that the St. Lawrence project cannot possibly be of the slightest use to Canada or the United States in any crisis this year or next year. . . . The President has chosen an unfortunate method of reviving a favorite project. . . ."

March 25: "Congress must consider both the difficulties involved . . . and the alternatives. . . . There can be no question that the St. Lawrence project captures the imagination. Some day it may be desirable. . . ."

June 7: "We are confronted with a vast diversion of manpower and materials needed in carrying out the defense program. . . . The more this St. Lawrence project is studied, the more it is to be hoped that Congress will not be stampeded into giving the President his way. . . ."

July 5: "Canada . . . has reserved the right to wait for a more propitious time. . . ."

July 6: "But the question which arises, so far as power is concerned, is whether the steam-power plants could not be built far more speedily, and with less diversion of labor. . . ."

September 18: "Can we afford to divert 27,000 skilled and semiskilled men. . . ?"

October 20: "The St. Lawrence is merely one source of power and by no means the best. Nor is it low-cost power. . . . The argument for the erection of steam plants . . . becomes stronger than ever."

Not one of these arguments varied an iota from the propaganda sheets put out by the Edison Electric Institute, the power and light trust press bureau. This is just one of the millions of coincidences which make newspaper reading so interesting.

With the smaller newspapers of the state there were other coincidences. Following are some of the newspapers which, according to M. C. Steele, FTC investigator, received what is known in the trade (or profession) as "good will" advertisements from the Niagara Falls Power Company:

Buffalo Express, $2,787.60
Buffalo Courier and *Buffalo Enquirer,* $4,438.30
Buffalo News, $6,075.36
Syracuse Herald, $3,299.38
Syracuse Post Standard, $3,286.28
Syracuse Journal, $2,786.28
Syracuse Telegram, $2,221.10
Rochester Times Union, $4,362.11
Rochester Democrat and Chronicle, $4,237.32

Rochester Herald, $1,305.18
Rochester Journal, $3,471.10
Hammondsport Herald, $1,305.18
(Senate Document 92, 70th Congress, Report of the Federal Trade Commission to the U. S. Senate, part 63, page 151.)

John L. Lewis opposed the St. Lawrence for selfish reasons of another sort. He, the coal and the railroad lobbies, believe that cheap power for the public will hurt their own businesses. To bolster his position Lewis, in the *United Mine Workers' Journal,* quoted the following newspapers as attacking the President's 1941 request to the Congress to start the St. Lawrence project immediately:

New York Times, New York Sun, Long Branch (N.J.) Record, Pittsburgh Post-Gazette, Philadelphia Bulletin, Springfield (Mass.) Union, Shreveport Times.

Columnist Rodney Gilbert (Heptisax) of the *New York Herald Tribune* sneered at the President. Roy Howard's bellwether in the Scripps-Howard chain, the *New York World-Telegram,* declared there was "a strong opposition based on sound argument" (July 15, 1941); the *Chicago Tribune* declared, "the scheme, far from promoting America's military preparation, will retard it"; the *Wall Street Journal* also opposed the idea.

The *Tulsa Tribune* ran a quarter page ad, paid for by the Public Service Company of Oklahoma, a private utility, based on the *Reader's Digest* condensation of Friedrich Hayek's book "The Road to Serfdom," a copy of which it had sent to every home it served throughout the state—*Reader's Digest* having supplied it and other corporations with tens of thousands, if not millions, of reprints at about cost price. The *Tulsa Tribune* ad, besides boosting Hayek and *Reader's Digest,* shows a cartoon with America at the parting of the ways. On the left, "The Road to Serfdom" which ended at a black place labeled "Socialism"; also the following smaller roads: "Planned Economy," "Tax Free Cooperatives," "Authorities" (meaning TVA, etc.) and "Government Ownership." The road to the right was labeled "Proven for 150 years" and ended in a bright place called "Freedom." America was represented as a citizen carrying a bag marked "The Priceless Jewels of Individual Liberty."

The American press knows every dirty trick in the history of journalism by which it is able to fool all the people most of the time, and one of them is to make it appear that propaganda is straight news. Thus it can, when it wishes, run column after column of testimony, interviews, public statements, Congressional reports, all of which are true, factual, documented, honest perhaps, and all of which aim at one goal: giving only one side of a controversial argument. This it does in the matter of the St. Lawrence. For examples:

New York Herald Tribune, November 8, 1945, news item headed: "St. Lawrence Seaway Plan Held Needless. Lackawanna Head, Union Leader, Term It Peril to Rail Earnings and Jobs."

New York World-Telegram, June 24, 1941, news item headed: "Seaway Opponents Hold United States May Bear Full Cost of Plan. See Canada Not Yet Definitely Committed to Completing Share."

There are millions of these items.

On the same dirty side of the journalistic picture there is not only suppression of the news, but there is burial alive. Just one example will suffice:

On June 18, 1946, Senator Murray of Montana denounced activities of the power lobby whose light had not been dimmed by hoary age or its effectiveness sapped. "In the appropriations bill that we are now studying, that lobby has been and is playing a big hand."

Senator Hill of Alabama, according to the *Times,* "outlined 'a widespread, vicious and unprincipled lobbying and propaganda campaign' against TVA and similar developments."

A new investigation of the power trust was asked.

The *New York Times* on June 19 ran about 7 inches of this big news. It did not suppress the story. That day the *Times* had 44 pages. Of all the 44 the least important is page 43, and it is on that page, sandwiched exactly between a weather map and the radio listing that this front-page news is actually buried.

In the 1930's the power trust propaganda bureau, the NELA, claimed it had just exactly four-fifths of 80% of the American press in its control.

In the 1940's because of the usual advertising and other controls about the same percentage of the American press came out for the power interests.

"Administration plans for a preliminary survey of the St. Lawrence River with a view of its development as a defense power project are assailed by three-fourths of the commenting newspapers, chiefly on the ground of expense and because of the time involved." Thus wrote David Lawrence (*United States News,* November 1, 1940).

In Congress, as in the press, members who were somehow tied to interests greater than that of the nation found all sorts of reasons for opposing St. Lawrence, just as many once found all sorts of reasons for favoring human slavery. An oversight in a public document nails at least one Senator as a friend of the power companies.

On the first day of the Irrigation Committee's hearings in 1945, Senator Murray, speaking for the Missouri Valley Authority, which would save at least $100,000,000 for the citizens of that basin, got into an argument with Senator John Overton of Louisiana. The printed record, page 27, records:

Senator Murray: "Take my state, for example. The power companies are against it (MVA)."

Senator Overton: "Off the record, more power to them."

Overton had intended his "Off the record" remark to remain off the record, but the stenographer recorded every word as spoken and Overton failed to cut it out of the proofs. Overton's history of opposing public light and power developments, including the St. Lawrence, is public. The foregoing oversight is confirmation.

In the vote of August 11, 1944, twenty-five Senators were for the Seaway amendment to the Rivers and Harbors Authorization Bill, but 56 opposed it; again party lines were broken as they always are on most important legislation affecting the general welfare.

Among the opponents of St. Lawrence were Styles Bridges of New Hampshire*; Bailey, Byrd and the late Senator Bilbo, the first two known to have voted in favor of special interests before, and the third merely a KuKluxer; George of Coca Cola fame; McKellar, irresponsible enemy of TVA; O'Daniel, spokesman for the Christian Americans, Fight for Free Enterprise and other native fascist organizations of Texas; Wheeler of Montana, the renegade liberal; the *Chicago Tribune* supported "Curly" Brooks; Taft, Wherry, and Hawkes, the former head of the United States Chamber of Commerce, and leading Senate spokesman for free enterprise.

Senator Bridges was "Chief Senate spokesman for the power companies," according to *PM,* March 21, 1941. Bridges was accused of trying "to slip a foot in the doorway behind which lies the whole vast world of atomic power."

Fewer than one thousand men block the St. Lawrence development and block the progress of America.

They own the power and light corporations, they maintain the lobbies in Albany and Washington, they control the press, they are members of the Senate—and they are united for one purpose: the greatest profit for the smallest number, instead of the greatest good for the greatest number, which is American democracy.

* *The Nation*, April 12, 1947. Columnist Joseph Alsop linked Bridges to the power lobby—*New York Herald Tribune* February 14, 1947.

CHAPTER 4

NAM-TO-PRESS-TO-CONGRESS

IT IS IMPOSSIBLE to overestimate the value of Senator Aiken's public declarations, in the House and on the platform, that a mere thousand men stand in the way of progress on the St. Lawrence. It is a fact, as this volume should help prove, that the same thousand stand in the way of all progress. But, unfortunately, it is also true that the political action which an enlightened public would take when truth becomes known, has not been taken, because the old "conspiracy of silence," long ago reported and always sneered at by the conspirators themselves, prevents intelligent counter-action.

The American people do not know their enemies. They do not know the names, the instruments, the techniques, the power of the few. They do not know who the electric light and power interests are although they have been named in Congress; they do not know the part the House of Morgan still plays in industry; they do not know the names of the 8 great banks which control much of America; they do not know the lobbyists. And so long as they do not know, so long as the press (abetted by the radio) continues to suppress the news when the enemies of America are actually named, it will be impossible for a nation of readers and listeners to take action against them.

It is more than a conspiracy of silence. The press and radio and other means of mass communication not only suppress the news, they also serve special privilege in other ways, because in every major challenge between private gain and public good the press aids the exponents of the former because of the community of interests which now exists.

To illustrate, here are examples of two decades. The 1934 report on the *New York Tribune* publishers, Whitelaw Reid's estate, listed stocks and bonds worth $16,210,809, including power and light, Standard Oil, Mexican investments, banks.

The estate of Joseph Medill Patterson (as reported in the

New York Times of May 17, 1947) listed $10,923,366, including holdings in AT&T, Brown-Foreman Distillers, Chrysler, General Motors, Standard Oil and duPont.

The respectable *New York Herald Tribune* and the yellow *New York Daily News,* whose policy was deliberately gauged to the mental age of 12 by Captain Patterson, do not deviate from the service of big business, the auto makers, the oil corporations, the duPonts, the NAM, the free enterprise system, the protection of the status quo and the furtherance of profits at the expense of the welfare of their own millions of readers.

It is not necessary, however, for the publisher to be a stockholder. He may or may not be indebted to his smalltown banker but he is always dependent on his advertiser, and the advertisers today are directed by the public relations departments of the great advertising agencies, which also plot the political action of big business.

No one has challenged and no one can successfully challenge the community of interests of business and the press.

Big business, as a part of the public well knows, is pretty well represented by the National Association of Manufacturers and the United States Chamber of Commerce, and its affiliates in thousands of cities and towns.

The public does not know—because the press has suppressed the facts—that there is a sort of general staff of billionaire firms which is one of the most powerful if not the most powerful economic and political force in the United States; nor does the public know of the 207 firms which actually direct the NAM, or the fact that the NAM was the chief founder of the USCofC, or the scandal in 1913 when the NAM was shown by a congressional investigation to have bribed members of the House of Representatives and also office boys, or the most recent scandal when the NAM was accused by forthright members of the House and Senate of writing a bill which was passed by a great majority in both chambers.

These are the most powerful of the secret rulers of America, and so long as the press keeps them secret it will be difficult, if not impossible, to restore in a real sense what the

NAM advertises as "the American way of life," or American democracy.

The super strategy board or general staff of the rulers of America, the Special Conference Committee, was first named by the Committee on Education and Labor of which Elbert D. Thomas, senator from Utah, was chairman, Senator La Follette chairman of the subcommittee "to investigate violations of the rights of free speech and assembly and interference with the right of labor to organize and bargain collectively," and Robert Wohlforth secretary. At the time the hearings were held, and in 1939 when the Committee's report was published, the press suppressed the news. In 1947, speaking against the Taft-Hartley bill, aimed to destroy the Wagner Act and all the gains labor had made under the New Deal, Senator Thomas again attacked the Special Conference Committee, and again the entire American press betrayed the American people by complete suppression of the news. (See 1947 *Congressional Record*, pp. 4401-4416.)

On both occasions it was shown that the strategy board of twelve billionaire corporations sets policy, from the employment of spies, gangsters, "goons," strikebreakers, tear gas and machine guns, to the writing of legislation which comes to Congress under the names of Representatives and Senators. In 1939 the La Follette-Thomas report showed that members of the Special Conference Committee and the NAM were the chief users of force and violence, spies and machine guns, in the fight against labor; and in 1947 Senator Thomas declared that the passage of the Taft-Hartley bill would restore a situation which would again make such usage possible.

Who are the twelve billionaire corporations, the super governing body of American industry—and politics? The Committee headed by Senator Thomas listed them as follows:

American Telephone and Telegraph Co.: W. S. Gifford, president; E. F. Carter, vice-president; E. S. Bloom, president (Western Electric Co.); W. A. Griffin, assistant vice-president.

Bethlehem Steel Co.: Eugene G. Grace, president; J. M. Larkin, vice-president.

E. I. duPont de Nemours: Lammot duPont, president; Willis F. Hartington, vice-president; William B. Foster, director of service department.

General Electric Co.: Owen D. Young, former chairman; W. S. Burrows, vice-president; G. H. Pfeif, supervisor of personnel.

General Motors Corp.: Alfred P. Sloan, Jr., president; John L. Pratt, vice-president; Donaldson Brown, vice-president.

Goodyear Tire and Rubber Co.: E. J. Thomas, general superintendent.

International Harvester Co.: A. A. Jones, assistant to vice-president; George J. Kelday, manager of industrial relations.

Irving Trust Co.: Harry E. Ward, president; Northrop Holbrook, vice-president.

Standard Oil Co. of New Jersey: W. S. Farish, chairman; W. C. Teagle, president.

U. S. Rubber Co.: L. D. Tompkins, vice-president; C. S. Ching, director of industrial and public relations.

U. S. Steel Corporation, the biggest of the billionaire Morgan corporations.

Westinghouse Electric & Mfg. Co.: A. W. Robertson, chairman; F. A. Merrick, vice-chairman; W. G. Marshall, vice-president; E. S. Clelland, director of personnel.

(Source: Senate Report 6, part 6, 76th Congress, 1st session, pp. 89, 91, 92, 97; also Part 45, p. 16781.)

The general staff of the 12 corporations meets informally and agrees on a program which is always anti-labor. Since 1935 it has had as its chief objective the destruction of the Wagner Act, the symbol of the New Deal era, one of the few short periods in American history when legislation was enacted consciously under the "general welfare" clause of the Constitution.

The informal decision is passed on to the directing group of the NAM, and from there to organizations and corporations throughout the nation, so that within a few days a great campaign gets under way, a vast propaganda covers the country, four or five million dollars worth paid for by the NAM, but ten or twenty or a hundred times that amount furnished free by the newspapers, magazines, radio and others who have the same community of interests.

In almost no time at all at least 90% of the American press echoes the "party line" of the 12 billionaire corporations, and the 16,000 members of the NAM.

The Special Conference Committee gives the signal, the same "sounding of the 'la' " which Mussolini explained he used for his journalistic orchestra, the press of the entire Italian nation, and immediately all the hacks in America get to work, and scores, if not thousands take up the *delenda est* campaign: the Wagner Act must be destroyed.

The cartoonists of most newspapers are just plain old-fashioned newspaper prostitutes. In fact, they are the last of the bordello era of journalism. The editorial writer may have something of a free voice; the columnist could be free—except that he is aware that sycophancy pays $50,000 a year and iconoclasm lands one in the poorhouse; but the "artist" is given blunt orders, and since his medium is graphic he cannot, like the editorial writer or the columnist, qualify what is to be said and protect himself. It is the strength and weakness of the cartooning art that it is more incisive, more onesided, more powerful, than the editorial viewpoint it illustrates; and thus it comes about that the same press which via its editorials and columnists presents the NAM or Chamber of Commerce line with discretion and camouflage, usually presents a cartoon in which graphic bluntness more often than not makes it a falsehood.

Honest reporting is turned into dishonesty. The editor sends out a good union reporter to interview Mr. Wilson of General Electric or Mr. Wilson of General Motors, an honest report is made, and the honest report is printed. But the editor will never at the same time publish an honest report of a contrary nature from the head of the electric or automobile union at either General Electric or General Motors, and in this way the public is fooled by what appears to be straight uneditorialized unbiased news. This is one of the oldest tricks in journalism.

The radio acts in exactly the same manner. The public does not know that Mr. Henry J. Taylor is himself a manufacturer nor that when he talks for General Motors he is talking for the main financial backer of the NAM, one of the most persistent enemies of union labor in the United States. These are the facts and a strictly honest radio would so announce them.

The public does not know that Lowell Thomas, as well as Fulton Lewis, Jr., at one time or another received pay from the NAM and that neither of them has ever deviated from the NAM-anti-labor line. It does not know that Lowell Thomas, who is supposed to give the news straight—a newscaster in contrast with news commentators—is just as biased and prejudiced as the latter, that he worked for one of the heads of the NAM, the Pew family of Sunoco and Sun Shipbuilding, and that his neat compliments to the Pews (until 1947, when he changed to Procter & Gamble) were a pay-off, as are his sneers against labor unions.

The "big" commentators on national hookups are in the pay of big money, in the pay of the thousand men who run the country, and while it may be possible for them not to speak the propaganda pieces of the NAM and similar peak organizations of industry and finance, it is not expedient. In 1946 and 1947 the liberal press reported the dismissal of newscasters and news commentators at about the rate of one a month. Perhaps it is just another coincidence that without exception the score of men who have been put off the air are those who did not propagandize for free enterprise and big business, and who did not attack labor, or sneer at all liberal ideas.

In the business of manufacturing public opinion, one of the usual methods is the introduction into the appendix of the *Congressional Record* of the editorial opinion of hometown newspapers as well as those of Washington and New York. Sometimes vast sections of the body of the *Record* itself are given over to quotations from the press of the land, all of course substantiating the viewpoint of the member of Congress who reads or inserts these editorials.

In turn, the newspapers reprint the Congressman's views. And when sufficient "build-up" has been created by press, radio and congressional oratory, a bill is drafted to meet the call of "the people of the United States," and debate begins.

The press takes sides. And shortly afterwards it is no surprise to find that an honest public opinion poll confirms the views of both the press and the framers of the bill in Congress. The poll, actually, has become a barometer of propaganda and prejudices of newspaper and radio commentators, rather than a test of enlightened thinking.

The voters will never learn from any of the means of mass communications that one of the sponsors of the bill introduced "on their behalf" is also the benefactor of a huge election fund, the major contributors to which are also the leading members of the NAM or the local chamber of commerce.

The public will never realize that from the first proposal, to the campaign in the press and radio, to the eventual passage of a bill in Congress, there has been a behind-the-scenes activity on the part of a few who have acted entirely for their own benefit and who have been successful because of their overwhelming power.

This statement is easily documented.

The history of the National Association of Manufacturers as revealed by the Thomas-La Follette investigation, shows that it was reoriented in 1933, shortly after the election of F. D. Roosevelt, that its chief objective, the destruction of the labor movement, was never lost sight of, and that its policy was to fight laws favoring the unions.

The first Wagner bill failed of passage. The Wagner Act became law July 5, 1935, and was immediately declared unconstitutional—not by the Supreme Court, but by the corporations. The NAM believed it unconstitutional and the most powerful publicity organization in the hands of the NAM, the American Newspaper Publishers Association, echoed the views of big business. Some corporations, however, obeyed the law they did not like, but newspaper publishers were advised to break it. "If the NLRB issued an order in this case, Mr. Hearst will not comply with it," said Elisha Hanson, who is attorney for Hearst, the International Power and Paper Company and the ANPA. In October, 1936, Mr. Hanson sent this bit of advice to his newspaper clients: "Publishers from now on should flatly refuse to have anything to do with the NLRB other than to notify it it is without power under the constitution to interfere with their business. . . . No order of the Board . . . will, if it be contested, be upheld in the courts."

The decisive test was made in behalf of Big Business by the Associated Press, the great news service, which had fired Morris Watson on the charge that he was organizing the Newspaper Guild. On April 12, 1937, the Supreme Court ruled against the NAM and ANPA and in favor of American democratic procedure.

From then on until the convening of the next Republican Congress, in January, 1947, the Special Conference Committee and the NAM spent a frightened decade lining up all the powerful forces in the nation to use every pressure, including the press, to emasculate or weaken the Wagner Act.

Not one day in those 10 years passed without a news item, a headline, an editorial, a radio mention attacking the Wagner Act. The *New York Times,* for example, published an average of 12 editorials a year advocating a change in this law for the benefit of business. The owner of the *Times* states frequently that he is a "liberal." Newspapers with less pretensions indulged in the usual frauds of journalism while fighting to destroy what has since become known as the Magna Carta of labor.

The destruction of the union labor movement had become the main objective of the NAM at its 1903 convention in New Orleans when it was but 8 years old. According to the La Follette investigation the NAM itself said that this "marked the first declaration by a representative national body for the open shop as a cardinal policy."

In 1932, just after the election but "before the progressive policies of the new administration had been crystallized in legislation," the "Brass Hats," a group of wealthy businessmen, reorganized the NAM for the purpose of protecting corporate interests.

Immediately after the passage of the Wagner Act, but even before the President signed it and made it law, the NAM called a secret session of its leaders, the heads of the few companies which controlled it, to consider five Administration measures: the Wagner Bill, the tax program, NRA, a plan to protect industry, and social security. According to the La Follette report the NAM also opposed the Banking Act, the Utility Holding Company Act, and similar legislation. It began its great many-million dollar propaganda campaign after it failed to stop the reforms by lobbying; it aimed "to render public opinion intolerant of the aims of social progress through legislative effort." In other words, a few men decided by the expenditure of millions in advertising and publicity and through the use of the press and other mediums to so change public opinion in the United States that it would use its pressure against measures aimed for its own benefit. The concluding part of the Thomas-La Follette report states:

"Finally, the committee deplores the failure of the NAM and the powerful corporations which guide its policies to adapt themselves to changing times and to laws which the majority of the people deem wise and necessary."

The United States Chamber of Commerce likewise opposed not only the Wagner Act but each and every piece of social legislation the New Deal planned for the restoration of the nation and the necessary benefit of the majority.

It is true that in 1933 the NAM went into immediate action against social welfare whereas the Chamber of Commerce surprisingly supported the President and his policies. It was a short honeymoon.

The break came in the May, 1935, convention. In a fireside chat Roosevelt had just outlined five reforms: The Social Security Bill, Extension of NRA, Elimination of Public Utility Holding Companies, Regulation of all Forms of Interstate Transport, and the Omnibus Banking Bill.

The Chamber met and denounced four of the five FDR

"musts." It opposed social security because "within a decade there will be a tax burden amounting probably to as much as one billion dollars a year"; it asked that NRA expire as per schedule in June; the elimination of holding companies (which are largely light and power, dominated by the House of Morgan) was called "destruction of enterprise," "violation of fundamental principles" that would mean a loss to investors; transport regulation was approved; the banking bill was denounced as "political dictatorship." In June the Chamber denounced the Wagner Act as "a dangerous measure" and said the country could not pay the "staggering" costs of social security.

From that time on the Chamber assisted the NAM in its twelve-year fight against the Roosevelt program of social legislation and especially the Wagner Act.

Of the thousands of examples which document the charge of collaboration between NAM, press and Congress, here are a few samples:

1937: "Wage Bill Junking Urged by Chamber"—*New York Times* of August 15. The U. S. Chamber of Commerce stated that "Attention should now be given to changes in the National Labor Relations Act rather than to making any additions to it." The NAM and the press, especially the *New York Times,* followed this line: changes, rather than repeal.

1937: Dec. 7. Lewis H. Haney, professor of economics at New York University and daily Hearst columnist (believe it or not), in an address to National Industrial Council (affiliated with NAM) urged the "scrapping" of the Wagner Act, said wages were inflated, denounced strikes.

1938: *Editor & Publisher,* April 23, reported convention of advertising men at which Lee Bristol, maker of patent medicines, urged revision of Wagner Act.

1941: *Los Angeles Examiner* (Hearst), June 17, reported address by W. D. Fuller, president of the NAM (and president of the Curtis Publishing Co., publishers of the *Saturday Evening Post* and other magazines). "Fuller would amend Wagner Act, enforce laws," said part of the headline.

1943: *Saturday Evening Post* in a big editorial answered

readers' questions, May 15: "5. Would you repeal the NLRA? (Answer) No, although it looks as if the War Labor Board might achieve the same result. We should, however, favor amendments to the Wagner Act giving the employer the right to point out that some labor unions are run by racketeers. . . ." The big magazine press as well as the newspapers followed the NAM line.

1944: January 21. Federated Press reported address by H. W. Prentis, Jr. (who was listed as an enemy of American democracy by Attorney General Jackson,* and who is an ex-president of the NAM), telling the National Industrial Conference Board they must work for "legislation to remove the Wage-Hours Law, the Wagner Act, the Norris-LaGuardia Anti-Injunction Act, the Sherman Anti-Trust Act and other laws affecting labor management relations."

1944: May 20. *Editor & Publisher* concluded one of its many anti-labor editorials: "We repeat that Congress must revise our labor laws."

1945: July 2. The *New York Times* used its "labor editor," Louis Stark, for one of its almost daily "think pieces" or camouflaged editorials passed off as news items. Head: "STRIKES SPUR DEMAND FOR LABOR LAW CHANGES." If this news item had stated that the demand for a change in the Wagner Act came from the corporations and the NAM, it would have been a fair item.

1945: October 26. "NEW LABOR POLICY URGED BY MOSHER." *The Times,* as usual, gives a column to every NAM president who speaks against the Wagner Act.

Throughout the year, as before and after, the various native reactionary organizations continued their attack on the Wagner Act. Sample: Committee for Constitutional Government (denounced in Congress as America's No. 1 fascist organization) sent hundreds of thousands of leaflets headed, "What's the Matter with America?" the first line of which said: "Labor unions are wrecking the country." Theme: change the Wagner Act.

In 1946 it became clear that after the death of President

* *Law Society Journal* (Mass.), Nov., 1940.

Roosevelt and the end of the war, a great period of reaction would set in, which could be exploited by certain interests. They did not fail the opportunity.

In January the newspapers permitted an organization which signed itself "Society of Sentinels, Detroit" to publish a huge "Open Letter to President Truman" which urged the end of OPA; the preservation of the United States as "an island of freedom, so that liberty may not everywhere perish from this earth"; and the destruction of the Wagner Act. The newspapers failed to state that this advertising was paid for by General Motors men and other big industrialists.

On March 22 the great *New York Times* approved the Case bill, which labor called "one of the most vicious" and a "labor slavery" bill.

The entire issue of NAM's weekly *News* of May 18 was devoted to urging Congress to enact this Bill, and also to destroy the OPA. (When OPA finally was destroyed, but before it was estimated that as a result every person in the country would have to pay $250 more for his living in 1946, the NAM boasted it was the power behind congressional action.)

On June 11 the Kiwanians and the U. S. Chamber united in urging what the *Times* called in its headline the next morning "Fair Labor Curbs." The weekly cartoon of the NAM's *Industrial Press Service* of July 22 showed workers sleeping on the job, thanks to the Wagner Act. On August 13 the *Times* ran another editorial against the Wagner Act.

In September the Committee for Constitutional Government began a campaign of millions of letters and pieces of "literature" to smash the Wagner Act. It sent out items by Professor Willford I. King, one of its paid lobbyists and a member of the staff of New York University, and ex-Congressman Sam Pettengill of Indiana. Of the frightening propaganda, the railroad weekly *Labor,* said: "The way to save America, according to this precious outfit, which apparently is collecting immense sums from the gullible rich, is to destroy trade unionism. You will remember Hitler and Mussolini took the same position."

On October 11 the *Times* printed, for perhaps the twentieth time, the same old program of the NAM board chairman, Ira Mosher, on how to smash labor. The *Times* knew it was printing old stuff, and old stuff is never news unless the owner of the newspaper wants it to be news. So it appeared again.

Just before the election the NAM got many of its corporation affiliates to circularize big business with an appeal for money for its publicity campaign in press and radio against labor. Here is a sample letter:

November 4, 1946

[Name of recipient withheld]

As you have supported the NIIC [the NAM's propaganda dept.] in the past, you are aware of what the NAM public relations program is doing to combat the unsound Robin Hood economics of those who think the way to make the country prosperous is to make jobs by regimenting business, stifling competition and confiscating profits [sic]. . . .

The NAM has a public relations program that is getting results. No doubt you recall the recent nationwide NAM campaign to make labor equal with management before the law. Most observers believe that we will get remedial labor legislation as a result of this fight—which is being aggressively continued—at the next session of Congress. . . . . .

[Signed] Frazer A. Bailey, Chairman,
NAM Development Committee."

Following the election, the press and the Congress were unanimous in declaring that the first order of business would be labor legislation. The *Times'* head of November 9 was: "Wagner Act Faces Move for Revision in Next Congress." Soon this was the unanimous opinion of the press of the United States.

Columnist David Lawrence said that "some amendments to the Wagner Act are long overdue" (November 12). "Senator Hawkes Hits Wagner Act" reported the *New York News* November 15, without stating that Hawkes is a previous president of the Chamber of Commerce, the head of Congoleum Nairn.

And so it went.

Congress was to meet January 3. The month of December was therefore vital in the anti-labor tactics of Big Business and its little helpers.

It would be impossible in the space available even to list the items illustrating the campaign. But the following samples are important because the very same alignment of powers occurs on every issue in which the public interest is involved. Reaction called upon the press, radio and all sorts of organizations and spokesmen to do a job, and the job was done, just as it has been done in the past and as it will be done in the future unless the public—against whom the job is directed—learns how to protect itself. This is part of the December record:

December 1. United Press, serving more than 1,000 dailies, carried what it termed "Senator Wiley's labor-reform program," practically nullifying the Wagner Act.

"NAM WILL PROPOSE A LABOR PROGRAM," reported the *Times*.

December 2. "ABOLISH LABOR BOSSES, KIWANIS SPEAKER ASKS" (*World Telegram*). Quoted Kiwanis International committee chairman George Stringfellow that "Wagner Act has created a labor monopoly."

Tool Owners' Union, a big business outfit including exposed fascists, Coughlinites, and labor baiters used a page ad in the *New York Times* and many papers to collect money to fight labor.

December 3. Fred Perkins, Scripps-Howard chain columnist, reported Senator Ball's plan to destroy unions.

December 4. "CASE DECLARES CONGRESS MUST ACT ON LABOR." Congressman Case of South Dakota, elected with part of the $53,700 fund raised by duPont, Pew and other heads of the NAM, is one of the main agents of the NAM line in Congress. This was an AP report used throughout the nation.

At the opening of the NAM convention, Executive Secretary Weisenburger demanded changes in the Wagner Act, declaring it was "bringing America dangerously close to open revolution."

December 5. If anyone doubts the NAM-press-Congress

line-up against labor (and the general welfare), the headline this day was a complete giveaway. It was: "SENATORS BALL, BYRD AT NAM SESSION TO OUTLINE CONGRESS PLANS." Two leading senators rushed to the NAM convention to promise big business they would lead in the attempt to destroy the effectiveness of the Wagner Act and 14 years of liberal-labor legislation.

December 6. The NAM *News,* published daily during convention, carried this head: "NEW LABOR LAW TO BE SEVERE ON UNIONS, SAYS BALL."

Columnist Mark Sullivan, who writes about a hundred anti-labor columns a year, attacked the Wagner Act, said the "climate" had changed November 5 when the GOP won.

President William K. Jackson of the United States Chamber of Commerce over American Forum of the Air attacked the Wagner Act as unfair to employers.

The fakery and hypocrisy of the press which had headlined a sudden liberal policy by the NAM ("LIBERAL PROGRAM ON LABOR, ECONOMY ANNOUNCED BY NAM," *New York Times,* December 5) was exposed by the liberal daily *PM* which pictured the *New York Herald Tribune* headline ("NAM ASKS LABOR CURB TO REBUILD U S") alongside the *Times* head.

The National Legislative representative of the United Autoworkers, Irving Richter, in his report published this day stated:

"The top Republican leaders did more than just VOTE the NAM line in the last Congress. They originated and militantly pushed a program for big business. They had two great advantages over the Democrats: First, they knew exactly what they wanted—the greatest possible profit for the Wall Street crowd, regardless of consequences to the general population. . . ."

December 7. Columnist Stokes reported: "The extreme right in this country is operating now more actively and more openly than ever. It was emboldened by the recent election. . . . This element which is powerful because it is so well entrenched financially, showed its teeth at the annual convention of the NAM. . . . It is certain that there is going to be labor legislation in the new Congress. . . . How drastic and punitive it is will depend upon whether the Republican party leadership follows the extremists represented in the NAM minority or whether it takes a more moderate course."

It should be noted that Stokes is frequently suppressed by his Scripps-Howard chain and other papers, and that his voice, and articles in the liberal-labor weeklies showing the NAM-press-Congress line-up against the welfare of the public, do not reach one hundredth the readership of the commercial press, its brasscheck columnists, editorial writers, cartoonists, financial editors, reactionary radio commentators and other makers of public opinion.

"A sweeping revision of the Wagner labor relations act" was being drafted by Representative Howard Smith of Virginia, another of the NAM voices in Congress, reported the *Herald Tribune.*

December 8. *New York Times:* "From many sources last week came demands for revising the Wagner Act." GOP chairman Carroll Reece was quoted as saying, "Labor legislation was still the first and foremost problem facing the new Congress." "CURBS ON LABOR LIKELY DESPITE LEWIS RETREAT"—*Herald Tribune.*

December 9. United Press item: "CONGRESS DRIVE FOR STRIKE CURB SEEN BOLSTERED."

Life magazine devoted an entire editorial page to an attack on labor. "Merely by revising parts of the Wagner Act" was a solution, the usual NAM solution. Also favored revising, amending Norris-LaGuardia anti-injunction law. And the whole NAM program.

December 11. "LABOR CURBS WILL BE FIRST CONGRESS JOB." Washington report to *New York Herald Tribune.*

December 13. "STUDY LABOR CURBS ON POLITICS"—*New York Sun.*

Page ads in many papers paid for by Wall Street broker, E. F. Hutton, stated: "We want the Wagner Act reviewed."

December 15. "DEBATE ON LABOR LAWS CENTERS ON WAGNER ACT"—Louis Stark in the *Times.* "EARLY WAGNER ACT REVISION IS SHAPING UP IN CONGRESS"—*Herald Tribune.* "To call Senator Ball a reactionary, as some of the labor press now does, is fantastic," wrote the reactionary ex-liberal Mark Sullivan.

December 16. NEA (Scripps-Howard) columnist Peter Edson: "GOP REVENGE REACTION RIDES HIGH." A joint statement by top labor and management spokesmen, including NAM and Chamber of Commerce, for peaceful labor settlements was called "too late" by Congressman Clarence Brown of Ohio who "expressed impatience to get on with the job of amending the Wagner Act"—(*AP*). "CAPITOL IS COOL TO LABOR PEACE PLAN" —(*AP*). "Under the Wagner Act we have had more strikes than ever before," wrote Lawrence Fertig, listed as "writer on economic affairs" in Scripps-Howard papers.

December 18. Two-page ad in Pew's *Pathfinder,* and other publications, paid for by The Conference of American Small Business Organizations, which states: "We will draft necessary legislation to amend the Wagner Labor Relations Act." This is one of the few open and honest statements by big business as to who drafts the anti-labor legislation which Congress passes.

December 19. Columnist David Lawrence (who also publishes *United States News*) attacked the Wagner Act, said it would be repealed unless some labor leaders agreed to amendments. *Trends,* a Wall Street newsletter, reported Ball, Byrd and Smith writing anti-labor laws.

Two to three solid columns were given over by big newspapers to the "10-Point Labor Harmony Plan" of General Motors' chairman, Alfred P. Sloan (*New York Sun*). The ten points did not vary from the 1933 NAM program or the *New York Times* perennial anti-Wagner Act editorials.

December 20. The Smith Bill was announced, the press giving it a fine play. Senator Taft announced debate on February 15.

December 23. Senator Taft, one of the wealthiest business men of Ohio, announced he was the best man to head the Senate Labor Committee. Columnist Marquis Childs stated Taft favored reviving the Case Bill.

December 24. The *New York Herald Tribune* reported

that Taft would outmaneuver the liberal Republican Aiken for the committee chairmanship, and that Taft, in discussing the CIO claim, via the Nathan report, that industry could raise wages 25% without raising prices, declared: "The solution for the country is lower prices, not higher wages."

There was a brief interlude for Christmas week. But in January, 1947, with the opening of Congress, the vast national orchestra of press, radio, public speakers and Congressmen began their thundering but harmonious playing of the Wagner Act Blues.

The Magna Carta of labor was to be sabotaged—not repealed—in exactly the way the NAM planned it in 1935.

So much for the overt campaign. When Congress met in January, press and politicians agreed on one thing: first action would be a labor bill. And a labor bill soon came before the House and Senate, sponsored, respectively, by Representative Fred A. Hartley, a man with one of the worst voting records so far as labor, liberal and pro bono publico measures are concerned, and one of the best records so far as subservience to corporate wealth and power are concerned; and the ubiquitous Senator Taft, the Ohio business man.

In April, when the committees of both legislative bodies were writing a compromise measure, fearing that the President would veto the House version as unconstitutional as well as unfair and punitive, the conservative leaders of rival labor unions for once agreed on a statement. Philip Murray of the CIO, William Green of the AFL and A. J. Whitney of the Railroad Trainmen denounced the Taft-Hartley "slave labor" bill as a fascist measure. All three agreed that it followed the early action against unions taken by Hitler and Mussolini. The press, as usual, suppressed or buried the fascist references.

Coincident with the release of the report of the Commission on Freedom of the Press—see last chapter—in which the newspapers were accused of failure to serve the American people, they proved the charge by suppressing one of the most important news items of the time.

If the reader will take the time and trouble to visit his

library, he will find in the *Congressional Record* of April 15, 16, and 17, 1947, in the debate on the Hartley Bill, the evidence of a dozen members of the House that this measure was originated by the NAM, sponsored by the NAM, and finally written by representatives of the NAM. In fact, on pages 3731 to 3733 he will find in parallel columns the NAM original and the Hartley Bill, officially introduced by Representative Blatnik of Minnesota. He will find named the lawyers and lobbyists accused of writing the bill: Theodore R. Iserman of the Chrysler Corporation and friend of Senator Ball; William Ingles, the $20,400 a year lobbyist for Allis Chalmers, Fruehauf Trailer, J. I. Case and Inland Steel; one Jerry Morgan, who serves several corporations; and Mark Jones, an industrial promoter vaguely connected with the Rockefeller interests.

If our country had a free press—if at least a small percentage of its 1750 dailies was honest—the matter would have been played up for exactly what it was: one of the most sensational news items of the congressional session. The facts were there, the matter was documented, and it was privileged. Not only did a final total of 18 members of the House, but later on, in May, five members of the Senate, Republican and Democratic alike, repeated the charges. Nevertheless, serene in their confidence that few if any papers would break their conspiracy of silence on matters affecting the general good of the greatest number of Americans, the press suppressed the news.

Sixty years of bitter struggle by the majority of the people of the United States to end costly strikes, violence and bloodshed, culminated in the destruction by reaction of the great gains of the New Deal of the Roosevelt Era. The NAM, the press, the Congress, the radio oracles, the columnists, the magazines, the one thousand rulers and their tens of thousands of paid agents, were again successful in gaining the day for the economic royalists, the money changers Roosevelt declared he would drive out of the temple. They were back—not in the temple, perhaps, but surely in the press, the radio, and in Congress.

PART TWO
BIG MAGAZINES

CHAPTER 5
THE MAGAZINE PRESS

The general distrust with which a healthy-minded people regards its newspapers does not extend to the other half of the press—the extraordinarily powerful group of popular magazines. It is quite natural that the *Fortune* Poll should ask the public—as it did in 1936—what it thought of its newspapers, and arrive at the not surprising conclusion that at least 26%, or about 30,000,000 persons, had their doubts. *Fortune,* however, did not ask the public what it thought of the integrity of its million-dollar making million circulation big brother, *Time,* nor of *Time*'s rivals and colleagues.

Much more important is the fact that whereas there has been at least a little criticism in many places, from the presidency to the liberal weeklies, of the entire newspaper press, the news services, and their false concepts of freedom of the press, there has been almost nothing said about the weekly or monthly magazines. It is as if critics and the organs of enlightenment no longer regard the magazine press of importance in the formation of public opinion and the guidance of American affairs.

Such an explanation would be based on the history of the great truth-telling (or "muckraking," as its enemies later called it) magazine era of the first two decades of the Twentieth Century, and the eventual emasculation or suppression of free magazines by the industrial and financial interests. Darkness and sweet romance descended upon the magazine world—the great muckraker, *Everybody's,* actually changed its name to *Romance Magazine*—and from the First World War to this day there has seldom been reason to look into a popular magazine for important news and great exposés which the newspaper press, retreating before the advance of the most selfish forces in the nation, had abandoned without a fight.

The great powers were not satisfied with their complete victory over the magazine press. (Its documented history is told in "Crusaders for American Liberalism" by Louis Filler, Harcourt, Brace & Co., 1939.) Trash may indeed be the opium of the people, but it was not the real aim of the magazines to stupefy the public, merely to suppress the facts, merely to nullify, to create a wasteland. The great powers slowly but universally turned the magazine press into an agency for the propaganda of their own ideologies. The House of Morgan, whose direct interest in newspapers is almost nil, branched out into the magazine field. The Harknesses, the Harrimans, the Astors, the last private banking house of Brown Brothers, and some of the leaders of the National Association of Manufacturers came quietly into the financing and control of most of the million-circulation magazines, until today it may be said—as the table appearing later shows—that the topmost ranks of Big Business and Big Banking are represented in the control of the weeklies and monthlies which reach twice as many people in America as the newspapers.

This control is partly open, partly secret, but whether open or secret, it is not known to the millions. It is true that the United States Post Office requires an annual statement of owners of weeklies as well as daily newspapers. When Milton Stewart of the Commission on Freedom of the Press complained that "it is impossible for us, without the power of subpoena, to find out who runs the various media—radio, newspapers and movies," the well-paid apologist for the press, *Editor & Publisher,* replied (December 1, 1945): "Mr. Stewart obviously is unaware of the Act of Congress, August 24, 1912, . . . requiring newspapers and magazines to publish a statement of ownership, management and circulation every year. If Mr. Stewart would check he would find a record of the chief executives, names and addresses of all stockholders and bondholders having more than 1% interest for all newspapers."

If Mr. Stewart did check a number of magazines and came upon the name A. K. Lockett, it is very likely he would give it no special attention, and it can be presumed that the millions not in the profession would ignore that name entirely. Nevertheless, it is Mr. Lockett who represents the House of Morgan in the management and control of several of the most powerful organs of public opinion in the country.

It might also be pointed out to *Editor & Publisher* that at the time Frank E. Gannett was heavily indebted to the International Power and Paper Company, the *Brooklyn Eagle,* in publishing its statement of ownership, did not reveal that not 1% but 40% of itself was mortgaged to an outsider. Nor did Mr. S. E. Thomason of the *Chicago Journal* reveal the fact that his paper also was in the same financial situation. The law of the land states that publishers must tell the facts of stock ownership or be fined and sent to the penitentiary. However the law does not mention loans.

Moreover, International Power and Paper was at least 60% a public utility, a vital link in the chain which formed the great Power Trust. Back of the $600,000,000 newsprint, power and light corporation were the most powerful banking houses of the United States, chief being the Rockefeller Chase National Bank, represented by Albert H. Wiggin, chairman of its board and director of International Power and Paper; and the Morgan group through the Bankers Trust Company, whose Owen D. Young was a member of the reorganization committee which in 1928 set up the holding company. Through Mr. Young the group became allied with the Mohawk-Hudson Power Company, a great factor in the fight of many decades against public power, and against the St. Lawrence Seaway in particular.

At one time or another International Power and Paper owned a substantial interest in the *Brooklyn Eagle,* the *Chicago Daily News,* the *Knickerbocker Press and Evening News,* the two Gannett papers in Albany, Gannett's *Ithaca Journal-News,* the *Boston Herald,* the *Boston Traveler, Chicago Jour-*

nal, Tampa Tribune, Greensboro (N.C.) Record, Augusta Chronicle, Columbia (S.C.) Herald, Spartansburg Journal (published by Harold Hall and William La Varre)—and tried, for $20,000,000, to buy several metropolitan newspapers.

It may, of course, be just a coincidence that almost the entire press, and almost every paper which had any dealings at all with the Rockefeller-Morgan-IP&P-Mohawk-Hudson combination, opposed and still opposes public power, and will fight any attempt to benefit all its readers by the passage of the St. Lawrence legislation.

But it is no coincidence that the power trust spent up to $25,000,000 a year on newspapers and magazines, and that the press, with so few exceptions that these could not sway public opinion, repaid the trust for its open bribery, its open advertising, or its other pressures. The corruption of the newspapers is now generally known. Somehow or other the part the magazines played in control of public opinion has been overlooked.

Nevertheless, the evidence is official. Martin Insull testified on the campaign of "goodwill" advertising,—advertising not intended to sell anything but to obtain the goodwill of the publishers for the power trust:

> "The National Electric Light Association starts out with a campaign of its own, running a certain number of advertisements in the *Saturday Evening Post*. That campaign cost the NELA 50 odd thousand dollars."

> "In its program to gain 'public goodwill' . . . the utility industry instituted an essay contest in the schools. . . . Early in September, 1924, the national advertising of this contest began in the leading magazines of the country, including the *Saturday Evening Post, Literary Digest, Ladies' Home Journal, Collier's, American, Cosmopolitan* and *Good Housekeeping*."

> (U. S. Congress, Utility Corporations, Report 71-a, Senate Document 92; 70th Congress, 1st Session.)

The 73 volumes of reports, exhibits and index explain in detail the dealings with numerous magazines, the propaganda the utility trust put over on the American people, and the part the magazines played in doing it.

With some of the newspapers it was necessary to bribe the

editors and publishers. But with the big magazines it cannot be said that anything unethical or illegal took place. The magazines, unlike many newspapers, were in the direct ownership or control of the same persons and corporations which had a community of interest not only with the NELA but with the private profit business system.

The NAM is the peak association of big business. It is not only the most powerful private organization in the country, it is the spokesman and chief propagandist of free enterprise. Although the public, or perhaps only 99% of the public, does not know it, through its members the NAM, in addition to being a dominant power in the newspapers—as Monograph 26 shows—is also a dominant power in the magazines, and, moreover, it has the following connections:

Walter D. Fuller: President of the Curtis Publishing Co., one of the reorganizers and present director of the NAM, also president (1947) of the National Publishers' Association.

William B. Warner: McCall's, Redbook and other magazines, ex-president reorganizer and director of the NAM, president (until his death in 1946) of the NPA.

Malcolm Muir: President of McGraw-Hill, publisher of many industrial magazines, also *Business Week* and *Newsweek* (*Time*'s chief rival), another link in the NAM chain of magazine influence.

J. Howard Pew: President of the Sun Oil Company (Sunoco). The Pew family also owns the Sun Shipbuilding Company and other industrial enterprises. Their publishing interests are: the *Farm Journal,* with almost 3,000,000 circulation, and *The Pathfinder,* the first of the newsweekly type of magazines. In addition to being among the largest contributors to political campaigns, the Pews also dispensed money to a dozen organizations including the *Crusaders,* a leading native fascist outfit, and the Sentinels of the Republic, the anti-Semitic affiliate of the American Liberty League.

The National Publishers' Association through its members has always had control of many magazines and has been more closely allied with the NAM than the American Newspaper Publishers Association, nevertheless so quiet has been its operations that there is not even a mention of this powerful group in the Monopoly Investigation report which exposes the ANPA.

The NPA and the ANPA, with their 50,000,000 daily newspaper and 100,000,000 weekly and monthly magazine circulation, form the most powerful opinion-creating force in America.

Many of the activities of the ANPA are publicized; it meets annually, and although its main sessions—when it discusses strikebreaking and how to fight its own employees, including the Newspaper Guild—are still secret (no freedom of the press when the press itself is concerned!)—it cannot be said that the ANPA is a blushing violet. As a lobby it was tremendously powerful in Washington.

On the other hand, the magazine publishers conducted a powerful lobby but sought no publicity and preferred to remain behind the scenes. And inasmuch as the newspaper and magazine press pretty well control the facts, they have pretty well kept the American people in ignorance about the lobbying activities.

Thanks to an anonymous person who once made public a confidential memorandum circulated among the members of the NPA, a light is thrown upon the activities of the organization which shows it up clearly and unequivocally.

It was the year 1934. A New Deal had been promised and was under way to achievement. One of its first and most important provisions was a labor law which would free the majority from the oppressive controls of the minority. Another was a bill to save the health, and incidentally the pocketbook, of the people by enforcing purity in food and drugs—and also in the advertising of commodities. Social Security at last became a national issue.

On July 16 of that year, the magazine publishers issued a memorandum of what their rôle had been in fighting social legislation. It said in part:

"This has been a most unusual year in the publishing field

and the National Publishers' Association has due cause to be proud of its operations during the year in the interests of the entire publishing industry.

"Wagner Labor Bill. This legislation would have been very costly to all publishers whether or not they operate their own printing plant. We took a very active part in killing this legislation.

"Tugwell Pure Food and Drug Bill. As originally proposed, this legislation would have been a serious blow to all advertising. Your committee and executives were finally successful in modifying this legislation.

"Unemployment Insurance. This bill provided for a tax of 5% on all payrolls. Its seriousness speaks for itself, and your representatives aided in preventing its passage."

The National Association of Manufacturers had fought the same bills; the American Newspaper Publishers' Association had fought the same bills, both more or less in the open, the newspaper press by poisoning the public mind with false news, half-truths, bias and misinformation. The magazine publishers worked in secrecy.

The head of the NPA was one of the men who not only reorganized the NAM but one of the Brass Hat clique which in 1933, after the beginning of the New Deal, turned the NAM into a labor-fighting outfit: William Bishop Warner, publisher of *McCall's, Red Book* and other magazines.

The Crowell Publishing Company, publishers of *Collier's, The American Magazine,* and *Woman's Home Companion,* was represented in NPA by A. D. Mayo.

The Curtis Publishing Company (*Saturday Evening Post, Ladies' Home Journal*) was represented by P. S. Collins, spokesman for President W. D. Fuller, one of the inner powers of the NAM.

The Luce publications (*Time, Life, Fortune*) were represented by Roy Larsen, publisher of *Time.*

The U. S. Chamber of Commerce's magazine, *The Nation's Business,* was represented by its editor, Merle Thorpe.

Malcolm Muir represented the McGraw-Hill Publishing Company.

It should be noted that the magazine press as well as the newspaper press—and the NAM and all other forces of reaction, including a large part of Congress—continued to fight the Wagner Labor Act which succeeded despite their efforts; that they were able to destroy the Tugwell Bill largely, especially the parts dealing with advertising; and that they continued to fight social security even when the tax was set lower than 5%.

The enemies of public health displayed themselves during the various pure food and drug bill hearings, but inasmuch as they included both the magazine and newspaper press, there was no one to laugh at them, to criticize, to denounce them as "un-American."

In case there was any doubt about what their editorial policy should be, the National Publishers' Association sent every magazine in the country a directive in 1933 saying:

> "The directors of the NPA Inc., realizing that there is imminent danger in the passage of the socalled Tugwell measure as embodied in Senator Copeland's Bill S. 1944, are definitely opposed to it in its present form."

The special NPA committee formed to protect "publishers' interests"—their only interests were money, via advertising, and these interests were in direct opposition to public interests —included the Curtis Company's Fred A. Healy; the Crowell firm was represented by Lee Maxwell; the Luce interests by R. L. Johnson; and spokesman for the publishers was the representative of the *Ladies' Home Journal,* Charles Coolidge Parlin, who thought that by insisting on calling it the Tugwell Bill, at a time the press had red-baited Tugwell, half the battle to destroy it was won. A great part of the campaign was to say the bill would "sovietize" America.

Mr. Hearst's contribution to the campaign was to use not only his *Good Housekeeping* magazine and his *American Druggist,* but to found a new publication, *Drug World,* all devoted to cooperating with the NPA, the Proprietary Association and the NAM members fighting public welfare. Here again, as has been shown elsewhere in the text and will be shown in future chapters, all the powerful elements were leagued against the public.

One of the men who told the truth—in a book some time

later—was Kenneth Crawford (then a leading liberal journalist, later a reactionary, now a member of the staff of a magazine, *Newsweek,* belonging to the NAM-NPA set-up) who wrote ("The Pressure Boys," p. 83):

"The National Publishers' Association, trade association of the slick magazines, the American Newspaper Publishers Association, whose time is spent protecting the freedom of the press to do what it pleases, regardless of the public welfare, the National Editorial Association, which does the same thing for the weeklies, and many individual journalists did their bit against the Tugwell Bill. Among the most effective of the individuals was David Lawrence, publisher of the *United States News,* who dutifully spread the propaganda that the bill would require a doctor's prescription for the simplest household remedy. Anna Steese Richardson, Good Citizenship editor of the *Woman's Home Companion,* made a 12,000-mile lecture tour preaching Proprietary Association doctrine."

The league against the public welfare included both wings of the press, magazine and newspaper, who saw their income hurt if advertising were made as honest as the labels on medicines, and since these editors and publishers controlled the news, the public could not get the facts, let alone organize to protect itself.

The Monopoly investigation pointed out (Monograph 26, p. 183) that "the original Food and Drug Act of 1906" which the corrupt press had fought but not defeated "was amended several times, but no fundamental revision of it was attempted until the Copeland Bill was introduced in 1933." It was the so-called muckraking or free magazine press, led by *Collier's,* which had made possible the Harrison Act in 1906, and it was a corrupt press, now including magazines, which 27 years later tried to kill the laws. Secretary of Agriculture Henry A. Wallace said of one of its provisions that it would "hamstring its administration so as to amount to a practical nullification."

Monograph 26 continues (p. 184): "One of the chief factors involved in this legislation was the very general interest of Congress. . . . Almost every legislator has in his district some interest, aside from consumers, affected by the legislation. The Vick Chemical Co. of North Carolina, and the Lambert Pharmacal Co. of St. Louis, were represented in the crusading zeal of Senators Bailey (N.C.) and Clark (Mo.) to combat bureaucracy. . . .

"Another important factor was the little publicity given to the legislation in the press. Newspapers had apparently been led to believe that it was a menace to advertising. . . .

"Business pressure was brought to bear during consideration of the Food and Drug Act to maintain the value of advertising to business, without regard to the consumer's interest."

Significantly enough the Monograph, which names the Proprietary Association, two senators, the conspiracy of silence on the part of the newspapers, fails to mention the magazine press at all, not from lack of courage but from lack of knowledge, confirming my statements that the NPA, in contrast to the NAM and the ANPA, aims at secrecy.

In concluding its study of the pressure group, however, the TNEC recognized its powers. "In these fields," it said, "as in others, the superior resources of business place it in a strategic position, and it is difficult for farmers, consumers, and even small distributors to imprint their own desires on public policy. Here as in other segments of public policy, the electorate needs the facts, if it is not to be unduly influenced by the superior show of strength from business."

CHAPTER 6

THE MORGAN HOUSE AND MAGAZINES

THE MOST INTERESTING FACT which can be discovered in any investigation of ownership and control of the great magazines of the United States is the powerful participation of the House of Morgan.

It is apparent from the evidence available that great financial interests are confident that they can control the newspaper press through various means, but that the magazine press is not so easily manipulated, and nothing but hidden financing is strong enough to direct the policies of this once great liberal means of public communication and enlightenment.

This attitude on the part of the several banking houses now in the magazine business is no doubt the result of the great fight between the "vested interests" and the public welfare which took place in what is generally known as the muckraking era. It was the magazine press, and not the majority of newspapers, which from the turn of the century to the end of the First World War produced for the amazement of the American people, the most sensational and documented series of exposés of corruption in the nation's history.

When it began it had the sponsorship of all people who had the general welfare at heart, but as the probes went deeper and further, and seemed to spare none of the hidden powers, the politicians as well as other spokesmen for money, business and profiteering, turned savagely upon the really free press and destroyed it.

Theodore Roosevelt tried to do it with one word. The "progressive" who had at first aided the courageous journalists and investigators, now denounced them as "muckrakers," and the venal newspaper press, which had previously abdicated its only reason for existence—the duty to print the news—now turned upon the magazines, which had supplanted them in this work and heaped muck upon them, repeating TR's quotation from Pilgrim's Progress ad infinitum. A dissenting opinion was expressed by the governor of New York (and later Chief Justice of the Supreme Court). Charles Evans Hughes said:

"When there is muck to be raked, it must be raked, and the public must know of it, that it may mete out justice. . . .

"Publicity is a great purifier because it sets in motion the forces of public opinion, and in this country public opinion controls the courses of the nation." (From an address to the Manufacturers' Association, 1906.)

Every underhand device was used by the financial and industrial masters of America to destroy the magazine or muckraking or free press. Bank loans were called, paper supply was stopped, publications were bought outright or their owners somehow bribed, and every inducement, financial and otherwise, was offered many of the investigators to cease and desist. Suits were filed to harass publishers, the United States Post Office was enlisted by the corporations and their bankers to help destroy the magazines, and even President Taft became a party to this undertaking. Louis Filler in his "Crusaders for American Liberalism" concludes:

> "The movement to put a stop to exposure was systematically begun by those who felt that they could no longer tolerate interference in their affairs . . . the destruction of the magazines was deliberately planned and accomplished in short order—in the case of individual organs, within a few months.
>
> "It was not enough for the trusts to develop private publicity bureaus, nor even to influence the independent press. So long as the muckrakers were at large and had a forum, they were dangerous—more dangerous than the Socialists, who scorned reform."

Wall Street, the trusts, "frenzied finance," both houses of Congress, robbery of the people, the Rockefeller Standard Oil conspiracy, the despoliation of the natural resources of the nation, were subjects for the magazines, and were without question more important than two comprehensive series of exposés which appeared in *Collier's,* "the national weekly": the patent medicine swindle—which had corrupted the newspapers—and the exposé of the *newspapers* themselves. But, in attacking the corrupt press *Collier's* may have done a bolder thing than *Everybody's*, *Hampton's*, *The Arena*, *Metropolitan*, *McClure's*, *Cosmopolitan*, *The Ladies' Home Journal*, *Harper's Weekly*, and all the other famous rivals, all now dead or silenced.

The United States reeked with corruption; the newspaper press had failed the people, and the reason obviously was control via advertising, by the covert—and overt—powers. The muckraking era was eight years old when *Collier's* in 1910 published its series on the daily newspapers—the first such action in the country's history.

The patent medicine exposé started in 1905. On November 4th, *Collier's* in an article titled, "The Contract of Silence" indicated that the press of America was corrupt, inasmuch as at least 99% of it had sold out to the makers of poisonous or useless patent medicines. The contract referred to was a simple little clause which appeared in red ink on the advertising contracts of cough and consumption cures, and even cancer cures. It said simply:

> "It is mutually agreed that this contract is void, if any law is enacted by our State restricting or prohibiting the manufacture or sale of proprietary medicines."

The press saw to it that no laws were passed.

It should also be noted that the journalist who obtained a copy of this contract, which according to President F. J. Cheney of the Proprietary Medicine Association made of the press a legislative tool of the quack medicine trust, was young Mark Sullivan of the *Ladies' Home Journal*. That writer has now become the mouthpiece of the most reactionary forces in the country, and the magazine is now owned by the Curtis Publishing Company.

Collier's passed into the hands of the Crowell Publishing Company which then had as one of its directors the head of the press, publicity and public relations department of the House of Morgan: Thomas W. Lamont. This was the first step of the Morgan firm into the publishing field. Since then, the firm has taken many others.

Very little has been said about this, naturally, since it is apparent that there exist few avenues for the publication of either facts or criticisms of this situation. Perhaps the most incisive, complete and bitter report is that of the noted iconoclast of the world of education, Porter Sargent, who in his privately printed book, "What Makes Lives," devotes a great number of pages to the power of the Morgan house in politics, the colleges, and the press. Of the present head of the Morgan empire he writes:

"Mr. Lamont, having stepped into the shoes of Charles Perkins, the first publicity man for Morgan, has since that time had much to do with the printed word. Newspapers, magazines, publishing houses, have been bought into, their policies changed. Books about to be published have been modified or censored. Walter Millis' 'Road to War' before publication was purged of the part Morgan played. The September, 1939, issue of *Harper's*, dealing with international topics, led to a call-down from the banker directors, and the publication of many pro-British and reactionary articles followed. Writers of books, once bold and free, are now cautious and avoid interference which they know would come. Such writers find a ready market for their wares. Those who do not conform seldom find publishers.

"All this is a tendency of the times, in which many have participated and which perhaps is supported by public opinion. But no man in the country has been more influential in determining editorial and publishing and educational policies these past twenty years than Thomas Lamont. He will prove a most interesting subject for some future biographer who can trace the influences upon him from Charles Perkins, and his influences through his partners, colleagues, friends, on boards of publications, philanthropic foundations, educational establishments. He has had position, opportunity, to influence the minds of the present generation through what was taught and read as almost no other man." (Pages 171-2)

"From a mere newspaper reporter, Lamont has come to perhaps the most influential place in the country, brains of the House of Morgan. . . .

"From the Crowell Publishing Company, Mr. Lamont testified, he wants only dividends. From Harvard he expects no dividends, of course, except the feeling of prestige and influence, and the knowledge that he is keeping things safe for the kind of democracy he approves. Some might call it plutocracy. . . .

"Mr. Lamont has played so influential a part in the financial, publishing and educational activities of the country during the past quarter century that we may regard him as a symbol of our times. . . .

"If we are to understand how our mental content is as it is, why we know certain things and are ignorant of others, why what we call our opinions are as they are, it is necessary to understand how the information that has come to us has been controlled, why certain kinds of facts have been withheld or slightly twisted.

"As publicity man for the House of Morgan and the whole system that they stand for, Mr. Lamont found it desirable and necessary to protect that system by controlling what is published and taught. He and those who have been inspired, employed, or instigated by him, and others who stand for the same thing, have been effective in so doing.

"So the muckrakers were suppressed, the newspapers were reduced, brought into safe hands, writers were controlled, books privately censored, publishing houses bought into and influenced, peace societies and philanthropic and educational foundations linked up with financial houses and the universities by interlocking directorates, our university teachers kept looking forward to pensions, young recalcitrants dismissed or set in their places, the preparatory schools dominated." (Page 202)

While the House of Morgan was represented on the Board of Directors of the Crowell Publishing Company two of the greatest and most powerful magazines of the muckraking era, *Collier's* and *The American,* changed their policies. (The other Crowell publications were *Woman's Home Companion* and the defunct *Country Home*—like the Curtis firm it also had its woman's magazine and its farm magazine.) The three popular magazines now published by the firm have a circulation of a little under 10,000,000 and therefore about 50,000,000 readers, which is a majority of the literate adult public of the country.

CHAPTER 7

MORGAN EMPIRE AND LUCE EMPIRE

AFTER THE MUCKRAKING ERA, the new owners of the magazines formulated a new policy: the magazine press must be made a safe and sane agency for the propaganda of big business, the bankers, the employers, the status quo, reaction, and what later became known as "free enterprise." In other words, the new bosses ordered a complete reversal of policy.

The best known illustrations of influencing it are that of the campaign of the National Electric Light Association, which spent $25,000,000 a year informing the American people that private ownership of power and light was to its benefit; and the annual campaigns of the National Association of Manufacturers, each costing several million dollars. In both instances documentary evidence has shown that "canned" editorials and even "canned" news items went along with the advertising, and that the American people were fooled—not a few all the time, or all a part of the time, but all the people all the time. In this job of fooling the people the magazine press did even a better job for its masters than the newspaper press.

Under the new policy of making the press a defense agency of money and power, the House of Morgan extended itself into more and more powerful magazines. But the greatest stroke of luck it ever had was with the newsweekly *Time*—and the successive Luce publications, *Fortune* and *Life*.

In 1923 two comparatively penniless journalists, Henry Luce and Briton Hadden, presented a brilliant plan to people with money. E. Roland Harriman approved and so did Harvey Firestone; the Harkness family put up some money; so did Dwight Morrow, one of the Morgan partners; but another Morgan partner, H. P. Davison, was one of the most enthusiastic backers. Luce and Haddon raised only $86,000 to get out the first issue of *Time,* and it was mostly Wall Street and reactionary talking money.

Time's statement of ownership, required by the United States Post Office, shows that in 1935 among the owners of 1% or more of stock were:

Henry P. Davison, 23 Wall Street, New York
Edith H. Harkness and William H. Harkness
Estate of Briton Hadden
Henry R. Luce (See Appendix 14 for full list)

The 1939 sworn statement is somewhat different. It includes:

Brown Bros., Harriman & Co., 59 Wall Street, New York
J. P. Morgan & Co. (Account of Henry P. Davison)
New York Trust Co. (Accounts of Edith and William Harkness)

The other Luce enterprises show the same ownership. For example, the statement filed by *Life* includes Brown Bros., Harriman & Co.; J. P. Morgan & Co., for the account of Henry P. Davison, and the usual names.

Although published annually, apparently these statements are not read by the public, and rumors circulate. Letters by the score arrived at *Time's* office questioning the Morgan interest, and *Time* was forced to explain (in 1937) in its Letters-to-the-Editor department, as follows:

"In 1922 (before *Time* was published) and in 1925, Time Inc. raised a total of $148,000 by the sale of preferred and common stock. Of this amount Mr. Harry P. Davison subscribed something less than $10,000. Since then the preferred shares in question have been retired, Mr. Davison has become a Morgan partner and his common shares have been registered in the name of J. P. Morgan & Co. for the account of Henry P. Davison. His holdings amount to less than 3% of Time Inc. stock now outstanding. Some 54% is owned by its editors, writers, business staff and their immediate families.—Ed."

The small investment of the Harrimans, Harknesses, Brown Bros., and the Morgan partners in the Luce publications paid dividends equal to a strike in gold or oil. In 1936 *Time* grossed $12,900,000 and had a net profit of $2,700,000. In 1940 *Time's* net was about $5,000,444. Members of the editorial staff, however, wrote me that "Luce is nobody's stooge. Of course *Time* will never do anything against the interests of the House of Morgan, but then neither will most other magazines without a penny of Morgan money in them."

This view, from inside the *Time* office, is confirmed by facts which have been revealed and by any study of the actual text of the three major magazines Luce publishes. Any reader can do what the writer has done: look through the pages of *Time, Life* and *Fortune* for all references to the House of Morgan and compare them to established facts.

Nothing in the history of the Morgan Empire has been as sensational as the evidence produced by the Nye-Vandenberg investigation into the munitions industry implicating the great banking house in America's entry into the First World War. And nothing in the history of the Luce publications so reveals their effort to protect Morgan as their treatment of the news on this subject—from 1934 even to the present time.

On December 14, 1934, shortly after it had gotten under way, the munitions investigation committee, headed by Senators Nye and Vandenberg, produced the most damning document in modern history relating to the influence of bankers and war. It was the cable sent to President Wilson by the American ambassador to England, Walter Hines Page; it was dated March 5, 1917, almost exactly a month to a day before the declaration of war by the United States; and its most important paragraphs were:

> "The inquiries which I have made here about financial conditions disclose an international situation which is most alarming to the financial and industrial outlook of the United States."
>
> "If the United States declares war against Germany, the greatest help we could give Great Britain and the Allies would be such credit. . . . A great advantage would be that all the money would be kept in the United States. We could keep on with our trade and increase it, till the war ends."
>
> "On the other hand, if we keep nearly all the gold . . . there may be a worldwide panic."
>
> "Of course we cannot extend such a credit unless we go to war with Germany."
>
> "The pressure of this approaching crisis, I am certain, has gone beyond the ability of the Morgan financial agency for the British and French governments."
>
> "It is not improbable that the only way of maintaining our

present preeminent trade position and averting a panic is by declaring war on Germany." (For full text, *see* Appendix 8.)

A large part of the American press suppressed the news of the Page cablegram calling for a declaration of war in protection of the Morgan loans.

Beginning on its first news page, issue of December 24, 1934, *Time* reported to the extent of more than four columns on the munitions investigation. Its heading was "War-Without-Profit." There was no mention whatever of the Page cable. As for the banking house which was one of its owners, *Time* reported:

> "The (Nye-Vandenberg) Committee was out to regain its lost ground by making new sensations. Senator Nye decided to grab a sure-fire headline getter when he announced he would investigate J. P. Morgan & Co. because 'no exhaustive study of the munitions business is possible without a knowledge of its financial agency.'"

When Mr. Morgan finally came to the hearings it was 1936, and *Time* devoted seven columns to his defense. This was accomplished largely through the style in which its report was written: it began by saying the Committee had "set out to prove, if possible, that the United States had gone to war in 1917 because Wall Street's international bankers needed United States troops in the field to secure repayment of their Allied loans." It reported Senator Norris saying that "gold" was taking us into the war but countered that "when the history of 1914-18 was written it said plainly that the United States went to war because German submarines sank United States ships without warning, killing United States citizens," pretending that this childish statement was real history. Then it mentioned historian Walter Millis' charge: "The mighty stream of supplies . . . the corresponding stream of prosperity . . . the United States was enmeshed more deeply than ever in the cause of Allied victory." It then sneered at "any stumpster" who sought to accuse the bankers and change history. It called the Morgan issue "a scandalous question," concluded that "yesterday's scandal like yesterday's news, is hard to revive," but did not print the Page cable. Instead it devoted the major part of its seven columns to quoting and defending Morgan and other bankers.

From that day on, *Time* never has lost an opportunity to return to the subject, always defending Morgan and always attacking the investigation. Here are some sample *Time* paragraphs:

July 17, 1939: "The Nye Committee pumped J. P. Morgan, Thomas Lamont and their partners, trying to prove that they had helped to grease the skids that plunged the United States into war. There was no evidence that they had tried to."

September 4, 1939: "To hang any large part of the 'blame' on J. P. Morgan & Co. seems to *Time* to be first class politics and third rate history." (This is reply to a protest that its July item was a falsehood.)

November 6, 1939: "When Isolationist Nye of North Dakota made his third speech, Byrnes signaled for the attack himself, with an assault on Nye's recent change-of-front on the responsibility of J. P. Morgan & Co. for World War I." (Also quoted Senator Minton attacking Nye for making "more from his lectures on munitions than duPont has made.")

May 20, 1940: ". . . Uncle Sam became Uncle Shylock, the country heard that the holy crusade had been waged to make good J. P. Morgan's loans, that Our Buddies were the pawns of the munitions-makers, that the Road to War was paved with baloney . . ."

Finally, when the second J. P. Morgan died in 1943, *Time* as well as the rest of the press joined in a eulogy which of course suppressed facts of importance. The Hearst *Journal-American* and the rest of the chain, then in the hands of the bankers because of failure to pay interest on its bonds (now paid off), published a 6-column picture on an 8-column page; the *New York Times,* which alone among papers rivaled *Time* in Morgan sycophancy, devoted 8 columns to the obituary, and *Time,* March 22, gave Morgan three pages of praise. It failed to mention the Page cable, the Nye-Vandenberg disclosures, or the Morgan loan to Italy which saved Fascism in 1925, and other little news items of perhaps some interest. But it did say (under a self-conscious headline "NO BUCCANEER"):

"The United States for two decades had largely believed in a fairy tale of Marxist origin—the legend that international bankers sucked the nation into a war which was none of its business. . . ."

"Fairy tale" and "legend" are of course propaganda words, and "Marxist origin" is the old red-baiting technique by which truth is destroyed, by which Mussolini floated the Morgan loan, and by which six million men were murdered by Hitler.

The truth is that every historian has taken cognizance of the disclosures made by the investigating committee, not only the Page cable, but all the documents left behind by William Jennings Bryan, Newton Baker, Woodrow Wilson and other leading actors in the tragic drama of 1917. America's greatest historians, Charles and Mary Beard, and all the rest, are agreed that the Nye-Vandenberg findings, and not the propaganda paragraphs in *Time* and the *New York Times*, constitute true history.

Walter Millis: "American industry and finance, led by the Morgan firm . . . devoted themselves to extending the economic complex which tended . . . to thrust the nation more and more deeply into an economic alliance with the Entente and consequently nearer and nearer to war with Germany." (Note that another Millis paragraph and not this one was used by *Time*.)

Charles A. Beard: "We were confronting the alternatives of a domestic crash and a foreign war, when we entered the war."

William E. Woodward ("A New American History"): "By gradual and successive developments we were drawn into a war which was purely European in character, and which had no point of contact with American affairs, except insofar as American interests were represented by profiteers in war supplies and the lenders of money to Germany's enemies."

Dr. Harry Elmer Barnes (to the present writer): "You are entirely right about the bankers and the First World War."

(His documentation on this subject appears in "War in the Twentieth Century," pp. 77-80.)

No historian or fair-minded journalist would try to make a personal devil of J. P. Morgan & Co. (any more than any honest historian or journalist could whitewash the bankers, as *Time* has tried to do). The Nye Committee itself (as summed up in the *New York Times)* saw a larger reason for our entry into the war: "The financial interdependence between this country and the Allies, evidenced by loans amounting to $7,077,000,000 before the United States entered the war, forced its entry into the war." The *New Republic* (July 1, 1936) summed up the facts: "Essentially the Committee finds that the Morgans held a key position to influence government policy during the years of our own neutrality and used that position not to 'drag us in' but to steer us bit by bit into a situation from which there was no way out but war." Even more brief is the editorial statement of the *New York Post* (January 8, 1936): "We weren't 'forced' into the war by those (Morgan) loans. But we WERE drawn in by the economic circumstances of which those loans were a symbol."

Time's reportage on the House of Morgan for twenty years has been neither accurate history nor straightforward journalism. It has been propaganda, whitewash for the House of Morgan, one of its owners throughout all the years of its existence.

It would not be incorrect to say that *Time*—and *Life, Fortune, The March of Time,* and each and every Luce production—works for the Morgan Empire every day in the year. It is in every way part of the same free enterprise system, and although not controlled by a Morgan agent sitting at a desk in its office, it has a community of interest with the rest of the "$30,210,000,000 worth of United States railroads, utilities, industries, banks" which are under the Morgan-First National influence (as *Time* itself reported February 26, 1940). Both are parts of a system which they watch, nurture and expand, and which they speak for.

The illustrations of open propaganda and apologetics,

dictated or not dictated by Mr. Lamont, "the foreign ambassador of the House of Morgan," are many, but they merely highlight the relationship.

As, for instance, the "Wall Street Plot to Seize the Government."

The documentary evidence, which is referred to elsewhere, was pretty well suppressed by the newspapers, but the predecessor of the Dies Committee—the McCormack-Dickstein Committee—eventually confirmed the most sensational charges, concluded that there had been a plot and that certain American Legion leaders and well-known men of Wall Street, one closely connected with the House of Morgan, had indeed planned the first American fascist dictatorship.

At the mention of the magic name "Morgan" the Luce publications mobilized in defense. Everything from distortion to the usual "light touch" of the famous "bright young men" of the Luce employ, the usual sneers and the usual adjectival barrage by men well trained in semantics, came into play to protect the most sacred cow worshiped in America, the Big Money for which J. P. Morgan was first high priest.

For example (*Time's* first and second page story, December 3, 1934):

"PLOT WITHOUT PLOTTERS"

(There follows a bright little imaginary story of General Smedley Butler mobilizing 500,000 men, capturing Washington, the United States becoming a fascist state.)

"Such was the nightmarish page of future United States history pictured last week in Manhattan by General Butler himself to the special House Committee investigating Un-American Activities.

"No military officer of the United States since the late tempestuous George Custer has succeeded in publicly floundering in so much hot water as Smedley Darlington Butler. . . .

[There follows a history of episodes in Butler's life, told as if they were all planned for publicity.]

"General Butler's sensational tongue had not been heard in the nation's Press for more than a week when he cornered a reporter for the *Philadelphia Record* and the *New York Post,* poured into his ears the lurid tale that he had been offered leadership of a Fascist Putsch scheduled for next year. . . . .

"Thanking their stars for having such sure-fire publicity dropped in their laps, Representatives McCormack and Dickstein began calling witnesses to expose the 'plot.' But there did not seem to be any plotters. . . .

"Mr. Morgan, just off a boat from Europe, had nothing to say but Partner Lamont did: 'Perfect moonshine! Too utterably ridiculous to comment upon! ! . . . ."

Any reader comparing the testimony and the Committee report on this event, given in the appendix of this book, must conclude that the *Time* report consists of distortion and propaganda.

The case of the House of Morgan and World War I and the handling of the conspiracy uncovered by General Butler, and their treatment by *Time,* and other Luce publications, are but two of scores of instances illustrating the community of interest which exists between the banking house and the Luce press. The amount of stock all the men of Wall Street own in the Luce publications may be only a small percentage, but it pays a dividend which cannot be measured in dollars only.

The Luce press, like the entire big magazines press, angles the news—and therefore angles public opinion in America for the community of big business interests of which it is an important journalistic part.

CHAPTER 8

THE MORGAN EMPIRE: PRESS RELATIONS

IN 1923, long before he became head of the Morgan Empire, Thomas W. Lamont, its more or less secret prime minister, paid an income tax of $847,820. During the making of the Versailles Treaty, Lamont was a member of the Reparations Commission, an appointee of President Wilson's.

In 1925, visiting Rome, Lamont said (to Hiram Motherwell, of the *Chicago Daily News*): "It would be a lot easier to float a ton of lead in New York harbor than an Italian loan in Wall Street." All dictatorships were dangerous risks, Mr. Lamont stated (off the record) "and this one in particular, because it is a one-man show." He pointed out that Great Britain had never floated an Italian loan after Mussolini came to power "because the British bankers are careful and conservative."

Almost immediately afterwards Mr. Lamont's firm floated the $100,000,000 loan which saved Mussolini and Fascismo.

Mr. Lamont himself was able to write in defense:

"Ask any traveller. . . . When the present regime came into power towards the end of 1922, Italy seemed to be tottering on the brink below which lay communism and bolshevism. The industrial system had become badly disorganized through an epidemic of strikes, with workers seizing control of the factories, and with widespread unemployment. There had been a virtual breakdown of railroad and other government services and of civil and judicial procedure. Municipal administration as well was burdened with incompetence and extravagance. The finances of the central government were unsound; government debt was piling up and the deficits in the government's budget were increasing. . . .

"Considerable currency has been given to stories that the Italian government has distorted its account of revenues and expenditures and by some method of transferring charges to municipal accounts, has manufactured the surpluses which it has reported. These stories may be denied absolutely. I am satisfied that the central government exercises close supervision over municipal budgets and municipal financing, and that the improvement in municipal finance has measurably paralleled that in central Government finance. . . .

"That the government's budget is in fact balanced and has been for the past two and a half years, there is not the slightest doubt." (*Survey,* March 1, 1927.)

The very opposite was stated by none other than Mr. Mussolini himself who wrote (in his *Popolo d'Italia,* July 2, 1921) that "Bolshevism is conquered" and had not existed more than a year before the "March" on Rome. And Professor Salvemini, using official fascist documents, has proved the Mussolini budgets fraudulent from 1922 on.

Nevertheless, from 1925 to at least the day Mussolini, in the words of President Roosevelt, stabbed us in the back, the American people believed that the Duce had saved his country from the reds and was therefore deserving of American sympathy and Morgan money.

The opinion of the American people was directed as plainly as Mussolini himself directed public opinion in his own dictatorship. No daily dictatorial orders were given, but somehow the newspapers and the magazines and other forces which push people around were able to create and keep alive the "bolshevik myth" to the benefit of the House of Morgan.

In the *Saturday Evening Post* of May 29, 1926, the investigators will find the leading article entitled "After Mussolini—What?" by Isaac F. Marcosson, one of the first of threescore and ten American journalists who have written in favor of Fascism or Fascist leaders in the columns of this leading periodical of the Big Business system. It is most likely that neither the National Association of Manufacturers, nor the editor, nor Mr. Lamont himself, as much as suggested to Mr. Marcosson that a good rousing piece in favor of Mussolini would help preserve the Morgan myth and steady the Morgan bonds, nevertheless the evidence shows that the pro-fascist articles filled the pages of this magazine from 1922 on. (Latest propagandist for a Fascist dictator is Henry J. Taylor who in the *Saturday Evening Post* of August 19, 1944, wrote the same sort of stuff which Marcosson wrote in 1926, but this time the hero was the Duce of Portugal, Salazar.)

Another leading *Saturday Evening Post* writer, then known as Kenneth L. Roberts (and now better known as Kenneth Roberts, the novelist who has glorified American Tories and denigrated the American Revolution and the common people who fought alongside George Washington) wrote that "the Fascist movement" "was a greatly needed movement" because "it saved the nation from descending into a chaotic whirlpool of Communism." Mussolini was absolutely sincere and honest. "Mussolini's dictatorship is a good dictatorship."

The Rome bureaus of the Associated Press, largest news service of the Americas, the *New York Times,* most powerful paper in the country, the *Daily Mail,* the most powerful mass circulation British newspaper, and other vast avenues of public information were in the hands of the Cortesi family, who were personnae gratae to the Fascists. All members united in building up the Morgan myth. The House of Morgan itself used its own publicity department to propagate the great red-baiting falsehood that in 1922 Mussolini had defeated Communism, and was therefore worthy of financial aid. There is no doubt that the Morgan myth replaced authentic history.

Lamont took a loss of $2,000,000 in publishing the *New York Evening Post,* the one daily newspaper the House of Morgan has ever owned. Mr. Lamont also lost money on the *Saturday Review of Literature* (now in other hands). It was the opinion of the editor of *Editor & Publisher,* Arthur Robb, that the financing of the *Saturday Review of Literature* "has for nearly two decades given Morgan a strategic foothold in the book publishing," but publishers insist that although it might have been a foothold, it was certainly not strategic. Mr. Robb also wrote that "Lamont is also cited as a director of Crowell Publishing Co. and as a silent manipulator of the press, who can get almost anything he wants put in or kept out of newspapers." Mr. Robb, professional apologist of the press, did not deny this but stated: "That, of necessity, rests on assertion." (*Editor & Publisher,* January 22, 1938.)

It was during the Lamont ownership of *Saturday Review of Literature* that a disclosure was made which shocked the book publishing world.

Two sensational books exposing the munitions makers ("Merchants of Death" by Engelbrecht and Hanaghen, and "Iron, Blood and Profits," by George Seldes) had been written before the Senate Committee produced the Page cable which mentioned the Morgan loans to Britain.

The demand for a more up-to-date book was met by Rose Stein with her "M-Day," written under contract with Harcourt, Brace & Co., a leading publisher. Miss Stein not only quoted the Page cable but devoted many paragraphs to the House of Morgan, its Mr. Harry Davison (who had helped Henry Luce finance *Time)* and its Mr. Lamont, and the part loans played in bringing America into the war.

In the protest against a review written by Walter Millis, one of the many American writers who has followed the usual aging route of left to right, Miss Stein, remarking on his charge that she had used material which had not yet been placed on the public record, declared:

"It so happens that Thomas W. Lamont of J. P. Morgan & Co., in one of his several attempts to block publication of 'M-Day,' made the same charge."

The matter was taken up with the publisher who, in filing a disclaimer of an attempt to block publication, said in part:

"The publication of 'M-Day' was delayed about 4 weeks because of questions raised concerning it by Mr. Lamont, but it would not be correct to say that Mr. Lamont attempted to *block* publication of the book. Through the editorial offices of a New York publication, one of whose staff turned to Mr. Lamont as to one well acquainted with this field of literature for advice concerning the book, Mr. Lamont saw a set of galley proofs of 'M-Day.' After two preliminary telephone calls, raising certain questions concerning the book, Mr. Lamont, at our request, sent us a memorandum outlining his findings in 'M-Day.' His memorandum did not deal with the questions raised over the telephone but called attention to facts and statements in the book which he considered inaccurate and misleading. His written communication was, of course, a private one, similar to communications we frequently receive which call attention to alleged inaccuracies in a publication. After consulting with Miss Stein we published 'M-Day' March 19.

Charles A. Pearce,
Harcourt, Brace & Co." *

It is not unusual for publishers to submit page proofs to interested parties, friends or enemies. But in this case it was not Harcourt Brace which sent "M-Day" to Mr. Lamont. The editorial staff of the *Saturday Review of Literature* had received the proofs for the purpose of writing an advance review, but inasmuch as Mr. Lamont was the owner of the magazine he was able to get the proofs delivered to him instead of the hired reviewer.

Even more intriguing than the sympathetic ties of *Time, Life* and *Fortune* with the Morgan Empire is the journalism of the *New York Times*. The 3% interest, apologists can say, did not dictate the pro-Morgan policy of the Luce publications. But the policy has always been there. On the part of the *New York Times* there is no financial interest whatever; it is a community of interests.

Under both Ochs and Sulzberger the American thunderer has been more of a mouthorgan playing the tunes Morgan likes than even *Time*. And like the Luce publications, when the test came during the Nye investigation, the *Times* much more crudely, much more blatantly and much more carelessly than *Time* went to the defense and apology of the banker. The *Times* said that the senatorial inquiry had exonerated the House of Morgan and in reply Senator Nye declared that the olympian *Times* had published a falsehood. He demanded a retraction, and being a Senator he was able to get space for his reply.

The *Times* then gave over its letter columns to Mr. Lamont, who took on one and all of the critics of Morgan. At least, it did seem so to daily readers.

Actually, one of the facts not mentioned in Lamont's reply was the September 5, 1919, speech by President Wilson in which he admitted that the First World War was "an in-

* *The Nation*, April 15, 1936.

dustrial and commercial war" (*See* Appendix 9), a fact almost unknown to the American public although it had actually appeared in the text of the speech in the columns of the *Times* itself. There was great debate over a matter about which there could be no question at all, and my letter to the *Times* so informed the paper, as all it would have to do to end the controversy was to look into itself, issue of September the 6th, 1919, page 2, column 4. And having a forewarning that the *Times, w*hose face was black with the Morgan shoepolish, as Heywood Broun so often remarked, would not refer to historical truth because it would shed a certain light upon Mr. Lamont's propaganda, I asked other people to write in the facts from other towns. But the *Times* continued to let the debate rage in its columns, with Mr. Lamont always having the better of it, of course, because none of the letters revealing the truth was published.

The full story of the *Times*-Morgan-Lamont episode is told in my book, "Lords of the Press." Unfortunately, I could not there nor can I here give the text of an exchange of letters between Mr. Lamont and myself concerning my comment on the Page cable and President Wilson's St. Louis declarations. Mr. Lamont's letters are marked "personal." The important thing about the matter is that Mr. Lamont took up the subject with me, just as apparently he has taken up this and other subjects dealing critically with the House of Morgan with book writers, newspaper writers and others who may influence public thinking.

When Robert L. Duffus, a staff writer of the *Times,* reviewed Harold Nicholson's life of Dwight Morrow, a Morgan partner, remarking incidentally that "the financiers actually made us an ally of the Allies while we were still officially neutral" and that Morrow, in "helping to draw the country into the European war . . . had a part in decivilizing the world," Mr. Lamont protested, and of course the *Times* gave him all the space he wanted, as it has done frequently, and let him have the final word, as it does usually.

The fact that other daily newspapers are more sensitive

to the wishes of Lamont and the Morgan fortunes than the *New York Times* is understandable. Many are more in need of advertising or other support which Morgan can give, and can therefore not afford to be as critical. The *New York Sun,* for example, debased itself much more than the *Times* in reporting the Nye Committee findings, but the *Sun* is not only the mouthpiece of Wall Street, it was (and may still be) tied to the corporations through a huge mortgage (as a result of the Munsey will). Its financial editor, Franz Schneider, was on the Morgan preferred list; he was let in on the "ground floor," permitted to buy new flotations at less than their market value, a recipient of a cash present from Morgan but not a bribe.

As for the Crowell Publishing Co., it was as late as November 9, 1946, that Editor Chenery devoted a whole page to an indignant reply to charges of Morgan control of the firm. He concluded:

"The only item of fact in the malicious canard is that Thomas W. Lamont, a Morgan partner, is a minority stockholder."

Thirteen years earlier some surprise was occasioned in writing and publishing circles by the disclosure of Morgan participation in the Crowell firm, but ever since then it has been common knowledge that Mr. Lamont has had his say in the direction of Crowell and all its magazines.

Shortly after a Senate investigation named Mr. Lamont as a director of the house which published four popular magazines which then had a circulation of 8,000,000—or at least 40,000,000 readers—the following additional facts were disclosed:

1. That at the time (1933) Mr. Lamont owned the *Saturday Review of Literature.*

2. That the elder Morgan had installed George Harvey, publisher and politician and known as "the president-maker," as editor of *Harper's Weekly*—Harvey later edited the *North American Review.*

3. That the Morgan preferred list included journalists and public opinion makers.

4. That Mr. Lamont in the pages of *Collier's* wrote a 6-part biography of Morgan partner Davison, which turned into a glorification of the House of Morgan.

Apparently Mr. Davison was a nugatory character, hardly worth one issue of *Collier's,* for the major portion of the biography is devoted to the elder Morgan, omitting of course the entire story of the 5,000 carbines which Morgan sold to the government during the Civil War, the speculation in gold which Lincoln denounced, the corruption of the financial system which resulted in the 1907 panic, and the falsehoods told by the Morgan firm to Theodore Roosevelt by which United States Steel was able to absorb Tennessee Steel. In destroying the myth which Lamont had created in *Collier's*—whose readers did not know the author was also on that magazine's directorate—the liberal *Nation* said of the financier: "He was one of the greatest enemies our society ever had."

Commenting on the use of a publication by a Morgan propagandist, the *Nation* also said: "To hold such a man up to the admiration of the present generation, at this time, is an insult to the intelligence of the American reader. It shows the need of greater vigilance than ever, of keener scrutiny of the forces that directly and indirectly shape public opinion through the press, the magazines, and other means by which ideas are instilled."

When Mr. Lamont became chairman, or head of the Morgan firm, he gave over the job of publicity, press and magazine director, to a certain A. H. Lockett.

This name is the clew to a fact which, so far as this writer knows, has never before been published: the participation of Morgan in the control of *Newsweek,* the rival to *Time* and *The Pathfinder,* in the big money newsweekly field.

As late as 1944, *Newsweek* made no secret of the presence of Lamont's successor, Lockett, on its board of directors. The column listing editorial and business control of December 25, 1939, names the board of directors:

Vincent Astor (head of the Astor fortune, mostly invested in New York real estate), chairman.

W. Averell Harriman (of the railroad and banking Harrimans, of Brown Bros., Harriman & Co., and later Secretary of Commerce).

Malcolm Muir, of McGraw-Hill (publisher of numerous trade and scientific publications, and a leader of the National Association of Manufacturers).

Charles F. Bomer—and A. H. Lockett.

In 1941 the name of W. Averell Harriman disappeared, being replaced by E. Roland Harriman.

In 1943 the name of Vincent Astor disappeared, being replaced by that of Mary Cushing Astor.

In the May 28, 1945, issue, the name of Mr. Lockett is no longer carried. New names appear: T. F. Mueller, Roland L. Redmond; and in August of that year Vincent Astor is again listed as chairman of the board, while the name of Mary Cushing Astor is retained as a member.

No publication in America is so completely owned and controlled by the big money interests as *Newsweek*. And its policy shows it.

In the role of "public relations counsellor" of the Morgan Empire, Mr. Lamont has cultivated practically every leading newspaper man, journalist, magazine writer, novelist and molder of public opinion who showed himself willing to be cultivated. Mr. Lamont's outstanding success is the case of Walter Lippmann, the boy wonder of Harvard, the radical youth leader of his time, the renegade Socialist.

Of America's most noted columnar writer it has been written that after his round-the-world trip on the yacht of Thomas Lamont he came home a changed man. He has never been the same since. Mabel Dodge had said of the boy liberal that "Walter is never, never going to lose an eye in a fight," but it could not be foreseen at the end of the first decade of this century that in the 1930's Lippmann would be espousing "the comfortable idea that we are safe in the arms of Morgan," as Heywood Broun, a fellow Harvard traveler, wrote of his colleague.

Even the magazine *Time* was conscious of certain influences in the life of Lippmann, for after recounting that he was making $54,329 a year and owned three houses, it concluded that he was "more apt to be on intimate terms with Morgan partners, than with union leaders." And there is a certain grim humor in the fact that it was the son of a Morgan partner who wrote: "Walter Lippmann constitutes an American tragedy. Starting out as a radical and a socialist . . . Lippmann ended up by giving over his exceptional gifts to the service of reaction."

The author of this final indictment is Corliss Lamont.

How vast is Mr. Thomas Lamont's power in the American publishing field? This may never be disclosed. The House of Morgan is itself an advertiser, but this is not the sort of advertising which corrupts the American press. The corruption of the American press, the use of America's newspapers and magazines for reaction (and Fascism), as William Allen White pointed out, would come through the advertising agencies because of their new role as social, economic and political advisers to the corporations. Mr. Lamont and the House of Morgan today control not only many of the biggest corporations which advertise, but work through the biggest advertising agencies which are directing the political advertising of big business.

An investigation of the subject, producing volumes of evidence, would require congressional action. Meanwhile, from the obvious documentation, it is certain that Mr. Porter Sargent is understating the situation when he writes:

"No man in the country has been more influential in determining editorial and publishing and educational policies these past twenty years than Thomas Lamont."

CHAPTER 9

THE SEVEN BIG MONTHLY MAGAZINES

THERE ARE a score of magazines in the United States which have a circulation of a million copies or more. We read less books and more magazines per capita than any other civilized country.

The most circulated magazine in the world is *Reader's Digest* with more than 11,000,000 copies sold a month, and probably 50,000,000 readers.

The table of magazine circulation given at the end of this chapter includes the fourteen leading general circulation magazines, according to the advertising weekly, *Tide,* with two additions by the present writer. In the third column of the table is listed ownership, control or affiliation.

It will probably surprise the reader, as it actually surprised the writer when he had concluded his investigations and made this table, to find that with the exception of *Reader's Digest* and *Look,* every big magazine in America is owned or controlled or affiliated with the biggest business interests of the nation, including the House of Morgan and the National Association of Manufacturers.

That the editorial policies of almost every one of the big magazines has been in accordance with the thinking and policy of the thousand men who also control most of America is pretty obvious. The magazine press is no more a free press than the newspaper press.

The Reader's Digest. A great tragic paradox of our time is the *Reader's Digest.* It is not owned by any corporate or corrupting interests, nor does it invite corruption by taking advertising and coming into contact with the public relations propagandists of the multi-millionaire advertising agencies. It is rich, successful, free of all fetters and influences, and nevertheless it is as reactionary a force in America as any publication.

Since I have already told the story of the *Digest* in my book, "Facts and Fascism" (pp. 158-183), I shall not repeat it here. The main fact is that the *Digest* is not a digest. It was originally. Today, as the magazine investigating committee of the National Council of Teachers of English showed documentarily in its huge report (which was suppressed), the majority of *Digest* articles are either "originals" produced by *Digest* editors, or their editors' articles planted elsewhere, or sundry items purchased by the *Digest* and planted in other magazines so that it can say it skims the cream from all others, digests it for the public. The political, anti-labor, reactionary, controversial and pro-big business articles which fill a large part of *Reader's Digest* are nearly always originated by the *Digest.*

If the *Digest* honestly had remained a digest, it could still have had an editorial policy, evidenced by the items it selected to reprint. This would have been more difficult to criticize. But, as it is now run, its claim to being impartial is an insult to all honest people.

The policy of *Reader's Digest* has always been anti-labor, always reactionary. It was not until *In Fact* exposed the magazine in 1942 that its owner, DeWitt Wallace, took pains to introduce an occasional article by a labor leader, notably Philip Murray, or even a rare honest liberal, all for the purpose of confusing people who had protested. The DeWitt Wallace policy is similar to that of the French restaurant-keeper who also protested a belief in the equalitarian 50-50 principle: in making a stew for his customers he used one rabbit—and one horse.

Scientific and elaborate studies have been made of the contents of the *Digest,* year after year. The pro- and anti-labor articles have been counted, measured for space, for passion. College students, teachers, scientists have engaged in this work, and the result has always been the same: the *Digest* has been found to have a decided editorial policy, just as any commercial magazine; it has been found to favor the ruling minority, spearheaded by the United States Chamber of Commerce and the NAM, and that it has never been fair to the vast liberal, democratic American majority.

The most elaborate study of *Reader's Digest* was made by the National Council of Teachers of English, which was deeply interested because the *Digest* is used in thousands of high schools of the nation.

More than a year was spent on research, with hundreds of teachers participating. The most important conclusion reached by the NCTE was that the *Digest* is not a digest."

This conclusion is important because the basis for use of this magazine in the schools is its claim to digesting the magazines of the country. If it is not a digest, it has no reason for special favor in the halls of learning.

The National Council of Teachers of English discovered that the majority of articles in the *Digest* either originated in the editorial offices of the magazines, or were bought and "planted" in other magazines, then reprinted. The report begins by stating that it will present no conclusions, but this is an instance where the facts speak for themselves very clearly.

The report shows that the magazine most favored for "digesting" is the *American Mercury*. The *Mercury* was at one time edited by Paul Palmer, now a *Digest* editor, and Lawrence E. Spivak, who remained as editor when Eugene Lyons took Mr. Palmer's place. Mr. Lyons has now been employed in the editorial department of the *Digest*, and placed elsewhere.

An investigation of the contents of the *American Mercury* during the Palmer-Spivak regime discloses the important fact that the first writing in favor of an American fascist party and movement appeared in this magazine. The writer was Lawrence Dennis, who used some of the same material for his book "The Coming American Fascism" (Harper & Bros., 1936), and who was later among the group indicted on the charge of conspiracy to commit sedition—the only "intellectual" in the lot, as the newspapers reported. (The Government dropped this case in 1947.)

Mr. DeWitt Wallace, editor of *Reader's Digest*, indignantly denied all charges that he himself was in favor of some of the things Hitler and Mussolini had done, as *In Fact* charged in 1942, and said statements attributed to him were "unadulterated lies." He could not, of course, deny the numerous articles he had selected which favored fascism—one in particular defending Franco, and another pointing out what was good in Nazi Germany.

In 1947, following a statement by Mr. O. John Rogge, the government's prosecutor in the trial of the alleged seditionists, Mr. Wallace was forced to admit that after Dennis had published his overt fascist articles in the *American Mercury* he had been hired for editorial work on the *Reader's Digest.*

Throughout the course of the war the Nazis made considerable use of articles in the *Digest* because they were good for propaganda purposes. The Nazis quoted *Reader's Digest,* with full credit, in the magazine *O(verseas) K(id)* which was distributed free to American prisoners of war. *Stars & Stripes* reported that the 805th Tank Destroyer Battalion had had canisters fired at it from Nazi 105mm guns, and that these contained reprints of *Reader's Digest* articles. And the present writer has copies of *Der Westkaempfer,* issue of January 30, 1945, containing one of the many anti-Russian articles the *Reader's Digest* printed which the Hitler propaganda machine reprinted for the purpose of undermining the morale of the American soldiers.

The National Council of Teachers of English devoted itself largely to the editorial policy of *Reader's Digest* at home. It stated in its report:

"It has been criticized as being anti-Semitic, anti-Negro, anti-labor, anti-Roosevelt. It has been said that it does not support the war effort and the unity of the United Nations. How serious are these criticisms if true? . . . .

"Reading influences the lives of people. This is a reading problem. Teachers must judge how serious the criticisms of the *Reader's Digest* are and whether or not they are valid."

There follows page after page of the evidence on which the charges are based. Emphasis is placed on the fact almost the entire labor press of America has denounced the *Digest* as its enemy. For example, the National Council of Teachers of English report quotes the *CIO News* articles:

"There is proof aplenty that the *Digest* has sandwiched lies, distortions and dangerous halftruths between innocent human interest stuff and patter. In wartime this is a matter of grave concern because of the tremendous power of the *Digest* in moulding public opinion." (This CIO report, incidentally, was also used in a special edition sent to the hundreds of thousands of union men in the armed services, most of whom were getting free copies of the *Digest*.)

The National Council of Teachers of English report also notes that William L. Shirer in an article on the Nazi use of propaganda (*Harper's*, November, 1944) referred to the *O(verseas) K(id)* use of a *Digest* item as very effective on the morale of prisoners.

It notes that the Spanish fascist press, notably *El Espanol* of Madrid, reprinted one of the many Russia-baiting articles by Max Eastman, a *Reader's Digest* editor who had formerly edited communist publications.

The National Council of Teachers of English report further notes angry protests from a group of University of Puerto Rico professors and Puerto Rico schoolteachers sent to Mr. DeWitt Wallace because of the editorial policy of *Reader's Digest*, which is stated as "anti-labor, anti-Roosevelt, anti-United Nations and defeatist."

No one who reads the full report made by the Council can have any doubt about its report being an indictment.

Not only is it shown that the *Reader's Digest* is not a digest, but that it is a magazine with an editorial policy, and that policy is definitely reactionary.

Ladies' Home Journal: Cyrus K. Curtis of the Curtis Publishing Company, left a gross estate of $28,933,045 (*Editor & Publisher*, November 13, 1943). He left this although he had lost $42,000,000 in his newspaper ventures (according to the *Guild Reporter*, January 15, 1942). On the occasion of the demise of the *Public Ledger* a writer in *The Nation* said of Curtis and his newspaper partner, John C. Martin:

> "These men were without liberalism or vision, I had almost said without conscience, certainly without understanding of the real purposes of the American democracy, and were actuated only by the motive of piling up more wealth in addition to the millions that accrued from the *Saturday Evening Post* and the *Ladies' Home Journal*. They ruined the historic *New York Evening Post,* as they long ago killed the *Public Ledger*. . . . Their's is the point of view of big business, of the rich and the privileged. Their motto is America by big business, for big business, with big business."

Curtis left his holdings to his only daughter, Mrs. Edward Curtis Bok, and her son, Cary William Bok. But before and after his death the dominating influence in the Curtis Publishing Company was Walter Deane Fuller. It was he who made the *Ladies' Home Journal,* the *Saturday Evening Post,* and other Curtis publications the spokesman for the trade associations to which he belonged. He is a great orator, but his one theme throughout the fourteen years of the New Deal was decreased taxation for corporations. He was rewarded for this brilliant work in December, 1940, when the "Congress of American Industry," as the National Association of Manufacturers calls its annual meetings, elected him president for 1941. The duPonts, the Weirs, the Girdlers, the Sloans and the Pews were unanimous in honoring the great magazine man.

Among the many notable posts which Mr. Fuller holds are: chairman of the finance committee, National Association of Manufacturers; member of the Better America Committee of the NAM; member of the governing board of the NIIC, the propaganda agency of the NAM; a member of its program committee; and chairman of the NAM Committee on Cooperation with Education.

Mr. Fuller is also president of the National Publishers' Association, the magazine counterpart of the American Newspaper Publishers' Association.

The president of the Curtis Publishing Co. (*Ladies' Home Journal, Saturday Evening Post, Country Gentleman, Holiday,*

Jack & Jill, with some nine or ten million circulation) was president of the NAM, is president of the NPA, was one of the notables who revived the NAM, is now chairman or member of NAM committees and on the governing board of the NIIC.

No newspaper owner has ever let affiliations of this nature and their influence on what he publishes become known to his readers.

Woman's Home Companion: The magazines devoted to housewives without exception have entered the field of politics for the purpose of spreading the propaganda of their owners. Although *Woman's Home Companion* usually sticks to its muttons and other culinary subjects, it has followed its rivals, *Ladies' Home Journal* and *Good Housekeeping,* in promoting what all claim is the interest of the consumer and is actually the interest of the advertiser who seeks to make money by exploiting the consumer.

The propaganda line goes all the way to the fiction writer. To my knowledge there are no instances of big magazines in the United States permitting a fiction writer to tell a story in which a worker is right and an employer is wrong, but every one of the big magazines will permit a writer of fiction to use its columns to attack labor. Here, for instance, is an example from the *Woman's Home Companion* of May, 1943:

"Nonsense," said Bob. "Our people are satisfied. They need no unions."

The story is called "Murder For a Million" and is by Clarence Budington Kelland, one of the most noted writers of commercial fiction in the world. But he is also one of the most reactionary and one of the most popular, and therefore an effective propagandist.

In the July, 1943, issue, the main article is "Henry Ford Talks at 80," a good human interest story which was advertised with the headline: "Mrs. Ford was so interested that she used to sit up all night and hold the light for me." It had the woman angle. But it also had something else. It disclosed, for those who are in the business, that this magazine had joined the news services and the newspapers in getting and printing the annual Ford interview—with pictures. It is part of the Ford publicity campaign, it goes with Ford ads, and most publications taking this money obliged with this annual puffery.

In its issue of February, 1947, the *Companion* perhaps surprised its readers by what looked like a modern crusade against patent medicines. It featured, and advertised throughout the land, an article called "The Truth About Reducing Drugs," a powerful and valuable exposé of the thyroid, benzedrine and belladonna patent medicine men. To the profession it was just another rousing attack on the man-eating shark.

To keep up the myth of freedom and courage publishers, especially former radicals like Hearst and former crusading publications now owned by the corporations, frequently break out with attacks on fakers who do not advertise, or politicians who control nothing, or public enemies who are generalized and never named. The man-eating shark is the safest of all objects of attack, and so it was again in the case of the *Companion's* war with unadvertised thyroid pills.

But cosmetics are sacred. The House of Morgan, which helps direct the *Companion,* also directs a face cream corporation against which the FTC once issued a fraud order. No commercial newspaper or magazine mentioned that one.

McCall's: The case of *McCall's* is similar to that of its rival, the *Ladies' Home Journal.* Both were published for at least one year by men who were presidents of the NAM (which permits only one 12-month term) and both were bound to the NAM by publishers who are among the 25 great powers behind the NAM.

The NAM in 1935 declared itself for a "continuing campaign" against the Wagner Act, and when the case went to the Supreme Court it elected William B. Warner, president of *McCall's,* its own president. Mr. Warner, like Mr. Fuller, was one of the original financial backers of the NAM from the days of its "reconversion" in 1933.

Among the confidential documents which the La Follette Committee found in its investigation there is one stating that as late as 1937, during the reign of William B. Warner of *McCall's,* it was still the purpose of the NAM to break strikes, and to employ a new weapon, public opinion, for that purpose. The confession was then made that it is the newspapers and radio which make or break strikes today; and of course the powers which controlled the means of communications would naturally come out winners. Mr. Warner's prospectus for 1937 contained these lines: "Now, more than ever before, strikes are being won or lost in the newspapers and over the radio. The swing of public opinion has always been a major factor in labor disputes." (*See* Appendix 20.)

Mr. Warner went about raising the biggest fund in the history of the public relations committee of the NAM. He deplored the small amounts available annually until his time in office, and he was the first to achieve three-quarters of a million. However, the documents seized by the La Follette Committee reveal that in addition to a program of using press and radio to break strikes—by perverting public opinion to favor the employer—it was also the plan of the NAM to use pressure upon all the means of advertising to get space free for its propaganda. Being a publisher himself, Mr. Warner knew that the advertiser lays down the law, and he figured that he could get his fellow NAM leaders who are heavy advertisers to lay down the law to the newspapers, the magazines, the billboard owners, and the radio. Mr. Warner had only $750,000 to spend, but that money was used merely for campaigning: the news items, editorials, cartoons, speeches, pictures, and other NAM publicity achievements cost nothing. All that big corporations had to do was to tell the press and radio what they wanted. They got millions of free space and time. Mr. Warner wrote at the end of 1937 that he had obtained $1,250,000 in free billboard ads, 2000 pages of newspaper space, worth a million, free, and a million dollars worth of time over 270 radio stations. The La Follette documents are an exposé of corruption which no apologist has dared mention.

Good Housekeeping: At a time Mr. Hearst and his $200,000,000 publishing empire were in difficulties—and largely in control of the Rockefeller Chase National and other banks—some of the enterprises were earning big money. *Good Housekeeping* usually earns $2,000,000 a year. It was devoted to women's beauty and household affairs, also popular commercial fiction for which it paid large sums. It stated (in 1946) that "to a certain extent the ability to pay top rates insured a magazine consideration from the best writers. Good writers, like good workers of any kind, prefer to market their wares where the rewards are the greatest." The price of fiction is this Hearst magazine's measure of literature.

Inasmuch as *Good Housekeeping* keeps out of politics as a rule, there would be no reason for many words about this mass-circulation magazine were it not for an incident which illustrated the relationship of the NAM, big business in general, bad medicine, advertising, and the art of fooling the public.

Good Housekeeping had since 1902 guaranteed its advertisers. To many it gave seals of approval. However, federal authorities investigated both the advertising and the items advertised and charged that the former were frequently fraudulent, the latter frequently either fraudulent, harmful or useless.

Finally the Federal Trade Commission, after wrangling with the Hearst people for years, issued the following press release:

> "Hearst Magazines, Inc., 57th Street and 8th Avenue, New York, of which *Good Housekeeping* is a wholly owned subsidiary, is charged in a complaint issued by the FTC with misleading and deceptive acts and practices in the issuance of Guarantees, Seals of Approval, and the publication in its advertising pages of grossly exaggerated and false claims for products advertised therein."

A consumers' service organization, Consumers' Union, had tested many items advertised in the Hearst magazine, and bearing the Hearst seal, and found that frequently "products bearing one or another of the *Good Housekeeping* seals were inferior, or potentially harmful, or overpriced, or otherwise poor buys." In parenthesis it might be stated here that there is no relation between advertising and value, no relation between "brand names" and value, and very frequently the lesser known or the unknown and unadvertised article is greatly superior to the one on which millions have been spent to sell the public.

The *Good Housekeeping* case involved all advertising: therefore the entire newspaper and magazine publishing industry, and a large part of big business. It aroused all the elements which place profits above public welfare. The battle in behalf of the Hearst magazines was led by Robert Lund, a director of the NAM, its former president, one of its reorganizers, and the head of Lambert Pharmacal Co., makers of Listerine, which *Good Housekeeping* had advertised extensively. He had fought the Federal Trade Commission to a standstill. At one time the Federal Trade Commission announced that Lund had agreed to "cease and desist" from advertising Listerine as permanently relieving or curing dandruff, or killing dandruff germs, or getting "at the cause," or having "marked curative qualities." Consumers' Union and the then ad-less newspaper *PM* had published the news. In fact, *PM* gave it a page, whereas it may be safely said that of America's 1750 newspapers no less than 99% suppressed this news.

A secret meeting was held in the home of George E. Sokolsky, who was then on the *New York Herald Tribune* (later on the *New York Sun,* and syndicated by Hearst), who had once been secretly on the payroll of the NAM, working in the anti-labor field with Tom Girdler and Ernest Weir, two important men of the NAM.

Notables at the Sokolsky meeting were J. B. Matthews of the Dies Committee; F. J. Schlink of Consumers' Research—a private outfit not to be confused with the Consumers' Union; Henry F. Bristol of Bristol-Myers Pharmacal Co., a patent medicine man; Mr. Lund, and a representative of Young & Rubicam, one of the Big Four of the advertising world.

Some of the heads of the biggest business organizations in the world, the patent medicine men, advertising's spokesman, and one of the top seven magazines got together and planned what to do. Matthews declared he would get the Dies Committtee to issue a terrific smear against all public welfare organizations; Sokolsky outlined plans for publicity; the businessmen decided to swing the magazine and newspaper press into line by withdrawing advertising from those which did not toe the line; and the meeting dispersed. Within a few days the front pages of the newspapers carried one of the hundred or more Dies Committee sensations—and falsehoods. Among the organizations redbaited were all which had favored pure food and drugs and decent wages and decent prices, notably: League of Women Shoppers, Consumers' Union, Committtee for Boycott against Japanese Aggression; New York Consumers' Council; Farmer Milk Cooperative. The newspapers did a great job for Hearst's *Good Housekeeping* and the vast and complex business enterprises associated with it. The powerful interests associated with patent medicines showed they could reach all the way into the NAM and into Congress itself. That they affected most of the press also was no surprise.

American Magazine: When the Crowell Company got hold of this magazine, which had been the great muckraking monthly to which Lincoln Steffens, Ida Tarbell, Finley Peter Dunne and other writers contributed, they changed its character—just as other wealthy interests made *Romance Magazine* out of the crusading *Everybody's.* The *American,* instead of being caviar to the general, was to become opium for the people. Its policy was to repeat over and over, many times each month, and year after year, the Horatio Alger, Jr., story of how the poor and unfortunate boy (and sometimes girl) made good—good meaning good money.

For years the *American* poured out its dope. It did not engage in political propaganda, as did *Collier's,* the other general magazine of the Crowell house. It seemed to realize the fact that it was nothing but a mouthpiece of the gilded status quo of the Morgan Empire when in an advertisement (*Time,* February 3, 1941) it said of itself: "Among magazines, the *American Magazine* is a particularly shining example of that discontent with status quo which has made this the most progressive nation on earth." But lest anyone think this was morganatic treason, it hastily added: "Latest proof of this is a revolutionary contribution to advertising. . . ." In that department at least there was no stale status quo of sterility and stagnation; there was in fact revolution! The *American* would cut pages five different ways to let advertisers get better position!

In 1944, the yellow press, led by the Newspaper Axis (Hearst-Howard-Patterson-McCormick) headlined the news of Senator—and Vice Presidential candidate—Truman's November, 1942, article in the *American* in which he had attacked "selfish fights for power, the endless bickerings and dissension" in the Roosevelt regime which placed America "in danger of losing the war in Washington." This same press, of course, did not explain the circumstances of the Senator's writing the article or tell the whole truth. This was that the Senator had indeed written a criticism for the purpose of speeding the war effort, but the magazine had misused it for smearing the Democratic administration. Truman did not try to kill the article when he asked for an injunction, he was merely trying to get his correct version printed and not the "unapproved version of his views cooked up by the magazine." Stated the future President:

"The *American Magazine* came to me and asked if I would consider writing an article on the situation as it existed in production.

"I scribbled out an outline, and sent it for checking of facts to the staff of the Special Senate Committee to Investigate the National Defense Program of which I was chairman. Then my wife, who was acting as my secretary, went over it with me.

"The *American Magazine* men rewrote the article and sent it back to me. I scratched out things I didn't like, eliminated the $40 words and sent it back to them.

"Then word came to me that the magazine was planning to publish an article differing from the one I had approved, and I applied for an injunction. . . . That made the magazine change its mind. The article was finally published as I had approved it."

This attack, frequently with the use of ghosts, against the Roosevelt policy continued. In April, 1945, the *American* ran an article by Senator Byrd on "The Government's Waste of Manpower." In March, 1946, it ran another of its anti-labor articles ("Labor's Feather Beds—What They Cost You") and the railroad workers' organ, *Labor* (February 16), quoted the former director of the Office of Defense Transportation on it under the subhead "Lie Exploded by (Joseph B.) Eastman." On September 15, 1946, *In Fact* published exclusively a confidential memorandum from the editor of the *American* giving a line on its political policies. It says in major part:

OFFICE OF THE PUBLISHER

THE AMERICAN MAGAZINE

(Confidential)

The attached memorandum from Sumner Blossom, editor of The American Magazine, *was originally intended solely for the information and guidance of our own editorial staff. It is of such potential interest, however, that I have obtained permission to give it limited circulation among some of our business friends, with the understanding that it is not to be further circulated or quoted.*

INTER OFFICE MEMORANDUM

THE AMERICAN MAGAZINE

To: Members of the Editorial Staff
From: Sumner Blossom

Information reaching me leads me to believe that we will have a period of communist dictated labor unrest in the United States beginning, perhaps, in September of this year. This information suggests that communist dominated unions of American workers will strike and threaten to strike at a time suitable to Moscow. The purpose is two-fold:

First, Moscow wants to be able to say to the rest of the world that Russia is solidly going this way, while "the decadent democracies are torn by internal unrest and strife." This will give Russia a talking point in her international negotiations of the next year. Russia realizes only too well that as our domestic problems increase our voice weakens in the councils of the world, and as our voice weakens Russia's chances of getting her own way increase.

Second, while Russia certainly does not want war at this time she is realistic enough to recognize the possibility of conflict in the future. Her government dominated publications have noted with increasing satisfaction the sharp reductions in our armed services, and have urged the immediate withdrawal of our troops from "all friendly countries." Some of the countries named are the Philippines, France, China, Belgium, Holland, Iceland, Greece, India and Indonesia. It has even been suggested that our failure to make such withdrawals would be evidence on our part of "aggressive imperialism."

I am not suggesting that I think war between the United States and Russia is inevitable. I am saying, however, that Russia has a definite international program, which, at this moment, she intends to carry through, and is prepared to go to war eventually if, in her judgment, her ends can only be accomplished in that way. As a step in her long range program she is centering her major attention this fall on the United States. It is not unlikely that at the same time there will be some strife in the United Kingdom, because the British, too, have communist dominated unions.

It is my belief that the situation in this country will be touched off by the maritime strike. There is good reason to believe the leaders of the seamen's unions might not have so readily acquiesced to the demands of Phil Murray for a truce with the steamship operators this spring had the timing been better. As I understand it, when President Truman threatened to use the Navy to move the merchant ships, and the union leaders countered with a request for support from foreign unions, they were informed that this support could not be forthcoming until, at least, the fall. When the truce was reached the leaders of the unions involved made it quite plain that the settlement was not at all satisfactory to them and indicated that the truce was nothing more than that. . . .

[The next three paragraphs deal with strikes, John L. Lewis, Earl Browder, the possibility of Lewis, Murray and Green being "on one side and the communists on the other" in nationwide strikes, and related ideas.]

It is my belief that if a series of communistic strikes comes, and our government adopts the policy of compromise or conciliation because of the coming elections, we will have taken one more step towards the loss of our present system. If, on the other hand, the government meets the challenge head-on, using whatever means are available to break the strikes, and our Congress enacts legislation to prevent their recurrence, we will have washed out the possibility of Russia wearing us down by a process of attrition.

Once again I remind you that Russia does not want war today. She, like every other nation in Europe and Asia, has suffered heavily in the war. We, alone, have enough weapons and stamina to fight a major war today, but we are demobilized. Russia is rebuilding and expanding her industry today and looking to the future.

All of this is why we published the article "Communism is Un-American" by Cardinal Spellman in our July issue. And this is why we propose from time to time to carry articles of similar import.

Cosmopolitan: Being a Hearst publication, this magazine is used for Hearstian purposes, as are all the newspapers, news services and other magazines owned or controlled by the Lord of San Simeon. Many people recognize Hearst newspapers for what they are, few connect the magazines with Hearst's yellow journalism.

A poll of Washington correspondents, the upper bracket of American journalism, while voting the *Chicago Tribune* the worst paper in the country, placed ahead of this individual journal the entire chain of Hearst papers. Hearst got 714 points, and the *Chicago Tribune* was second with 455. (*See* Appendix 10.)

Still more interesting was a poll conducted in many parts of the country which showed that 27.3% of the persons asked considered Hearst a bad influence for America, only 10.7% considering him good. In those cities in which Hearst publishes newspapers the vote was much higher: 43.3% of all asked said Hearst was a bad influence, 10.5% said he was good, 46.2% did not know.

The *Cosmopolitan* had been one of the powerful muck-raking magazines of the early part of the century. In 1910 it published the last series of articles against graft and crooked politics. This was written by Charles Edward Russell, and the concluding chapters, which Hearst then approved, declared that only the Marxian idea, socialism, would put an end to corruption. Today the *Cosmopolitan* and all the rest of the Hearst publications devote much of their space to fighting the Marxians.

It is for this reason that the Nazi propaganda ministry found the *Cosmopolitan* useful during the Second World War.

The British Monitoring Service of Axis Radios included in its report of February 9 and February 12, 1942, references to a Hearst news service and the *Cosmopolitan,* as follows:

NAZI RADIO February 9, 1942
Summary

E. D. Ward (Edward Delaney)

"an American citizen who cannot be connected with National Socialism," reviewed the Berlin press of the day. . . . Ward quoted the Berlin press, which is printing excerpts from an article in the . . . *Cosmopolitan* magazine. . . . Ward showed the satisfaction of the papers (*Voelkischer Beobachter,* etc.) with the *Cosmopolitan* article. . . .

* * *

A talk—"THE TIME BOMB"—in English, speaker's name not given.

This was a lengthy quotation from an article in the December issue of *Cosmopolitan* magazine, written by Eugene Lyons.

Lyons, the speaker said, showed the Red Conspiracy in the United States. There is a Stalinist Fifth Column in the defense industry and everywhere. Lyons points out the defense stoppages caused by the communists. The communists have organized a net of underground sabotage.

And this is the picture of the development the Nazi speaker gave on the basis of Lyons' prophesy:

An OGPU ruling America; agitation by communist soapbox orators; riots; rebellions; and then the American citizen will suddenly awake into the bolshevik paradise. The time bomb is ticking everywhere in the United States, thanks to "Franklin Stalino Roosevelt."

On February 9 "E. D. Ward" . . . remarked that the Berlin press was now printing excerpts from an article . . . in the February issue of *Cosmopolitan* magazine. . . . An hour later there was a complete talk in English . . . which dealt with an article in the December issue of *Cosmopolitan* written by Eugene Lyons. . . . It is extremely significant that Berlin shortwave radio seems to be using more and more Hearst material. . . .

The Lyons article is a typical piece of Hearst Russophobia which warns America against the far-reaching bolshevik menace. . . .

NAZI RADIO February 12, 1942
Summary

Jane Anderson—talk in English—"Truth Will Prevail"—8:15 P.M.

The only remarkable point in this talk was the reference to (and reverence for) the INS (International News Service, the Hearst press agency), which the speaker said had "always maintained the highest standard" of news reporting. . . .

It should be noted that the Eugene Lyons quoted is a former United Press correspondent who in Moscow was at first redder than the reds; he propagandized for the communistic way of life and had an answer for every criticism of his doubting colleagues. He was fired by his employer, Roy Howard, who accused him of faking a news story, and he in turn denounced Howard, but a decade later he had become such a Soviet-baiter that he was able to write propaganda against Russia not only for Hearst but for his former personal enemy, Mr. Howard.

Miss Jane Anderson, who praised the Hearst news services, was herself an employee of this same organization. For making the broadcasts, one of which is quoted above, she was indicted for treason, along with Donald Chandler of the *Baltimore American,* another Hearst newspaper, and Robert Best, the Vienna correspondent of the United Press.

The entire Hearst newspaper press published a whole series of propaganda articles by the Nazi leaders.

* * *

From the foregoing pages, which ought to be elaborated into a stout volume by one of the University presses, it will be seen that a few men, whose interests are identical with that of the National Association of Manufacturers, control the big magazines. Here is a summary of the situation:

LARGEST CIRCULATION MONTHLY MAGAZINES *

Publication	*Circulation*	*Ownership, Control, Interest or Affiliation*
Ladies' Home Journal	4,166,937	W. D. Fuller of NAM
Woman's Home Companion	3,543,977	Crowell, J. P. Morgan
McCall's	3,425,357	Warner of NAM
Good Housekeeping	2,533,478	Hearst
American	2,480,568	Crowell, J. P. Morgan
Cosmopolitan	2,045,930	Hearst
Redbook	1,547,094	Crowell, J. P. Morgan

* Figures from various issues of *Tide,* the advertising magazine, 1946-47. *Reader's Digest* circulation, 11,000,000; 9½ million printed in English; 7 million sold in the U. S. and Canada—"Little Wonder," by John Bainbridge.

LARGEST CIRCULATION, WEEKLIES

Life	3,904,363	Luce, J. P. Morgan
Saturday Evening Post	3,396,236	Fuller, NAM
Collier's	2,837,627	Crowell, J. P. Morgan
Look	1,911,405	Cowles
Time	1,194,708	Luce, J. P. Morgan
Liberty	1,168,932	Atlas Corporation
Newsweek	605,573	Harriman, Morgan, Astor

MISCELLANEOUS †

Farm Journal (monthly)	2,700,000	Pew of NAM
Pathfinder (fortnightly)	1,000,000	Pew of NAM

† These circulation figures have been reported at various times.

CHAPTER 10

THE SEVEN BIG WEEKLIES

AMONG the seven big monthly magazines there is not one devoted to news, or national affairs, politics, or the general welfare: the four leaders cater exclusively to women, the fifth is a general magazine, the remaining two are for the most part dispensers of fair to middling fiction. On the other hand, all the seven big weekly magazines are aimed at the manufacture of public opinion.

Their 15,000,000 circulation may reach as many individuals as the total newspaper circulation of 50,000,000. No one questions the fact that the public has more faith in magazines than in the daily press, and for this reason the seven may be said to constitute a great power in public affairs.

In no less than four of the seven there is an interest by the House of Morgan; another is directly linked with an official of the NAM, another is owned outright by Atlas Corporation, and only one is not directly ruled by the big money: it is *Look,* published by Cowles, and subject merely to advertising and big business pressures, as is every publication which feeds on the same rich sources.

Largest in circulation, if not in influence, is *Life,* the Luce picture weekly which in 1947 claimed 5,000,000 circulation and, because it featured pictures, which even illiterates could understand, and not reading matter, which required some literacy, it claimed not the usual five, but seven, "readers" for each copy. With *Time*'s million circulation and at least 5,000,000 readers, and *Fortune*'s 20 readers for each $1 copy, and the *March of Time* playing in 9,000 theaters to 20,000,000 persons, Luce can very well claim that almost the entire literate adult population, and a huge segment of the illiterate, are his audience.

All the Luce avenues of communication have been traveled by his reactionary views. The most revealing document in the history of Henry Luce's political development is his address to the graduating class of the University of Chattanooga in which he proposed the rule of nations by an aristocratic elite. ("Education and Aristocracy," University of Chattanooga, April 21, 1936.) The idea is not new. It was heard in Greek and Roman days, and it was given considerable circulation when Benito Mussolini declared that his guiding light was the philosopher Pareto.

At the very same time Mr. Luce was preaching the "aristocratic elite" to colleges, Mr. Lawrence Dennis was preaching the rule of a fascist elite in the pages of the *American Mercury*. (Ten years later Prof. James Burnham was to revive the theory of the rule of the elite in Mr. Luce's *Life* magazine. Mussolini did not hesitate to liken his adaptation of the theory to Hitler's *Der Fuehrerprinzip*, but there is no evidence in the writings of Messrs. Luce, Dennis and Burnham that a similarity at least exists.)

Mr. Luce also used the pages of *Life* as a sounding board for an aggressive American imperialistic program which had obvious similarities to various fascist programs, and which he called patriotically "The American Century."

In his June 9, 1941, issue Mr. Luce published one of the many articles written by the late Chicago packer and former ambassador to Belgium, John Cudahy. It was in the form of an interview with Hitler, and it pleaded the Nazi cause.

In his report to his chief at the Department of Justice, Mr. Rogge elaborated on the plan at Hitler headquarters of planting Hitler interviews in the American press for the purpose of influencing world affairs. Mr. Rogge's report details the planting of one such article in the Hearst papers. The Rogge document states that Otto Dietrich of the Propaganda Ministry and von Ribbentrop decided to perpetrate a "kolossal" hoax on the people of the world by telling them, at the time the Nazi forces were marching into France, that Paris would not be occupied, that Britain would not be attacked, and that all Hitler wanted was an equivalent of the Monroe Doctrine.

The false interview with Hitler was written in the Propaganda Ministry, the Rogge document states, and was then planted on the dean of the Hearst correspondents, Karl von Wiegand. The Rogge report states: "Von Wiegand began his account of his alleged interview with this: 'With the German Armies Nearing Paris, June 14 (1941)—"The Americas to Americans, Europe to the Europeans." This reciprocal basic Monroe Doctrine, mutually observed, declared Adolf Hitler to me here. . . .' "

This is but one of the scores of Hitler, Mussolini, Franco, Salazar and other interviews with fascist heads of states which have been planted by the fascist propaganda bureaus in the world press. If Mr. Luce did not know that the Cudahy Hitler interview was one of the scores arranged and inspired for propaganda purposes, then he is probably the only editor ignorant of the facts of life.

But Mr. Luce apparently did know that there was a purpose in this Hitler interview because he published at the head of it a disclaimer which said in part:

> "This spring *Life* commissioned John Cudahy . . . to write a series of articles about Nazi Germany and its war aims. Two weeks ago he was accorded an interview with Adolf Hitler. . . .
>
> "*Life* is well aware of its grave responsibility in printing this article at such a critical time. It does so because it is confident its readers can intelligently recognize this interview for what it really is—an essential part of Hitler's political strategy of 'softening up' the U.S. with large denials of aggressive intentions.
>
> "*Life* suspects that Hitler chose this particular time for his interview because he hoped it would undercut the President's speech. . . ."

The Hitler item appeared in *Life* before the United States was actually at war with Hitlerism. Throughout the war the newspaper and magazine press with the exception only of three nondescript publications which were suppressed, supported not only their own countries, but all the Allies regardless of their systems of government.

In 1947, however, men in public life and certain newspapers were calling for a third World War, this one to destroy the former Ally of the United States, and the nation which did most of the fighting and suffered most of the losses in World War II. Former Governor Earle of Pennsylvania publicly stated he favored immediate use of the atomic bomb to destroy the Soviet Union.

Historians, however, will discover that the first clarion call for a holy crusade of the Western Democracies for the third World War was sounded while the second was still in progress, and that it appeared in the pages of a Luce publication.

The author was William C. Bullitt, onetime ambassador to Moscow, and onetime ambassador to France. The date was September 4, 1944. The editorial introduction called Mr. Bullitt "a special *Life* correspondent" who had gone to Italy where "he was granted interviews with well informed and authoritative personages, among them Pope Pius XII." There was more than an inference that Bullitt was quoting the Pope as favoring what was euphemistically called a holy crusade and what may some day become an atomic struggle in which not only the U.S.S.R. but also the U.S.A. will be destroyed.

This proposal to divide the world into a Western and an Eastern bloc, and to fight it out for control, was later taken up by Winston Churchill, whose writings were purchased by *Life* and the *New York Times,* and eventually by leaders throughout the world. Mr. Luce may therefore point with journalistic pride to the fact that one of his publications was the first to propose World War III.

Almost all the Luce writers of note follow the Luce line, just as all Hearst writers must obey the daily orders which come over the teletype to Hearst newspapers and magazines from the Lord of San Simeon. Ex-Ambassador Bullitt is not an exception.

The salient facts in the more recent history of this Luce writer are revealed by his onetime colleague, Ambassador Dodd, in his book, "Ambassador Dodd's Diary." Dodd was one of the few men in American diplomacy who stood up to Fascism. He had a difficult time.

The Dodd Diary tells how Bullitt sent Marcel Knecht, editor of *Le Matin,* to him to propose a Franco-German alliance aimed at joint action against Russia. Dodd was asked to use his good offices with President Roosevelt to approve this plan. Other pressures were brought on the Ambassador to Berlin. In his published Diary, Mr. Dodd says:

"I felt compelled to report the account [of Bullitt intrigue against Russia and for Germany] as given me by the French Ambassador [to Berlin, Francois-Poncet]. Later, or about the same time, when the new Italian Ambassador came here directly from Moscow, we were told that Bullitt had become attracted to Fascism before leaving Moscow . . ." (Page 372).

The Dodd Diary declares that the Chamberlain government in Britain and the Nazis and Bullitt favored dividing the world, with Germany dominating all of Europe. Japan was to control Asia. Bullitt told Dodd he favored Japan seizing the Siberian peninsula and Vladivostok. When Dodd protested that this would deny Russian access to the Pacific, Bullitt replied, "That makes no difference." Dodd wrote in his diary: "I was amazed at this kind of talk from a responsible diplomat. . . . The President must know the man's mentality, but if so, how could he have appointed him ambassador to Soviet Russia."

There are other references in the Dodd Diary proving that while Bullitt was in Moscow he intrigued with the French, Germans and British there to form alliances to destroy Russia.

His main job, however, was to destroy the Franco-Russian treaty. Dodd says (page 309) that Bullitt condemned "cooperation between England, France and the Balkan states in the hope of bringing Russia into a moderate policy and keeping the peace of Europe." Bullitt also "went to a strategic person in the French government" and "defeated the Russian negotiations" for a loan. Dodd concludes: "it seemed unusual for an American ambassador to Russia to defeat Russo-French negotiations."

This intrigue by Bullitt reached a climax when Bullitt left

Moscow and went to work in Paris for the defeat of the French treaty with Russia. Ambassador Dodd (page 372) had to report the Bullitt intrigue to Roosevelt, and to correct the assumption Bullitt gave in this undercover job that he, Bullitt, was acting for the President. "My position is difficult. . . . I cannot resign," wrote Dodd, now inclined to believe "the Washington newspaper story (saying Bullitt) is in full sympathy with Nazi ideas" (page 372).

The Bullitt and Cudahy articles in the Luce press are but two examples of whole series of similar items which appear year after year—all of them signed by big names, all of them preaching a reactionary philosophy.

Mr. Luce also employs in his three leading magazines a host of bright young men, many of whom have graduated from these offices in the past twenty-some years and sought an outlet for their views elsewhere.

From the writings of Luce men now appearing in other magazines and in books, the reader of Luce publications can learn that there is considerable strife in the home offices, just as there is in the Hearst and Howard offices. There is apparently daily talk of suppression, and of editing of articles to suit the known viewpoint of the owners. In other words, nothing is different in the Luce offices than in the offices of most of the major newspapers of America.

Foreign correspondents who have graduated from *Time, Life* and *Fortune* have stated publicly—in books, in magazine articles, and over the radio—that their reports have failed to appear, or that their statements have been so edited that a wrong impression was given the reader.

When *Time-Life* correspondent Richard Lauterbach wrote "These Are The Russians," a book which pro and anti reviewers alike agreed was factual and objective, *Nation* reviewer Alexander Kendrick pointed out that "if *Time* and *Life* had printed half of what he [Lauterbach] had sent them (and what appears here) even Mrs. Luce might have learned something about the 'inscrutable' and 'mysterious' Russians she seems to want so badly to fight. . . . For instance, Mr. Lauterbach has a chapter which he calls 'The World From Moscow,' and which *Life* refused to print, although it was intended as an answer to William C. Bullitt's *Life* article, 'The World From Rome,' which Mr. Luce liked so much. . . ."

Again, there is the case of William H. White and Annalee Jacoby, whose reports from China apparently contradicted the pattern in Mr. Luce's mind—Mr. Luce was born in China, knows there are two Chinas, one fascist, the other anti-fascist, and years ago decided which China he wants triumphant. Therefore, when Luce published a special leading article on China, he did not use the materials supplied by White, "a correspondent of the highest reliability," and printed the Kuomintang and other views. Luce used material supplied by Lin Yutang and Congressman Walter H. Judd, whose statements are also disproved by the former head of the OWI office in China, Richard Watts, Jr. (*New Republic,* December 3, 1945). Watts states that Luce tossed aside "the careful, factual reporting of one of his ablest correspondents because it does not happen to fit in with the political line of the boss," and suggested that other excellent foreign observers, notably Jack Belden, John Hersey, Charles Wertenbacker, Robert Sherrod, Will Lang, John Scott, Lauterbach and White are frequently used as window-dressing, whereas other reports, "less plausible," are "rewritten and recolored in the home office" and "set the authentic tone and express the Luce party line."

In other words the Luce magazine press does the same as the ordinary newspaper press.

By a rare coincidence, the Luce line in China is in complete conformity with the policy of the House of Morgan, which has a large interest in Chinese loans.

Time: A large percentage of the 5,000,000 persons who read 1,000,000 copies of *Time* every week are under the impression that they are getting something better than the newspapers; they believe that this magazine gives them a fairer and more honest report of the events of the world, is a better guide to the formation of their opinions and views. But it can be stated on the authority of none other than the editors of *Time* itself that *Time* is biased and prejudiced.

On July 14, 1941, *Time* stated in an editorial note: "*Time* makes no claim of being unbiased and impartial. Its editors make no bones about their bias. . . ."

Of course *Time* added that this was "bias in favor of democracy and other prejudices which they share with their fellow Americans."

It concluded: "But *Time* does set as its goal to be fair in reporting and never to take sides in partisan affairs."

The evidence, however, is clear that the first part of the editorial statement is true: *Time* is biased and prejudiced. As for the second part, it is a matter for every reader to judge from the facts.

Time is reactionary. *Time* is anti-labor. *Time* is anti-liberal. The evidence in almost every issue proves this. And a study of all issues from 1923 to date also shows that in every controversy in which the House of Morgan was named, *Time* was on the side of the great banking institution, just as in every news item in which there was a pro and anti NAM position, *Time* was for the NAM's point of view.

Time, admitting that it is biased and not impartial, has been biased against Russia for almost a quarter of a century; and has been partial, although a study of its columns compared to the study of the pages of the *New York Times,* 1917 to 1920, made by Charles Merz and Walter Lippmann ("A Test of the News," *New Republic* supplement, August 4, 1920), shows clearly that *Time* has never printed scores of absolutely false items such as Merz and Lippmann found in the *Times,* nor is *Time*'s bias as virulent as that of the *Times.*

Mr. Luce's editorial policy is also evidenced, at least to people in the same trade, by the persons who are chosen, year after year, to glorify with long and glowing articles. Mussolini, Franco, Mannerheim, have been the recipients of the Luce equivalent of a medal of honor, and even Hitler himself, whose signed articles in America appeared only in the Hearst newspapers, was treated at least cautiously.

When *Time* chose Hitler for its "man of the year" there was considerable excitement in the editorial office, and more than the usual weekly rewriting of the main feature item. The chief argument among editors was whether or not the article was too anti-Nazi.

The following paragraph was inserted, after editorial conference, in the second draft: "What Adolf Hitler & Co. did to Germany in less than 6 years was applauded wildly and ecstatically by most Germans."

However, since an editor forgot to cut a later paragraph in the original version, the inserted lines were soon flatly contradicted.

In the second version there also appeared the following phrase: "Hitler's . . . was no ordinary dictatorship, but rather one of great energy and magnificent planning . . . magnificent highways . . . workers' benefits. . . ."

In the first half of the thirties *Time*'s foreign editor was Laird S. Goldsborough, who was also assigned by Luce to produce the famous July, 1934, issue of *Fortune,* the greatest glorification of Italian fascism ever to appear anywhere in America.

In the editorial introduction the editor wonders "whether fascism is achieving in a few years or decades such a conquest of the spirit of man as Christianity achieved only in ten centuries." This nonsense about "the spirit of man" was merely covering up near-slavery, near-starvation, and exploitation of millions of workers for the enrichment of the employers who subsidized Mussolini—which is what every honest journalist knew fascism was. Here is the concluding editorial paragraph: "But the good journalist must recognize in Fascism certain ancient virtues of the race, whether or not they happen to be momentarily fashionable in his own country. Among these are Discipline, Duty, Courage, Glory, Sacrifice."

History of course has shown up Fascism to be a fraud. It is terrorism, degradation, murder. The July, 1934, issue of *Fortune* will remain, however, an important piece of documentary evidence in any future history of the relationship of the American newspaper and magazine press to foreign Fascism.

Goldsborough, descendant of an old aristocratic American family, was generally known as "Goldie" to his colleagues on the foreign news staff of *Time*. He resented bitterly the nickname with its Jewish implication. At the same time in the items he wrote he frequently referred to Leon Blum, premier of France, as "spidery Jew Blum," and used other expressions which were protested by many readers as anti-Semitic.

Quincy Howe, in his book, "The News and How to Understand It," points out that Goldsborough "had a schoolgirl crush on Mussolini" and used the anti-Semitic phrases about Blum "after Hitler came into power." Howe also states that "following Luce's marriage to Mrs. Brokaw *Time* stopped ridiculing the Jews."

This statement is disputed by several *Time* editors. It is obvious from the reading of *Time* itself that the only period in which it was slightly liberal was when Ralph Ingersoll was its publisher, and that even after Luce's marriage to Clare Boothe Brokaw phrases such as these appeared in the magazine: "heavy-jowled Jew Fleischaker," "smart Jew," "garrulous Jew" and "shrewd Jew."

It took thousands of letters of protest from readers—and all Luce publications are extremely sensitive to criticism in letters—before the practice of using anti-Semitic phrases such as the foregoing, was finally stopped.

The war in Spain—the fascist conspiracy that destroyed the democratic Republic largely by red-baiting it—caused trouble in *Time*'s office, just as it did in other editorial offices where even the use of the terms "Loyalist" and "Nationalist," "reds" and "fascists," were disputed by editors and writers. *Time,* during Goldsborough's turn as foreign editor, published considerable material favorable to Franco. Goldsborough wrote that Franco was soft-spoken, humorous, carefree, something like FDR, and that his program was "back to Normalcy," but Loyalist Spain was "government of mobsters," and the Loyalist soldiers defending Madrid were "shoemakers, cabdrivers, waiters" who were "prevented from scattering . . . by their officers standing behind them with cocked firearms. . . ."

As one of the score of American war correspondents who were actually in the defense of Madrid, the present writer must say that this is an outrageous perversion of the truth about one of the most noble and heroic episodes in the history of the fight for freedom of all peoples of this world.

The majority of *Time's* staff was anti-fascist. A party given to support the Spanish Republic in its fight against Hitler, Mussolini and Franco, was sponsored by the leading writers of the nation, including the following *Time-Life-Fortune* staff members: T. S. Matthews, later *Time*'s managing editor, Robert Cantwell, John Chamberlain, Allen Grover, Louis Kronenberger, Margaret Bourke-White, Mary Fraser. A little pro-Franco magazine called *The Sign* (April, 1938) threatened Luce with a boycott. Luce replied:

> "As to the 'party,' I can tell you that I did not approve of it and that my associates now know I did not approve it. We do not object to individuals in Time, Inc., editors or writers, sponsoring various causes.
>
> "This 'party' was the first of its kind to come to my notice and a rule covering such activities will presently be put in force in this company. (Signed) Henry R. Luce."

Saturday Evening Post: If every issue of this popular weekly had on its front page, in large type, instead of the little notice on an inside page, the fact that it is directed by Fuller of the National Association of Manufacturers, and that like the NAM it is devoted to defending corporate interests, then everything about this magazine, even its fiction, would require no further explanation.

The NAM furnishes the general staff of the armies of reaction of America. Equivalents of the NAM originated, or organized, or paid for the fascist movements in all of the Hitler Axis countries and in South America, and wherever reaction has gone to its last inevitable step, armed itself with bayonets, become fascism. If fascism comes to the United States, it will come as "Americanism," as Huey Long predicted, but it will succeed only if it is backed by the great financial and industrial interests, as history has shown in Germany, Italy, Japan, Spain, Portugal, China, Greece and elsewhere.

Meanwhile, the forces of reaction have at their disposal the great magazine press, of which probably the most effective member is the *Saturday Evening Post*. It is significant that the former president of the NAM is the present president of the house which publishes the *Post*. Mr. Fuller is still one of the inner circle which directs the policy of the NAM.

A comprehensive study of the contents of the *Saturday Evening Post* has been made, but it has not been published. The present writer has had access to the manuscript. A large part of it is devoted to analyzing a 6-month period of 1940, when the United States was still technically neutral, and no one had to hide his feelings. This analysis concerns chiefly the articles written by the *Saturday Evening Post* correspondent Demaree Bess, whom the Nazis treated with exceptional kindness. He was permitted to travel where others were excluded, he had the "cooperation" of high officials, and he went to occupied France, Holland and Norway. This despite the fact the year before he had been barred from Germany for an article Himmler did not like. Yet it was Himmler himself who gave Bess permission to return. A Gestapo agent visited Bess at a Paris hotel and offered to help him. Arrangements were made and Bess began to enjoy Nazi hospitality. Richard O. Boyer wrote in *PM* that American correspondents were not permitted to see anything for themselves, they were watched, "supervised," treated like prisoners. Not Bess. He went, he saw, he wrote. And the articles of 1940 may today be found in libraries.

November 9, 1940: "Germany's Wild Animal Circus"—An apology for Hitler's failure to end the war by September 1.

January 11, 1941: "Inside German Europe"—This article resulted in much protest and many cancelled subscriptions. A tremendous whitewash of the German occupation of Norway, and of Quisling, the traitor, who was later executed. The whole is a disgraceful defense of fascists.

February 1, 1941: "The Bitter Fate of Holland." Although

this article says the nation is not enjoying the Nazi occupation, it is written to try to show that it does not pay a nation to resist Hitler, because it will suffer terrible consequences if it does not surrender. Pro-Nazis are quoted with great effect, especially bankers, who want a Dutch-Nazi alliance, and non-Nazi businessmen everywhere are appealed to. A very effective piece of propaganda.

March 8, 1941: "They Took Sweden By Telephone." Not about Sweden but almost entirely an attack upon Russia. The plan of the article is to make Nazi Germany the lesser evil vis-a-vis Russia.

April 5, 1941: In an article on Poland, Bess perpetrates the most vicious of all his pro-Nazi propaganda pieces, this time in defense of the Nazi treatment of the Polish Jews, some five million of whom were enslaved, worked to death, or murdered in gas chambers and other new means of extermination. Bess has a Nazi explain the whole situation and whitewash the most terrible crime in the history of the world, genocide.

Thus the *Saturday Evening Post* which from the 1920's on had lauded Mussolini, Deterding, Hugo Stinnes, Ivor Kreuger, and many fascists, was obviously on the side of Hitler in the 1940's.

On August 9, 1941, the *Post* carried this line: "Japan's herioc four-year struggle for peace in China." An editor tried to convince *PM* that "that was sarcasm."

In its issue of September 11, 1940, the *Saturday Evening Post* worked another angle of yellow journalism. In attacking labor it invited the public in an ad to read its next number where it could "watch a columnist whip away at a CIO leader until Justice officials nab him on charges of forgery and larceny."

This is not the truth. No CIO leader has been "nabbed."

The *Saturday Evening Post* rarely retracts statements its victims call false, and there is no adequate law in the land against libelling groups, organizations, religious bodies, unions, and the like. Congressman Bruce Barton, himself an endorser of Mussolini and head of the advertising firm of Batten, Barton,

Durstine & Osborne, tried to pass it off as a copywriter's slip, but the *Post* finally apologized in small type on September 28.

It had previously published a long, smeary attack on the CIO, using the usual renegade liberal for the job. Again, it was a case of no actionable libel suit existing due to the United States not having a group libel law, as France, Canada and other democracies have. This time the *Saturday Evening Post* refused to publish the CIO's reply.

It used this same author for another typically *Post* smear, and the result was a libel suit by Dr. Jerome Davis against it and its writer, Benjamin Stolberg. The court decided that Stolberg and the *Saturday Evening Post* had printed a libel, and awarded Dr. Davis a sum of money. In February, 1945, the *Post* paid Gardner Jackson $1,500 for a libel against him written by Stolberg.

Of the *Post's* unceasing service to reaction by its compaign against unions, the Railroad Brotherhood organ, *Labor,* said (August 20, 1940): "The American people are being subjected to a blitzkrieg of propaganda. One of the most mendacious of the big berthas employed to smother us with misinformation is, of course, the *Saturday Evening Post.*"

In 1939 the *Saturday Evening Post* published a series of articles purporting to be the confessions of a "General Walter Krivitsky." One of them dealt with Spain. The present writer went to Spain (for the *New York Post*) in December, 1936, and stayed until May, 1937. All important statements made by Krivitsky as to events in that period were falsehoods.

The *Saturday Evening Post* did not inform its millions of readers that a known Hearst hack writer, Isaac Don Levine, was the ghost who wrote for Krivitsky. The *Post* did claim that the State Department had vouched for the authenticity of the "general," but *Time* magazine questioned this. "This week the State Department refused either to confirm or deny the authenticity of General Krivitsky," reported *Time* (May 22).

In February, 1941, the man who passed under the name Krivitsky committed suicide in a Washington hotel. The Associated Press suppressed news having an important bearing on this action, and many newspapers faked their stories, hinting at murder, assassination, "the long arm of the OGPU." Even the dignified *New York Times* used "Stalked by the OGPU?" in a subhead. In his last letter to his wife Krivitsky had written, "It is very difficult. I want to live very badly, but it is impossible. . . . I think my sins are big. . . ."

But what were his sins? Chief among them, apparently, was the outrageous lie against the Spanish anti-fascist Republic which was published in the *Saturday Evening Post.*

Just before he ended his life, he was trying to find someone who would publish the truth about that magazine. He arranged a meeting with an official of the League of American Writers on February 6th, and in an, at times, incoherent rush of words which showed he was already emotionally unbalanced, he said that Levine had not paid him for the articles in that magazine, that another ghost writer had "double-crossed" him regarding his book, that he did not have the money to pay his rent. "You know," he concluded, "I could raise plenty of hell if I wanted to tell all I know. There are lots of things in that story I didn't say ever. If Levine doesn't come across, I'm going to get some money: do you know who'd buy an article about the truth about the *Saturday Evening Post* stuff?" (On February 8th he went to see Levine at 1 Fifth Avenue, New York; on the 9th Levine left for Washington, giving as his address that of J. B. Matthews of the Dies Committee; on that same day Krivitsky went to Washington to talk to Levine; at 9:30 A.M., February 10th, Krivitsky's body was found in a quiet hotel. The press suppressed mention of the suicide note but gave the nation a sensational—and false—story, quoting Matthews as saying, "It's murder, all right." All the foregoing facts were given the Associated Press by the novelist who talked to Krivitsky on the 6th, but the Associated Press failed to print the news.) As for the *Saturday Evening Post,* it published a series of fraudulent reports, it spread fascist news regarding the Spanish conflict, and when the truth at last came out, it did not correct its Krivitsky series.

The *Saturday Evening Post*'s service to fascism began just

after the First World War, when Kenneth Roberts, Isaac L. Marcosson, and several other nationally known writers were hired to sing the praises of reactionary dictators, the greatest swindlers of the era, and tycoons such as Sir Henri Deterding, who financed a war in Baku to save his oil, and told the *Saturday Evening Post* that he favored the murder of all workers who refused to work—on his terms.

Nothing has changed but the names of the writers. Today leading reactionary writers include Demaree Bess and Henry J. Taylor. The latter is never named as the president of the Package Advertising Company, a business firm which in 1946 and at the date of this writing was under investigation by the Federal Trade Commission on the charge of monopolistic practices. Taylor also works for the Scripps-Howard chain and speaks over the ABC network (for General Motors.) Everywhere, Mr. Taylor spreads reaction.

One of the new names in the labor-baiting department of this weekly is the noted sea writer William McFee, who specialized on the maritime unions. In announcing one McFee article, Editor W. W. Stout of the *Post* boasted that it was authentic because McFee had had the aid of a genuine NMU-CIO official, a certain Jerome King.

What neither McFee nor the *Post* told 15,000,000 readers is that Jerome King is actually Jerome Madeiros, a murderer.

Moreover, Madeiros, before coming to the service of the *Post* and collaboration with the noted author McFee, was already notorious as a labor racketeer, a goon, a traitor to his union, and a crook. It was in a fight with union men that Madeiros killed a CIO worker, and was arrested, tried, and sent to the penitentiary for murder. When the *Post* and McFee were asked to state the facts, they refused. From that time on the noted author became known in labor circles as Fibber McFee. (Documentation: McFee article, *Saturday Evening Post,* September 21, 1940; Madeiros murder sentence, December 29; details in *In Fact,* February 10, 1941.)

* * *

From the larger viewpoint, the question of being a Democratic or anti-Democratic force in America, a noteworthy statement was made by Mr. Justice Jackson of the U. S. Supreme Court. Addressing the Massachusetts Law Society the then Attorney General traced the history of the nation as a democracy—in contrast to its being officially a republic—and named as openly anti-Democratic or fascist forces such examples as General Van Horn Moseley, Merwin K. Hart, H. W. Prentis, Jr., then president of the NAM, Lindbergh, the League for Constitutional Government (obviously Gannett's Committee for Constitutional Government) and the *Saturday Evening Post.*

The Nazis never missed an opportunity to use undemocratic and pro-fascist publications for their propaganda machine. They filled the airwaves with extracts from Hearst's *Cosmopolitan,* Lawrence Spivak and Eugene Lyons' *American Mercury,* the *Reader's Digest,* and the *Saturday Evening Post.* Here is documentary proof. On March 17, 1941, the foreign monitoring service of Columbia Broadcasting Company, which supplied radio stations and newspapers with news, sent out the following (which few, if any, used—the *Post* itself is a large advertiser):

"3/17 [1941]
CBS 21.-
NAZI QUOTES *SATURDAY EVENING POST* TO SHOW ROOSEVELT ALONE IS RESPONSIBLE FOR DECISION ON LEND-LEASE ACT

"Following the line set by earlier Axis broadcasts, E. D. Ward, former American press agent who broadcast by shortwave from Berlin, tonight said that Pres. Roosevelt and not the American people was responsible for the decision to pass the Lend-Lease Bill.

"Ward, whose true name is Edward Delaney, quoted extensively from the *Saturday Evening Post.* Here are several paragraphs of his broadcast which was recorded at Columbia's shortwave listening station. . . .

" 'Let me quote you from an editorial in the *Saturday Evening Post* of January 4th last. . . .

"[The quoted *Saturday Evening Post* editorial denounces the President, saying he alone and not the American Government is responsible for lend-leasing airplanes and other munitions, and alone is responsible for 'a military alliance with Canada.' Ward, who worked for Hitler, then continued as follows]:

" 'End of quotation from the *Saturday Evening Post.*

" 'And yet we are told that one man does not make the nation's decisions.

" 'Are the statements I have just quoted from the *Saturday Evening Post* of January 4th correct, or are they false?

" 'If they are false then that publication is guilty of the most monumental libel in the history of the country and legal proceedings should be taken to enforce a retraction.

" 'But have such proceedings been instituted? No. . . .'

EJ HS L 1:07 PM."

The *Post,* after Pearl Harbor, changed its line on world politics, but so far as the social and economic situation in America is concerned, so far as labor, the majority, and Democracy in America is concerned, it has not changed. It is still reaction's booming voice.

Collier's: By the usual tests—notably, editorial attitude towards labor, liberals, reactionaries and fascists—*Collier's* is very much like its main rival, the *Saturday Evening Post,* but never as crude, irresponsible and blatant. It will not have a Henry J. Taylor write a glowing blurb for a fascist dictator, but it will print the letters of Cardinal Spellman doing just that—even though they are not entirely truthful either. The Cardinal wrote that "Franco is a very sincere, serious and intelligent man." If this is true, it is a half-truth, worse than a lie. He could have stated that Franco is a very sincere, serious and intelligent murderer, as all the evidence of the Franco uprising against law and order, and the massacres then and later amply prove. The Cardinal is entitled to his opinion, and *Collier's* has full freedom of the press to publish not only that opinion but also statements the Cardinal made as fact which are not facts. *PM* devoted four pages on October 11, 1943, to pointing out the Cardinal's errors. *Collier's* of course did nothing about them.

On October 2, 1943, it attacked the maritime unions, defending the columnist Westbrook Pegler, who had previously libeled the National Maritime Union. At that time the list of dead of the seagoing unions was proportionately higher than the dead of the American air service, or infantry, or any other fighting outfit. The National Maritime Union's public relations director, Leo Huberman, sent *Collier's* a refutation of its (and Pegler's) libels, quoting United States Navy men, asking the courtesy of a correction. *Collier's* refused to reply.

In its issue of February 15, 1941, *Collier's* attacked Mussolini. By then the Morgan loan to fascist Italy was not worth saving. Six months earlier, when there was still hope, *Collier's* had published a piece of praise, reviving the 1925 Morgan myth that Mussolini had saved Italy from Bolshevism.

As for Mexico, *Collier's* continued to write articles attacking the regime—and its oil policies. "Bolshevik banditry" was one label *Collier's* placed on the restoration of the oil lands to the nation, as ordered by the 1927 constitution of the Republic.

On December 9, 1939, the leading editorial was: "Rewrite the Wagner Act."

These are but a few samples from a file of about a thousand items which prove either that *Collier's* has never moved an inch from the policy line of the NAM and the House of Morgan—which merely owns a small block of its stock—or all these thousand items add up to just so many coincidences.

Liberty: This magazine has passed through many hands. It was started by the *Chicago Tribune* and the *New York Daily News* heads, Colonel McCormick and Captain Patterson, respectively, at a time when a loss of ten or fifteen million dollars did not hurt them at all, due to the post-war tax laws. But they tired of losing money and the great Bernarr Macfadden took over the editorship and the losses. It later passed into the hands of Paul Hunter and Associates, and is now edited by Hunter but owned by Atlas Corporation which is bossed by Floyd Odlum.

In all these changing years *Liberty* has been consistent in only one policy: it has always been reactionary.

It was intensely so during the editorship of Fulton Oursler, now an editor of *Reader's Digest,* who had the cooperation in editorial policy of George Sylvester Viereck, who had been in jail at the time of the First World War for being a German agent, and who was sent to jail in the Second World War as a Nazi agent. At the time Viereck collaborated with Oursler at *Liberty* Viereck was known to be a Nazi. He wrote pro-Nazi articles which appeared in *Liberty* under Oursler's editorship. Correspondence between Oursler and Viereck was read during the latter's trial. In a document (Appendix to Appellant's Brief, U. S. Court of Appeals, D.C., No. 8204—filed May 4, 1942) there are references to this collaboration. On page 171 the following statement is made:

"Mr. Viereck was . . . advisory editor of the Macfadden Publications. Until New York's German Library of Information (the Nazi propaganda bureau) was compelled to close its doors, he was its literary advisor (stet).

"Many of Mr. Viereck's writings have appeared in *Liberty, Saturday Evening Post* and the Hearst newspapers. The author (is) the American correspondent of the *Muenchner Neuests* (stet) *Nachrichten*."

(Page 172)

"Q. Now, can you tell us what if any work Mr. Viereck did for *Liberty* Magazine and the approximate time?

"A. He did a great deal of work for *Liberty* Magazine for a period of some time shortly after 1925, I am not sure when, until two or three years ago, and I am not sure of that time.

"Q. Now, can you tell us what kind of work Mr. Viereck did for *Liberty?*

"A. He wrote original articles, he edited and prepared for publication articles to be signed by others than himself. Those were his chief activities for *Liberty*."

The questioner was the Assistant Attorney General Mr. Maloney, the witness was Mr. Oursler's assistant. The owner of *Liberty* at that time had been Macfadden, and the editor Mr. Oursler.

Like 99% of the publications living on advertising, *Liberty* was always anti-labor, editorially. It had other anti-labor uses. In the La Follette investigation of Violations of Free Speech and the Rights of Labor, Exhibit 86 is a letter from William H. Gray, field solicitor for Railway Audit & Inspection Company, which the La Follette Committee listed as a supplier of gangsters, stoolpigeons, racketeers and spies for strike-breaking corporations. The letter states:

"Note with interest what you have to say re the story in the *Liberty* Magazine, etc. I have been following that up, also the stories in the *Saturday Evening Post* as I get some very good talking points out of each magazine. . . ."

Exhibit 136 is the reply of Eugene Ivy, Atlanta attorney of this strikebreaking agency:

"I am sending you a clipping from the *Liberty* Magazine which I believe will be of much interest to you, especially that portion which relates to the Industrial Racket. I think it would be wise for you to be prepared on this subject with the information. . . . I suggest that you destroy this letter immediately. . . ."

Although at no time was there any direct NAM money in *Liberty*—as contrasted to the indirect money for the entire press, the annual $2,000,000,000 American advertising outlay, most of which comes from NAM manufacturers—the NAM viewpoint was about as directly followed as in the other popular magazines.

Oursler hired the hired man of the National Association of Manufacturers, George E. Sokolsky, to do one of the largest gilt-edge pieces of brasscheck journalism in defense of advertisers. It happened that Mr. Oursler's daughter one day asked him why he ran ads. "The things they say are not true. I don't believe a word of them," Oursler reported his daughter as saying. Oursler "decided to turn over the pages of *Liberty* to a defense of advertising. He thought of a man who could tell the story so that it would 'shine as truth.' " (*Nation*, December 24, 1938). That man was Sokolsky. (In its report on the NAM the La Follette Committee decided that it worked "in secrecy" and with "deceit" and hired professors, journalists, preachers, including this same Sokolsky.)

Liberty, like most of its rivals, carries a large amount of patent medicine advertising. Patent medicines usually harm you or rob you; about 99% of them are bad or worthless. The Federal Trade Commission issues fraud orders against patent medicine ads every day and all but a few newspapers in America suppress these news items every day.

Dr. Jesse Mercer Gehman in his important work "Smoke Over America" points out an outstanding piece of hypocrisy in the Macfadden magazines, including *Liberty*. Macfadden, "father of physical culture," wrote against the use of tobacco, but when he got *Liberty* from the *Chicago Tribune* he found that a large part of his income would be cigarette ads. He took them.

Under the Atlas Corporation ownership *Liberty* in its first fortnightly issue, February 1, 1947, finally did something neither the Brown Brothers, Harriman, Morgan or NAM magazines have ever done: it came out openly with its main feature article in praise of the National Association of Manufacturers. Written by one Henry D. Steinmetz, it began by saying that the speech, "See Here, Private Enterprise," delivered by Private Marion Hargrove before the Congress of Industry, "resounded in headlines throughout the country." This statement is not true. In publishing the speech in *In Fact* (December 31, 1945), it was noted that the text came from the *Congressional Record* (December 14, p. A6005) and that no newspaper outside the *Chicago Sun* had given it. From inquiries made by newspaper men throughout the country, at the request of the present writer, it appeared that neither the New York papers, nor the papers of any other city, nor the Associated Press and United Press carried the Hargrove address, although all other NAM speakers were reported.

Liberty goes on to say that among the activities of the NAM have been "plumping" for the Panama Canal and "the new pure food and drug laws." It may have dug the Panama Canal, but as for the pure food and drug law, it was a group of members of the NAM which killed the Tugwell Bill and emasculated the Copeland Bill which replaced it.

Again, it is stated that the NAM's publicity organization has been brought "at least on a par with the more powerful labor organizations." On the authority of Monopoly Investigation Monograph 26 it can be said that this statement also is false. The NAM's publicity department is many times as strong as that of all the labor organizations combined, obtains, say, a thousand times as much publicity, and perhaps more.

Again, taking the tests of policy, from reaction to fascism, from labor-baiting to red-baiting, it can be said that *Liberty* through its four varied ownerships has done a pretty good job of holding tight to the same old big business-NAM-sacred cow line.

As for the factor red-baiting, here is a gem from *Liberty:*

> "Bolshevism is knocking at our gates. We can't afford to let it in. We have got to organize ourselves against it, and put our shoulders together and hold fast. We must keep America whole and safe and unspoiled. We must keep the worker away from red literature and red ruses; we must see that his mind remains healthy."

The noted author who made this statement in *Liberty* was—Al Capone!

Newsweek: There seems to be no reason for the existence of this weekly: it is nothing better than a rewrite of what has appeared in the newspapers, and it is boring and dull. It seems incredible that a staff of some 50 newspaper people should succeed in producing, week after week, a thick magazine supposedly condensing and explaining the news, and doing it without a ray of brightness or intelligence.

Newsweek is the chief rival of *Time. Time* is bright, and has been accused of sacrificing accuracy frequently in order to be clever. Many persons have subscribed to *Newsweek* in the belief that it was less biased and prejudiced than *Time. Time* is bright, admits that it is biased; *Newsweek* is dull, but does not admit it is biased.

A good explanation for the founding of *Newsweek* is that its owners, bankers, Wall Street men, heads of the National Association of Manufacturers, were not quite satisfied with the reactionary prejudices of the big business newsweekly *Time.* They wanted something even more reactionary. No publication of national circulation is so openly Wall Street as *Newsweek.*

Like all corporation-owned magazines, *Newsweek* is anti-labor. The Full Employment Bill was dubbed "The Fool Employment Bill" by *Newsweek* editor Dr. Ralph Robey. Some time later he became a hired hand of the NAM.

In the service of Fascism *Newsweek* supported Franco and attacked the Loyalists of Spain. When protests were sent it, the then editor, Rex Smith, replied the term "reds" for the Republicans was used "for the sake of clarity."

Newsweek employed Major General J. F. C. Fuller of the British Army to write its military analysis. Repeated attacks by Walter Winchell resulted in the general being fired. However, it is a fact that General Fuller was one of the few Fascists outside Italy and Germany who openly admitted that fact. He was a member of the British Union of Fascists, a candidate for Parliament of this pro-Nazi, anti-Semitic organization.

In its August 2, 1943, issue, *Newsweek* still lauded Mussolini for saving Italy from "chaos, political decay, rising Communism." Twenty-two years earlier, in his own paper, Mussolini called these statements false. In 1925 they were part of the propaganda used for floating Fascist loans in Wall Street, and they are now part of the American mythology.

Almost every general criticism of the other popular weeklies applies to *Newsweek.* Its propaganda for banking, big corporations, the NAM's free enterprise, is more openly and more "honestly" stated than in *Time.*

Look: Look is the only one of the big circulation magazines of the whole United States which has been accepted, at times, by Liberalism. It has a circulation of 2,000,000; the anti-liberals have 98,000,000. Gardner (Mike) Cowles runs *Look.* Investigating the Cowles publications, Kenneth Stewart concluded (*PM,* May 28, 1944): they were "essentially honest, bright, fair, competent, interesting, up-to-the minute . . . they advance the best and most liberal elements in Republicanism . . . lack luster that might make them great as well as good—the spark of the human spirit, the flash of genius, the grand gesture."

Look is not a crusading magazine, nor is it liberal, in the sense that the *Nation* and *New Republic* are liberal. It is liberal only by contrast to all the rest. It might be fairer to say merely: *Look* is the only popular magazine which is not reactionary.

Conclusion

It is of course impossible to make a complete indictment of the magazine press in one short section of a book. Only a few examples have been chosen to illustrate the general theme: that the popular weekly and monthly magazines, which constitute a great power, are in the control of the same forces which run almost everything in the nation.

A complete study should be made of this situation. Very little has been reported. One of the most notable exposés was Dwight Macdonald's series on the Luce Empire in *The Nation* in 1937. On the other hand, a lot of nonsense, to use a mild term, has been written by all sorts of people, in an attempt to whitewash a very black journalistic situation.

There is, for example, Mr. Quincy Howe who in a book called "The News and How to Understand It," and devoted to a lot of muddying of clear waters—including statements about the present writer and *In Fact* which are not true, and which could have been corrected by a 5¢ telephone call—has the following to say of the Wallaces and *Reader's Digest:*

"Perhaps their avoidance of controversial, political issues accounts for the circulation," "perhaps it is their spirit of uplift." "No magazine in the United States has less outside control." *Reader's Digest* "uses that independence chiefly to promote general humanitarian causes of which most Americans strongly approve." "The editorial genius of DeWitt Wallace." "Good humor, sweetness and light."

And of the Morgan interest in *Time:* "But 'connection' is not 'control.' . . . Time, Inc., owes less to Morgan money, brains and influence than it does to the ability of its own executives. If money and influence could alone make a successful publication, bankers would be richer than they are and the publishing world poorer."

And of *Newsweek*: "*Newsweek* has become more and more the property of several well-to-do families—Harrimans, Astors, Whitneys, Mellons. These families do not impose their immediate interests on *Newsweek* any more than the Morgans do on *Time*. Few financiers control their publications as directly as the muckraking journalists would have you believe—and when they do the results are disastrous to all concerned."

Of Mr. Howe it cannot be said, as is usually done in the case of writers, and others who make statements which are childish, preposterous, stupid or propagandistic, that he is either a knave or a fool. Mr. Howe is neither. Mr. Howe was not born yesterday and he knows as well as the members of the staffs of *Time, Life*, and *Newsweek*, that not once in the history of these publications has there been deviation from the big money line, that all the magazines in which the House of Morgan, the Harrimans, the Harknesses, and the heads of the National Association of Manufacturers are interested are the defenders, propagandists and apologists for the so-called free enterprise systems these men of Wall Street and industry have established. Even some fools know this.

Mr. Howe is neither a knave nor a fool, and may not even be one of Upton Sinclair's brasscheck journalists whose morning breakfast consists of shoe polish. He is, however, one of Humbert Wolfe's boys. Mr. Wolfe wrote:

> You cannot hope to bribe or twist
>   Thank God! the British journalist.
> But, seeing what the man will do
>   Unbribed, there's no occasion to.

Mr. Howe is an illustration of a type.

There are, of course, honest but naïve souls who believe that we live in a world of a million coincidences, that this coincidental world is the best of all possible worlds, and that nothing is ever planned and certainly nothing is ever sinister.

Unfortunately, these honest and naïve persons, such as the editors, publishers and owners of *Editor & Publisher*, the *New York Times* and most newspapers, are also the men who to a great extent control public opinion. They are able to reach the millions. And they are able to tell the millions that there is absolutely no significance in thousands of facts such as these:

A member of the House of Morgan was one of the financiers of *Time. Time* has since its first issue defended the House of Morgan.

The Harriman, Astor, J. P. Morgan and other interests own and control *Newsweek. Newsweek* is anti-labor. (Just a coincidence.)

The two biggest advertisers are the automobile and cigarette industries, makers of the most highly priced and the cheapest of all items of general use or consumption. Annually each gives the newspaper press about $50,000,000. Not 1%, not 17 of the 1750 dailies, prints the numerous Federal Trade Commission fraud orders against the cigarette makers, or the auto makers' fraudulent 6% installment plan. (1745 or more coincidences.)

In the foreign field, next to the almost unanimous attack on Russia by the popular magazine press, the next most unanimous victim has been Mexico. In the early years of the Mexican revolution, there was great confusion in the American press, but as issues came into light, and the program of the "bandits" was seen to be the restoration of Mexico to the Mexicans—as distinguished from the "cientificos" and others who had sold their country to the oil, copper, silver and hacienda interests of the United States—the American press rose nobly to the defense of finance and big business.

Oil is at the bottom of the Mexican question, as of many other questions. The 1927 Constitution declares that the natural wealth of the sub-soil belongs to the people. Since 1927 corrupt Mexican interests, aided by corrupt American interests, have tried to alter or compromise this constitutional precept, and on each important occasion, such as a presidential election, the newspaper and magazine press of the "colossus of the North" has stood staunchly by the corrupting forces of both nations.

Collier's, the *Saturday Evening Post*, the *Atlantic Monthly* (under the previous editorship of Ellery Sedgwick, the defender of Franco Fascism), and such commercial magazines as *Mill & Factory*, published series of articles or special editions attacking the Mexican constitution, its liberal parties, its duly elected administration, and its general policies. The cannons of this magazine press were loaded with the same ammunition which the Standard Oil Company was distributing to the newspapers and other kept and venal organs. In contrast, most publications not taking Standard Oil advertisements or in other ways indebted to the Rockefellers, continued to report the Mexican situation fairly and honestly.

As for *Reader's Digest* it puzzles many because it takes no advertising, is not affiliated with big money. It does not seem to be out for the money, as all the rest are. Perhaps all its owner wants is great power. It is interesting to note that Mussolini among the dictators was also unique in having no lust for money.

It was Mr. Morgan himself who corrected a Senator who during the Munitions Investigation suggested that "money is the root of all evil." "It is 'the love of money' which 'is the root of all evil,' " said Mr. Morgan correctly. And you will find both money and love of money woven into every page of the history of Hitler and Hirohito, Salazar and Franco, Peron and other dictators. Mussolini accepted a French bribe of 50,000 francs (plus a monthly subsidy) because he wanted power, and as he himself said, power in a European country comes easiest via ownership of a newspaper press. Mussolini permitted the Italian national association of manufacturers and similar organizations to subsidize his seizure of power, but unlike Hitler, who permitted the German steel trust to do likewise, Mussolini kept no money, hoarded no money, did not enrich himself via money or live the life of a millionaire.

Money is woven into the pages of *Life, Time, Fortune, Saturday Evening Post, Collier's, Newsweek* and all the rest of the big magazines. Dwight Macdonald, no brasscheck writer, points out how year after year Luce and his magazines have become "more deeply entrenched in the industrial plutocracy" of his friends, Lamont, Davis and Morrow of the House of

Morgan. Moreover, "Time, Inc., is big business itself." It has enormous investments in industry. Can it be possible that the millions made annually by the Wallaces do not tie *Reader's Digest* to other millions, to the world of millions, as Mr. Howe would have us believe?

The newspaper press with its 50,000,000 and the magazine press with its 100,000,000 circulation have had, ever since complete commercialism set in, just after the First World War, a double objective in their editorial policy. In general terms this objective has been:

1. To make money.
2. To protect the system in which they prosper.

In thus pursuing these objectives in the period just before the Second World War, during it, and immediately afterwards, the most important service of the press has been suppression of the truth about the treason of big business in time of crisis and war; and directing public anger against the leadership of the enlightened public, the liberal and labor organizations.

PART THREE

BIG BUSINESS

CHAPTER 11

BIG BUSINESS IN THE WAR

In 1942 a fearless Senator accused the two largest industries of the United States of hindering the war effort. He actually made the charge of treason. He said: "The present grave lack of steel is the responsibility of the large steel companies which have sought to perpetuate their monopoly."

Oil and steel were essential to victory. On March 27 the Senator said: "Even after we were in the war, Standard Oil of New Jersey was putting forth every effort of which it was capable to protect the control of the German government over a vital war material.

"As Patrick Henry said, if that is treason—and it certainly is treason—then make the most of it.

"Yes, it is treason.

"You cannot translate it any other way."

The Senator who made these charges became President of the United States in 1945.

The charge of treason—the most sensational news item in the whole history of the Truman Committee's war investigations—was either suppressed or buried by most of the press, although it was forced to report the official findings, even to name names of corporations and officers who had sabotaged the war in one or more ways.

Liberal *PM* headlined the news "Standard Oil Accused of Treason." More surprising was the fact the *New York Daily News* also gave the item a two column head. On April 5, *PM* reported, under the heading "Press Protects Standard Oil," the vast effort by the American press to apologize for this alleged treason, to whitewash the Rockefeller corporation. *PM* accused the *New York Times* of publishing an editorial defense of Standard Oil which varied with a State Department finding; and it accused the newsweekly *Time* of "distortions," of so slanting the news that Thurman Arnold and the Truman Committee, instead of Standard Oil "turned out to be the culprits."

The pattern of Big Business during the Second World War is revealed not in one but in a score or more of Senate documents, reports of the Department of Justice, and other agencies which cannot be doubted or questioned. All the facts are easily procurable, they are libel-proof, and since they have not appeared in the newspapers or magazines of large circulation they are still important enough for several books. Unfortunately, no such books are being published.

A dozen or more could be written on the general subject, dividing it into three distinct phases:

1. The "sitdown" strike of the corporations which refused to go into production on both the defense program of 1939 and the first wartime program of 1941-1942.

2. Profiteering and robbery of the American people; manufacture and delivery of defective airplane motors, copper wire, bullets and other war materials, resulting in endangering the lives of American soldiers.

3. The secret cartel deals by which the biggest American corporations supplied nations soon to be our enemies with materials and information, and kept America unprepared. (Books on the cartels have appeared.)

Throughout the war, and even now, the truth about the whole business was suppressed—in the newspapers. We did not have to wait twenty years for great investigations which might startle the nation, just as the Nye-Vandenberg Munitions Investigation in the 1930's disclosed to the world the workings of the merchants of death, who profited on both sides of the fighting front. Every agency of government did its duty. The corporations which had been members of the Nazi cartels were named, the manufacturers who profiteered by selling defective cartridges and wire were exposed, tried, convicted and fined a few dollars, but thanks to the fact that the American press is free it used its special prerogative under the Article One of the Bill of Rights of our majestic Constitution to betray the best interests of the American people by keeping silent, while it devoted its headlines to a daily assault upon the laboring men and women who were producing the guns and tanks and planes and bullets to win the war.

There was total suppression. There was burial alive of the news. There was suppression of the names of the guilty in general news stories, and there was a well-paid campaign of whitewash which followed every official exposé of corruption and which was almost always accompanied by a great "public relations" advertising campaign in which accused corporations, having nothing to sell to the public, took pages in the newspapers and magazines to inform America how patriotic they themselves were and how well the free enterprise system was functioning—and winning the war by itself.

First of all there was the big business sitdown strike of the days of the defense program. Officially, Monograph 26 describes it in these terms:

> "In the 1940 defense crisis business displayed much the same attitude that it had shown 23 years earlier. Business would help the government and the people, but the basis of payment therefor would have to be fixed before the wheels would begin to turn. Profits, taxes, loans, and so forth, appeared more important to business than getting guns, tanks and airplane motors into production. . . .
>
> "It developed that business did not want to work for the country on the basis of a 7 or 8 percent profit limitation written into the Vinson-Trammel Naval Expansion Act in 1935, so these provisions were repealed. Thus the whole cost-plus basis of defense contracts which industry liked so well during the last war when it had practically a free hand in determining costs, went by the board in 1940 when the allowable items of cost were determined by the Treasury Department. . . .
>
> "Business is apparently not unwilling to threaten the very foundations of government in fixing the terms on which it will work."

Again, in Monograph 21 of the same TNEC investigation:

"Monopoly impairs democracy's ability to defend itself in time of war. National defense requires an expansion of output: monopoly seeks to augment its profit by restricting output and maintaining price. It thus obstructs the procurement of arms and supplies, increases the cost of defense, adds to the burden of debt and taxation, and undermines national morale. When the nation is attacked it may even turn the balance from victory to defeat."

The government reports called it "blackmail." The press suppressed everything it could.

The defense program merged with the war production program and President Roosevelt, determined that there must be no such scandals as followed the First World War, put all police powers of the government into action.

The assistant attorney general, the Tolan House Committee, the Truman Senate Committee, the Mead Committee, the Bone Committee, and several high officials of the Department of Justice did their jobs well and made their reports. They found several criminals, they frightened many others, and they indicted the Big Business or Free Enterprise system itself of everything from profiteering to treason; in fact, they continued when the war was over, in 1946 and 1947, to expose and indict monopoly, profiteering, the cartel system by which free enterprise was shown to be anti-free enterprise, and certainly anti-American; but throughout these years the public which reads the commercial press heard little or nothing of these matters of vital importance.

For example: Just after Pearl Harbor, the Assistant Attorney General, Mr. Thurman Arnold, issued a sensational report of the sabotage of the national program, the first report naming the practices which were later to be referred to as the treason of big business in wartime. Said Mr. Arnold:

"After a year of defense efforts we find consumers threatened with artificial price spirals, independent business threatened with destruction and agriculture forced to resort to price-raising methods in order to keep up with the procession.

"Looking back over 10 months of defense effort we can now see how much it has been hampered by the attitude of powerful private groups dominating basic industries who have feared to expand their production because expansion would endanger their future control of industry.

"These groups have been afraid to let others come into the field. They have concealed shortages by optimistic predictions of supplies, and talked of production facilities which do not exist.

"Anti-trust investigations during the past year have shown that there is not an organized basic industry in the United States which has not been restricting production by some device or other in order to avoid what they call 'ruinous overproduction after the war.'"

The nation was at war, faced with a rubber famine—which lasted for years because Standard Oil had suppressed the artificial rubber patents;—and an aluminum shortage, because the Mellon interests were in a cartel with the Nazis; a refusal by the steel interests to expand; a lack of magnesium; and so on down the industrial line. Fortunately for America, the Allied nations, notably Britain and Russia, were holding the military lines—at a loss of millions of men and homes and billions in treasure, while the United States spent two years getting into production and making the instruments for winning the war.

It is no exaggeration to say that this situation was more scandalous, more criminal, more treasonable, than the little deal by which the Krupps got one shilling on every fuse used on the Vickers hand grenades and the big deal by which certain supplies, shipped to Denmark by the United States, were transshipped to Germany with the connivance of the British Admiralty (as Admiral Consett later disclosed).

If the public had known, and if public opinion, or rather public indignation, counts for anything, and it can be all-powerful, the reaction to Mr. Arnold's disclosures would surely have resulted in a great speeding-up of our war program. Government seizure of the auto industry for that purpose was demanded by such leaders as Congressman Coffee, the Washington leader of the Liberal Bloc in Congress, Congressman Marcantonio of New York, and the international secretary-treasurer of the United Autoworkers, George F. Addes. Not a word in the newspapers about this, of course. Then came the

Arnold report. The burial and suppression in the press which followed is revealing.

To begin with, the second largest news service in America, the United Press, buried the news under seven paragraphs of unimportant Washington items, and it did this despite the fact the indictment was general. Later when Mellon and Davis and Duke of the aluminum cartel, the duPonts of General Motors, the Rockefellers of Standard Oil, and the Morgan Partners of United States Steel were named the story was also suppressed. Here indicted was the free enterprise system itself.

It was at this moment that Senator Truman for the first time used the word "treason."

In the metropolis, the New Deal paper, *PM,* played up the news, but the Hearst papers suppressed it entirely, as did the late Captain Joe Patterson's *Daily News,* while the olympian *Times* buried it somewhere in its vast wasteland. The *New York Herald Tribune,* which frequently publishes news the *Times* suppresses, did not have this item. The New York evening papers, including the *World-Telegram,* suppressed the news.

In Philadelphia, the New Deal paper, David Stern's *Record,* buried the news on page 10, the only paper to have any mention of it at all. The report had been released January 3, should have been in the Sunday papers on the 4th, in Monday papers both morning and evening. The *Philadelphia Inquirer* and the *Bulletin* suppressed the news.

The suppression in Chicago was most interesting. The *Tribune* was still fighting our going to war against Naziism and Fascism, still using every fair and foul tactic to throw muck on the Roosevelt administration, and might have made use of this report if its first duty—to advertisers—did not interfere. Not a trace of the Arnold story appeared in the final edition of the *Tribune* that Sunday.

The eight-star final sports edition of Hearst's *Herald-American* Saturday evening suppressed the news, although with the difference in clocks there had been ample time to set type and print the item received Saturday afternoon. Sunday, on page 4, column 3, this paper ran exactly three paragraphs at the bottom half of the page. Senator Truman's treason charge was omitted.

Colonel Knox's *Daily News* on Saturday printed the facts on page one, six paragraphs, which is not much. The *Times* did little better. It ran on its twelfth page a one-column head over an eight-paragraph item: "Arnold Charges Private Groups Held Up Defense." No Truman story. The only honest coverage was by Marshall Field's *Sun* which used the heading "Army Delay Blamed on Big Business" on page one, mentioned Truman as well as Arnold, and was one of the few papers of the whole country which returned to the subject with an editorial.

On January 15, Senator Truman released his report (Senate Committee Investigating National Defense) which for the first time named the corporations, notably General Motors, Chrysler, Ford, Aluminum Company and Bethlehem Steel. The report was so sensational it could not be ignored by even the most corrupt newspapers, but even the *New York Times* took the liberty of suppressing the names of every one of the corporations involved, although it spread the report on three inside columns in addition to four and a half paragraphs on page one. On the other hand, *PM,* which had no advertising from any of the corporations named, as did the *Times,* devoted four and a half solid pages to the Truman indictment.

There were of course a few honest papers throughout the country which printed the facts, as they usually do. The *St. Louis Post-Dispatch,* the *Christian Science Monitor,* among the nationally known dailies, the *Gazette* and *Daily* of York, Pennsylvania, among the smalltown dailies, but these newspapers—not 1% of the total of 1750—were not able to enlighten the whole nation and stir it to righteous anger.

On the other hand, the papers and writers began immediately their volunteer work for the big money. The main culprit in the Truman report was the auto industry, the largest advertiser of them all (tying for first place frequently with the soap makers and the tobacco vendors); and here is one of the items of whitewash, as written by the then Scripps-Howard and now Hearst columnist Westbrook Pegler:

"What the hell difference does it make now whether the maladministration in Washington, industrial inefficiency, economic caution or honest fear of a Socialistic coup in the motor industry or what combination of all these factors caused the enormous and irretrievable waste of materials and loss of time in the conversion of the motor factories toward production? . . . Naturally the motor companies were slow to abandon their regular trade. . . . I was in Washington when the CIO presented the 'practical, simple plan for utilizing and adapting the available machinery in the automobile industry for plane production.' . . . Possibly the magnates made a mistake in rejecting it as a Socialistic scheme intended to wrest the industry out of the hands of the owners, who, incidentally, are legion. . . . [Mr. Pegler apparently does not believe in the O'Mahoney report that 200 families own and control American industry; that the duPonts control General Motors.] The industry is sure to be Socialized now and God only knows who will get it when the war is over. . . . But, as capitalists and believers in private property their reaction was the only one that could have been expected of them."

The remarks of that leading social philosopher Mr. Pegler were not unique. In fact, it might be said that the same percentage of the press which attacked Mr. Roosevelt on each of his four campaigns, the press which was the enemy of the New Deal and which is always the enemy of progress and the friend of reaction (say some 90% of the newspapers, to be conservative), went quickly to the defense of each and every one of the industries, corporations and individuals accused of everything from neglect to treason. Advertising played a part. Said *Space & Time,* the newsletter of that profession (April 6, 1942): "Thurman Arnold has his say on what Standard Oil of New Jersey had done and had deliberately failed to do. . . . Standardmen William Stamps Farish and Frank Atherton took the stand to defend themselves. . . . Meanwhile McCann-Erickson Inc., the Standard advertising agency, well paid for its expert knowledge of which side the press is buttered on, is preparing an advertising campaign to do the necessary."

In the same report *Space & Time* notes that nothing will be done to Standard, one reason being its power which reaches into Government, into the Truman Committee itself. Tom Connally, of the Committee, had argued so bitterly with Senator O'Mahoney "that the latter was reduced in exasperation to muttering 'treason' under his breath," a remark first used by Truman. Senator Herring of Iowa also did his best for Standard. On the War Labor Board was W. C. Teagle, former chairman of the Standard Oil of New Jersey, and Ickes' Office of Petroleum Coordinator "is well stocked with Standard men . . . who have Harold LeClaire Ickes so beautifully surrounded." At the War Department was General W. D. Bryon, until then a Gulf Oil vice-president. Commenting on the revival of the phrase "merchants of death," *Space & Time* concluded: "There is nothing wrong with the idea as a device to identify the Farishes, Howards and Teagles as the legitimate heirs of Sir Basil Zaharoff."

On April 2, the *New York Times* devoted its leading editorial, a full column, to a rousing defense of Standard Oil, something Standard Oil could not have bought for a million dollars but somehow got for nothing. Newsweekly *Time* devoted two pages to this subject in its issue of April 6. On page 16 it said that, "Seldom has a United States business firm taken such a smearing as Standard Oil. . . . Thurman Arnold monopolized the nation's front pages; Standard was damned from hell to breakfast. But last week when the company finally got a chance to reply, its 'treason' turned out to be strictly of the dinner-table variety." And from there on, three columns of whitewash. Page 89 of the same issue of *Time* was an advertisement paid for by Standard Oil. *Time* got $8,000 for it. At this time, as always, Mr. Luce's other magazine, *Fortune*, ran a series of articles in praise of certain other corporations. Each of these articles coincidentally followed an attack by the Justice Department on the corporation as being part of the Nazi cartels, as, for example, Dow Chemical and Bausch & Lomb. Each of these whitewash pieces usually appeared within three months of the day the government made its accusation, or just the time necessary to get the material in print. Believers in a world of coincidences are welcome to this item for their scrapbooks.

Typical of the daily newspaper whitewash was the full page feature story by Jonathan Waldo in the *San Francisco Chronicle* (April 20) headlined "Treason Is An Ugly Word." It was illustrated with the trade-marks of Dow, Bausch & Lomb, and Esso, and said that the press had sensationalized Arnold's use of the word "treason"—whereas in fact and in truth not one paper in ten had headlined it, and more papers suppressed or whitewashed the firms than printed the real indictment.

Throughout May and June the ad-less newspaper *PM* reported that "Press Plays Esso Handout" and "Standard Gets A Good Press." The *Nation* said (August 17) that "even such a reputable and often courageous publication as *Time* magazine has played the game of apology and cover-up for Standard," and on August 31 *Time* showed its courageousness by publishing another full page of whitewash of Farish and Haslam and Standard Oil, who had now been able to "refute the charges" of the government, while on page 74 of the same issue appeared another of those $8,000 page advertisements, this one paid for by Esso.

In August, when the few liberal papers were telling a few liberals that "Standard's Alibi Collapses" and "Farish Refuted at Senate Quiz," the reactionary *New York World-Telegram* presented an eight-column headline dripping with whitewash: "U. S. Agencies Fully Advised on Rubber Patents, Farish Tells Senate." Even more venal was the series of articles whitewashing many of the accused war corporations which the Scripps-Howard chain published in 1943 under the title "Forging the Future." Their February 19 issue was devoted to one of the worst cartel offenders, and the heading was "Aluminum Co. Plays Dramatic War Part."

But the greatest effrontery of all was the use made of the venal press by Standard Oil itself. After it had been exposed and had failed to clear itself, it spent a fortune on advertising, and with its advertising went statements, reports, ideas for editorials and "news" items to all the papers of the country.

The McCann-Erickson advertising agency buttered the bread of the nation's press. Then, in September, 1942, Standard Oil of New Jersey collected a lot of the whitewash, reprinted it (with special permission; no one refused) in a booklet, and flooded the nation with copies. The cover reads "The End of a Myth (Editors Sum Up)," and an introductory note says that the case has now been "greatly clarified, as evidenced in representative newspapers." Quoted in the booklet were: the *New York Herald Tribune,* the *Boston Herald,* the *Evening Star* of Washington, the *Sun* of New York, the *Denver Post,* the *New York Times.* Representative newspapers!—representative of big business and the men who control America's future.

Significantly enough, the very newspapers which suppressed all charges and evidence of treason by the corporations were loud in headlining "treason" when an irresponsible Congressman, one Cox of Georgia, used that term in 1940 about the workmen at the shipyards at Kearny, New Jersey, who asked a few cents an hour more pay.

The greatest sitdown strike in American history was being staged at that time by the aviation industry (led by General Motors). The government had awarded $85,000,000 for 4,000 planes, but only 33 had been produced by August. "In the great capital sitdown strike of 1940, which delayed the signature of defense contracts and the start of work on most of them from May, 1940, until the beginning of October," wrote I. F. Stone in his book "Business as Usual," "the aviation industry was used as a front for the rest of business in its fight for special tax privileges on defense contracts. Unlike the strikes of labor, the sitdown strike of capital in the summer of 1940 had the support of the nation's great newspapers."

For the rest of the story (suppressed by almost all the newspapers) the reader is referred to the book just quoted and to pages 252 to 267 of "Facts and Fascism." Anaconda's defective wire, the Curtiss-Wright defective airplane engines, and the U. S. Cartridge Company's defective bullets are briefly noted, also the general charges against the Mellon Aluminum Company, United States Steel, the duPont General Motors, and the other leaders of the automobile industry, the rubber barons, and all the rest.

The defense of the nation had been entrusted to a few corporations. The major part of the many-billion dollar war budget was apportioned to 83 firms. Led by the great powers, industry, which later boasted it won the war, betrayed the nation—betrayed it for thirty billion pieces of silver. The evidence was given the country in government reports, but never reached the people. The press stood in the way.

The activities of big business interested a conservative Republican named William Allen White, one of the few honest editors of the nation. He tried to explain it in this way (in his *Emporia Gazette*, after a visit to Washington, in May, 1943):

"One cannot move about Washington without bumping into the fact that we are running two wars—a foreign war and a domestic one.

"The domestic war is in the various war boards. Every great commodity industry in this country is organized nationally and many of them, perhaps most of them, are parts of great national organizations, cartels, agreements, which function on both sides of the battle front.

"Here in Washington every industry is interested in saving its own self. It wants to come out of the war with a whole hide and with its organization unimpaired, legally or illegally.

"One is surprised to find men representing great commodity trusts or agreements or syndicates planted in the various war boards. It is silly to say New Dealers run this show. It's run largely by absentee owners of amalgamated industrial wealth, men who either directly or through their employers control small minority blocks, closely organized, that manipulate the physical plants of these trusts.

"For the most part these managerial magnates are decent, patriotic Americans. They have great talents. If you touch them in nine relations of life out of ten, they are kindly, courteous, Christian gentlemen.

"But in the tenth relation, where it touches their own organization, they are stark mad, ruthless, unchecked by God or man, paranoiacs, in fact, as evil in their design as Hitler.

"They are determined to come out of this war victorious for their own stockholders—which is not surprising. It is understandable also for Hitler to desire to come out of this war at any cost victorious for the German people.

"But this attitude of the men who control the great commodity industries, and who propose to run them according to their own judgment and their own morals, do not make a pretty picture for the welfare of the common man.

"These international combinations of industrial capital are fierce troglodyte animals with tremendous power and no social brains. They hover like an old silurian reptile about our decent, more or less Christian civilization—like great dragons in this modern day when dragons are supposed to be dead."

Although Mr. White was America's bravest editor and publisher, he did not name the troglodytes and silurian reptiles.

CHAPTER 12

DUPONT, HOOVER, AND HITLER

> "Finally, concentration of economic power emerges into concentration of political power, with the result that small groups of powerful interests control the State and National political life."—Committee on Small Business, House of Representatives.

THE MOST POWERFUL FAMILY in America is the duPont family. It is not unaware of its power.

In an office memorandum which the Munitions Investigation made public (during the hearing, September 18, 1936) one of its chief executives, Major K. K. V. Casey, speaking for the duPonts, said: "This is our country. . . ."

Under investigation at that very moment was the failure of the most important disarmament conference of the League of Nations to that date. When the testimony was concluded, Chairman Nye reported:

> "After the whole (Geneva) conference was over and the munitions people of the world had made the treaty a satisfactory one to themselves, we find that Colonel Simons (of the duPonts) is reporting that even the State Department realized, in effect, who controlled the Nation."

America's "merchants of death" diversified their business. In the Second World War they claimed, no doubt correctly, that their chief enterprise was no longer gunpowder and more modern explosives. Instead of being the leading American member of the Dynamit cartel, which had divided the world among five or six corporations, it had become the American member of the Big Three which divided the world for chemical exploitation: DuPont-Imperial Chemicals-I. G. Farben. There was more money in chemicals than in munitions, and the money came in every week, war or no war.

But I. G. Farben was discovered to be one of the great paymasters of Hitler and its chief owners the leading Nazis.

The cartel axis had armed Fascism, not the Democracies, and all the evidence pointed at I. G. Farben as one of the forces which inspired the Nazi war to dominate the whole world.

So, in June, 1946, when the shattered world went into conferences on atomic power and the duPont firm was accused of attempting to monopolize a force which would either destroy the universe—or free the inhabitants of the earth from want and fear—it again issued a denial, saying it had received only $1 from the American government for its patriotic part in atomic developments and owned no patent rights whatever. That was true.

"As for I. G. Farben," concluded the duPont statement, "the implication that the duPont Company had any connection with the German company of a nature detrimental to the United States or the United Nations, is just as far from the truth as Pravda's comment that atomic research was 'sold to private monopolies.' "

On January 6, 1944, the United States Government had indicted the duPonts and Imperial Chemicals Industries of Britain for forming a cartel with I. G. Farben of Germany and Mitsui of Japan. But this was not the first time that the duPonts had been under government investigation. The documentary evidence produced by the Nye-Vandenberg munitions investigation, and the La Follette-Thomas civil liberties investigation, and others, includes the following charges:

1. The duPonts secretly helped in the armament of Germany, and especially aided Hitler. Munitions Hearings, Part 12; for a full summary of this and Hoover exposé see *In Fact,* February 1 and 8, 1942.

2. The duPonts were aided in this work by the Secretary of Commerce, who was later elected President of the United States, with duPont among his largest financial backers. The man: Herbert Hoover (Part 9, Munitions Investigation, 73rd Congress—note especially pp. 2138, 2140, 2143, 2146, 2158, 2166-70, 2173-76, 2242.)

3. The duPonts control the largest auto firm, General Motors, which, along with the rest of the industry, refused for

months to convert to tanks and planes. (Documentation in *Facts & Fascism,* pp. 254, 262-264.) Also blocked standardization of tank engines. (*In Fact,* November 23, 1942.)

4. The duPonts are among the largest financial interests in the National Association of Manufacturers, which was organized for one purpose: to smash labor unions. (Part 6, report 6, La Follette Investigation; see Appendix 19.)

5. The duPonts were among the largest financial backers of the Liberty League, and its affiliates, which included the Sentinels of the Republic, the anti-Semitic wing of the first really important American Fascist movement. (Black Lobbying Investigation; see Appendix 22.)

6. The duPonts put more money into the presidential elections every four years than any other ruling American family listed in TNEC Monograph 29. The duPonts and A. P. Sloan, of General Motors, put up $9,000 or 17% of the $53,700 spent in the Republican campaigns in South Dakota.

7. The duPonts also helped arm Japan. Mitsui paid the duPonts $900,000 in 1932 for nitric acid-ammonia explosive formula. (Munitions Hearings.)

8. The duPonts, General Motors, and other American corporations conspired with Nazi representatives Baron von Tippleskirch and Baron von Killinger for a commercial and political alliance with leading businessmen and Republicans. (*Congressional Record,* August 20, 1942, pp. A3364-66; inserted by Representative John M. Coffee of Washington, from documents supplied by the author of this book.)

The foregoing "bibliography" of public documents may serve as an inspiration for someone who could find a publisher courageous enough to print a book on the DuPont Empire. Space here permits only a short summary of two episodes which, however, show the continuity of the DuPont Empire's international policy.

(1) The story of the duPonts, Mr. Hoover and Mr. Hitler.

The Versailles Peace Conference having failed to make peace, the League of Nations held conferences year after year for the purpose of disarming the world, planning some cures for its economic ills, and establishing international justice. In 1925, when rumors abounded that Germany was arming secretly, a disarmament conference was planned in Geneva.

In the course of the Munitions Investigation * it was revealed that the American Secretary of Commerce, no less a person than the future president, Herbert Hoover, sent the munitions makers telegrams to come to Washington for a secret conference to form a program for joint action against disarmament at Geneva. The duPonts and other powder and gun makers received copies. Here is the important paragraph from the Hoover invitation as received by Winchester Repeating Arms Company:

> "You are invited to send a representative to an informal preliminary conference to discuss the economic phases of the forthcoming Geneva Conference for the control of the International Trade in Arms, Munitions, and Implements of War. . . . It is important that the American representative at Geneva be fully posted as to the views of American manufacturers of sporting arms and ammunitions so that he may be able to safeguard their interests. . . . Draft convention being mailed you today." (Page 2138)

Testimony further revealed that the duPonts and others knew of the coming disarmament conference before the American people were told, and that they began having conferences with General Ruggles before his official appointment to the conference, and that they called on United States Government officials, especially Army and Navy men, before any word of the conference became public. The great munitions lobby went into action to sabotage disarmament, as later hearings proved.

On the witness stand Irénée duPont read a report made to him by his representatives at the Hoover conference:

> "The meeting was called to order by Secretary Hoover who suggested that the representatives present express their views, and that these views be put in writing and a committee be appointed to represent the interested industries at a later meeting, at which, it was hoped, that the delegates appointed by our Government to attend the Geneva Conference would be present. . . . It was the unanimous opinion of the representatives of the industry that there were grave objections to the proposed draft in its present form. . . ." (Page 2140)

* Evidence is from Part 9, Munitions Hearings.

DuPont admitted the lobbying—he called it "conferences" —with General Ruggles. He read a report made to him by his representative, Colonel Aiken Simons, March 25, 1925, 18 days before the public announcement that the United States would send a delegation to Geneva. Colonel Simons reported:

"As directed, I called on General G. L. Ruggles, Assistant Chief of Ordnance who is to go to Geneva. . . .

"General Ruggles stated that the United States was committed on the policy of cooperation in the limitation program, and that the following license plan seemed to be the most harmless . . . the War Department would take care that the Department of State protected such American industries. . . . To which I replied that this had not been done heretofore. . . . General Ruggles then suggested that the license be put under the Departmnt of Commerce (Hoover), which I agreed was better." (Page 2143)

Senator Clark asked:

"Does it strike you as singular that a delegate to the Geneva Conference, whose appointment was considered as being very secret, should be in close conference with your (duPont's) representative on the subject two weeks before his appointment was announced by the State Department?"

Irénée duPont:

"All I can say is that apparently he did."

Senator Nye asked duPont why he wanted the licensing placed in Hoover's hands. DuPont replied:

"I should think that the Department of Commerce would be more competent to handle a commercial transaction, probably, than would the State Department. . . ." (Page 2146)

Senator Nye:

"Mr. duPont, how extensive back in 1924 had been the contributions of the duPonts to the cause of the two political parties, the major political parties?"

DuPont:

". . . these records were all sent in to you."

Nye:

"The record is not complete . . . the total contributions to the Republican Party in 1924 were $34,096.64 . . . Do you sup-

PART THREE

BIG BUSINESS

CHAPTER 11

BIG BUSINESS IN THE WAR

IN 1942 a fearless Senator accused the two largest industries of the United States of hindering the war effort. He actually made the charge of treason. He said: "The present grave lack of steel is the responsibility of the large steel companies which have sought to perpetuate their monopoly."

Oil and steel were essential to victory. On March 27 the Senator said: "Even after we were in the war, Standard Oil of New Jersey was putting forth every effort of which it was capable to protect the control of the German government over a vital war material.

"As Patrick Henry said, if that is treason—and it certainly is treason—then make the most of it.

"Yes, it is treason.

"You cannot translate it any other way."

The Senator who made these charges became President of the United States in 1945.

The charge of treason—the most sensational news item in the whole history of the Truman Committee's war investigations—was either suppressed or buried by most of the press, although it was forced to report the official findings, even to name names of corporations and officers who had sabotaged the war in one or more ways.

Liberal *PM* headlined the news "Standard Oil Accused of Treason." More surprising was the fact the *New York Daily News* also gave the item a two column head. On April 5, *PM* reported, under the heading "Press Protects Standard Oil,"

Convention on the Trade in Munitions, it may be of interest to you to hear that on my recent visit to Washington I saw a copy of the convention finally signed at Geneva, and it is not nearly as bad as we thought it was going to be. There will be some few inconveniences to the manufacturers of munitions in their export trade, but in the main they will not be hampered materially. . . .'

"After the whole conference was over and the munitions people of the world had made the treaty a satisfactory one to themselves, we find again that Colonel Simons is reporting that even the State Department realized, in effect, who controls the Nation. . . ." (Pages 2166-7)

Chairman Nye:

"Here, after all, is very, very clearly demonstrated a fact or facts which make it clear that when our Government enters into negotiations with other governments looking to a particular agreement, it does not necessarily imply that all the departments of Government are in agreement. One department of government may agree to participate in a conference with others, but there is not an assurance in that offer that other departments are going to cooperate and that the Government as a whole will finally agree.

"In fact, there seems to have been in the case of this controversy here rather emphatic proof that irrespective of the wishes and the interests of the State Department to participate in a conference that would accomplish something really worthwhile as respects control in the sale of arms over the world, they were seriously hampered by the War Department, seriously hampered by the Commerce Department (Herbert Hoover) who responded to every beck and call of the munitions industry to see that there was an upsetting of the plans that were uppermost in the minds of those who were opposed to the work of the conference." (Pages 2169-70

As the Munitions hearings progressed it was evident that the munitions industry, headed by the duPonts, wanted to share the profits from the secret arming of Germany, in violation of all treaties. Here is some of the testimony:

Senator Vandenberg:

"I want to make a general statement . . . so that it will be understood what it is we are undertaking to do. We shall discuss the rearming of Germany and Austria. . . . We find ourselves with a direct interest in the fruits of the Versailles adventure. . . . If sinister influences have defeated the attempt at limitation in this instance (Geneva conference), we are warned against the menace. . . . Here was the greatest attempt in the history of the world to effect a disarmament control. . . . Certainly we can dismiss the supposition that these Allied Governments have permitted the rearming of Germany . . . because they wanted them to disarm. . . . The alternative proposition must be that forces, even more powerful than governments themselves, have had a stake in this outcome and have influenced it. We are hunting the possible identification of such forces. . . . There were and are two sources of profit, external to Germany, and the others which could exist in respect to the rearming of Germany. . . . One source could be those who made the direct sales. . . . Major Casey, did any of your company representatives in Europe report to you as long ago as 1924 or 1925 the existence of some sort of a secret French-British report on the rearming of Germany and Austria?"

Major K. K. V. Casey:

"I believe there was such a memorandum." (Pages 2173-76)

One more document provides the final proof that the Secretary of Commerce, Herbert Hoover, was of real help to the munitions makers. This document is Exhibit 831 in the Munitions inquiry. It consists of a report from Colonel Simons to the Winchester Repeating Arms Company of New Haven and other gun makers, and says in part:

"National legislation re: Arms and ammunition for export.

"In the Spring of 1925 it became known that an international congress was to be held in Geneva for the purpose of limiting the exportation of munitions and that it was probable that efforts were to be made by certain foreign elements to prohibit the private manufacture of munitions. On March 28, 1925, Mr. Hoover, Secretary of Commerce, telegraphed a number of American manufacturers. . . . This conference was presided over by Mr. Hoover. . . .

"We found Mr. Hoover very sympathetic and helpful throughout and with his assistance a call was sent to 36 other industries. . . . Resolutions were drafted showing the objections of the American manufacturers to the proposed international agreement. . . .

"It is believed that by the action of Mr. Hoover in appointing this committee and the committee's subsequent work, the Geneva Conference was prevented from adopting international agreements which would have been burdensome to American manufacturers, and so far as I know the committee has never been dissolved.

[Signed] Aiken Simons
[Dated] February 22, 1928." (Page 2242)

The final word by the chairman of the investigations:

"This letter finds Colonel Simons crediting Mr. Hoover as Secretary of Commerce with the put-out, and the committee with an assist, in that particular, in making a failure of that Geneva Conference. . . ."

The Nye-Vandenberg Committee also reported that before and after the arrival of Herr Hitler as chief of the German state, the duPonts were among the American firms helping in its rearmament.

German Big Industry began paying Hitler in 1923. (Fritz Thyssen of the Steel Trust gives all the details in his book, "I Paid Hitler.") What Big Business wanted was security against any attempt by the German Republic to make industry pay its share of the money and suffering which losing the war forced upon the German people; industry wanted light taxes, free enterprise (which is also the National Association of Manufacturers' slogan), and especially protection against any extension of the rights of labor (such as the Wagner Act in America, for example). Since Germany was nominally a republic in control of the Social Democratic Party, industry was afraid that labor would be top dog. It soon found that it could do business with the Social Democrats. But it could not fool the working people of Germany.

At this time Thyssen heard Hitler fool some working people. Hitler called his party N-A-Z-I, which is a contraction for National Socialist Workers Party, and he made promises of a socialistic nature and offered the workers control of the state. Thyssen knew this was a fraud and that Hitler would take money from Big Business. He started paying in 1923, just after the Hitler Beer Hall fiasco, and he got others to contribute later, so that in 1932, when Hitler's star waned and it looked as if a liberal coalition would keep control, the cartels of Big Business poured out millions and put Hitler in power in 1933.

The duPonts knew what was happening. Testifying before the Munitions Committee, Wendell R. Swint, director of foreign relations of the DuPont Empire, said he knew that the Krupps "had developed a scheme whereby industry could contribute to the [Nazi] Party Organization funds, and in fact every industry is called upon to pay ½% of the annual wage and salary roll to the Nazi organization." The great I. G. Farben also informed Swint that German industry was the backer of Hitler's Nazi outfit. Swint testified that Dr. Carl Bosch of I. G. Farben told him that it was "a question of Fascism and Bolshevism." Actually Bosch was repeating the Hitler propaganda, because at the time Germany was a coalition government ranging from the Conservatives on the Right, the Centrum (Catholic Party) in the center, and the Social Democrats on the left, all following a policy of appeasement of Naziism.

The Munitions Committee also obtained the information that even after Roosevelt had been elected, but before he took office, and while Hoover was still president, Felix duPont signed a contract with a Hitler agent who gave his name as Giera but who was actually the international spy Peter Brenner. This occurred February 1, 1933. At this time it was still illegal to send munitions to Germany but the duPonts appointed Giera for the purpose of smuggling them via Holland. The contract appoints Giera agent for Germany and Holland, "to negotiate the sale of military propellants and military explosives to purchasers located in that territory." Letters seized by the Nye committee show that Giera and Colonel William N. Taylor, duPont's Paris man, and Major Casey, discussed means of smuggling into Germany. Taylor is quoted by the Senate committee as saying it was easy to run guns up the Dutch rivers into Germany because there was no inspection, and "in view of the Taylor reports regarding active smuggling of arms into Germany via Holland the provision that the Giera agency covered purchases of military propellants and explosives in Holland . . . is most significant. Furthermore, the amazing contract, covering also the sale of military propellants and explosives, in Germany, contained no reservations whatsoever respecting the restrictions on such military material in Germany laid down in the Treaty of Versailles and by reference in the treaty between the United States and Germany."

Lammot duPont informed Harry (later Lord) McGowan

of Imperial Chemicals of the Giera deal, and on March 6, 1933, the British munitions lord replied that "our German friends . . . have not been idle. . . . I am sure that when freedom to manufacture is granted for home use . . . they will expect to have a permanent position in the business." But McGowan did not want duPont to horn in on his cartelized field, so he asked duPont to cancel Giera. DuPont paid Giera $25,000, and listed the money paid the spy as "expense money" in its income tax return. No one went to jail.

The duPonts immediately sent Giera, a German spy, to Japan to work for them, the Senate Committee disclosed. When Giera applied for a job to the duPonts he boasted he was a spy, had worked in thirteen countries, and for Germany against the interests of the United States in the First World War. He was one of the spies employed here by Captain Von Papen and Captain Boy-Ed from 1914 to 1917. After April 6, 1917, when the United States declared war on Germany, Giera, the German spy, "quit the Germans and went to work for us (duPonts) to save his neck," it was testified by Major Casey. (Munitions Hearings, Part 12.)

The evidence is conclusive that the duPonts participated in the arming of Germany and aided the Nazis, and that the duPonts had friendly conferences with Herbert Hoover, as Secretary of Commerce, regarding easing of the limitations on the munitions business while they were helping to arm Germany.

In 1928 the DuPont Empire contributed one of the big pieces of money to the campaign which elected Herbert Hoover president.

The curious thing about 1928 was that this was exactly the year the DuPont Empire and Anaconda Copper decided to subsidize the campaign of a Catholic liberal, Alfred E. Smith. (The religious issues and hatred raised in this campaign, like the religious issues raised against Lehman for Governor of New York, illustrate how much Nazi-Fascism we have in this country, but that should be the subject of another volume.)

However, although the duPonts were the big financial

backers of the Democratic party, they did not forget how Hoover had worked for them, and so they also became one of the main backers of the Republican campaign. They simply could not lose.

The Republicans raised $9,433,604 to buy the election for Hoover. But that figure does not tell the story. A handful of Big Businessmen did the paying. Exactly half, almost $5,000,-000, came from a few men each of whom put up $5,000 to $50,000, or more. In 1932, when Hoover, a discredited man, ran again, 112 persons who had profited by his presidency or hoped to profit, put up 40% of the millions for his campaign. (For documentation, see "Money in Elections," by Professor Louise Overacker.)

In 1928 Alfred duPont gave the Hoover fund $25,000; Lammot gave $10,000; T. Coleman $10,000; Felix was listed in the one to five thousand class. Alfred P. Sloan, of General Motors, gave $25,000 and the Fisher Brothers of General Motors and Fisher Bodies put up $100,000. In addition there are loans, and deficits which the duPonts helped pay.

(2) The full story of the duPont cartel deal with the Nazis appears in Monograph 1, Economic and Political Aspects of International Cartels, Committee on Military Affairs, 1944. It is noted on page 6 that "there was a gentleman's agreement between duPont and I. G. Farben by which each was to give the other first option on new processes and products," after which an interesting story is told concerning the use of acrylic products. For general use this plastic was being sold to commercial molders at 85¢ a pound; it was the identical stuff being sold to dentists at 45¢ an ounce, and there was danger that the latter would soon find out how they were being robbed. However, this was no great problem for free enterprise. If arsenic or another dangerous poison could be added to the plastic sold for 85¢, it could no longer be employed for dentures. And so it was decided to add 1% of the poison. (Page 19)

When war impended, the cartel began worrying about the future. The document reveals that the American members promised the Nazis they would restore the contracts and gentlemen's agreements after the war, no matter which side won. Where profits are, there is no fatherland. Regarding stock jointly owned in an Argentine firm, the document states:

> "DuPont supported Imperial Chemical Industries on this point [that stock could not be delivered to the Nazis in wartime] but assured IG that after the war it would endeavor to restore IG's participation.
>
> "The problems faced by a neutral in maintaining its cartel connections in wartime are illustrated by duPont's relations with ICI and IGF from 1939 to 1941 . . . DuPont agreed to withhold IG's information from the British. . . .
>
> "As the anti-Nazi policy of the United States became more apparent, some cartelized American companies reduced, though they did not abandon, their commitments to German companies.
>
> "DuPont, for example, continued during 1940 to negotiate agreements with IGF."

(The quotations are from pages 62 and 64.)

In 1941 there was a resolution adopted by the duPont Company which declared that dealings would "remain suspended until the termination of the present international emergency." Under the heading "forestalling seizure of enemy property," the document tells of assignments of patents in wartime, quoting from official duPont contracts, adding:

> "Nevertheless both parties agree to reassign all assigned patents and patent applications at any time."

Finally, the document states (on page 74) that the duPonts apparently had an understanding that many, if not all, of its cartel agreements would be resumed after the war.

The evidence of duPont undertaking to restore the Nazi cartel after the war was first presented by Assistant Attorney General Wendell Berge who (on September 7, 1944, before the Kilgore Committee) declared:

> "The danger is very real that the monopolistic firms of Germany will retain their power through the maintenance and resumption of cartel agreements. For instance, the I. G. Farben has had arrangements with duPont and with the British Imperial Chemical Industries for the division of the South American market. A report by the duPont foreign relations department to the duPont executive committee, dated February 9, 1940, states:

> " 'The duPont Co. informed I. G. that they intend to use their good offices after the war to have the I. G. participation restored.'
>
> "A communication from duPont to Imperial Chemical Industries later in 1940 states with respect to the obligations to I. G. Farben (termed in the communication 'former shareholders'):
>
> " 'I think we have all agreed that there is a moral commitment, if and when circumstances permit, for these former shareholders to become shareholders again but the basis on which this may be done will have to be discussed at that time.' "

At this point Chairman Kilgore interrupted to ask if the duPont-I. G. Farben commitments were similar to the Standard Oil-I. G. Farben commitments, which Senator Truman had held treasonable, and Mr. Berge replied: "That is correct."

Both Senator Kilgore and Mr. Berge insisted on the danger of the Standard Oil and duPont treaties to restore their deals with the Nazis. The conclusions of these men is best expressed by Mr. Berge's statement in his presentation of the evidence in the duPont case. He said:

> "As the military defeat of Germany grows near, we will see a determined effort on the part of the Germans to save their industrial power.
>
> "The Germans know that their best chance of preparing for another war will be through the maintenance of their monopolistic industrial firms. These firms have had agreements with British and American industry. If these agreements can be continued, revived, or renewed in the future, this country can win the war but Germany will have gone far toward the winning of the peace.
>
> "During the next few months we must be prepared to witness the exodus from Germany of political agents who will announce that they are ordinary business men. . . ."

The public does not know the facts, has never been able to get the evidence. The newspapers, by suppressing the real duPont story for generations, makes it easy for the duPonts to speak as if evidence does not exist.

CHAPTER 13

THE TOP OF THE PYRAMID

ONLY the older generation will remember the ogres of their time: old John D. Rockefeller, the man who had trimmed widows and orphans out of millions and whose armed forces shot down his workers at Ludlow, Colorado; and old John Pierpont Morgan, whose name was used as a synonym for Wall Street and the love of money which is the root of all evil.

In the course of time the curse was erased from the Rockefeller name, thanks very much to the most efficient use of a new arm, the public relations propagandist or plutogogue, as personified by Mr. Ivy Lee, the man who elevated press agentry from the sawdust of Barnum & Bailey's circus and the blackmail of department store advertisers.

As for "Morgan" and "Wall Street," the job of reconversion and rehabilitation was done so well, so secretly and so completely, that only the Populist remnants, then the Socialists, and later on the Communists, dared to use these terms in anything but a tone of reverence and respect, earning along with many crackpots and irrational fanatics the terms "crackpots" and "irrational fanatics" from the respectable press and respectable citizenry.

A whole generation has been spent in whitewashing Wall Street, gilding the name of Morgan. So restored to public favor have both become that they suffered no ill effects whatever in 1946 when the Department of Justice instituted an investigation which produced the evidence that six most powerful banking groups of the nation, headed by Morgan, Stanley & Company, hold a monopoly on the nation's commerce, manipulate gigantic corporations, railroads, utilities and banks, and so completely dominate big industry that the term "free enterprise"—which was also a semantic trick to take the curse off the ill-fated term "capitalism" after the breakdown of 1929—could become the homeric laugh of the century.

Times have changed. Within one generation we have seen the two most powerful chains of newspapers, Hearst's and Roy Howard's, change their politics and their social coloration, the former from a demogogical crusade against "the interests" and "Wall Street" and Morgan and the like, to an impassioned whitewasher of Standard Oil, great monopolies, once painted with horns and a tail; the latter from tribune of the people to attacker of the Wagner Act, and all the New Deal laws which helped labor. The *World* passed away. Its smaller brother, the *St. Louis Post-Dispatch,* continues to crusade and to speak for people, but it is as it has always been, a regional voice instead of a national clarion. The other chains, McCormick-Patterson, Gannett, and the newcomer, John S. Knight's string of five, do not crusade for the public welfare.

These chains and their colleagues which make up the opinion-forming press are today not only on the side of Wall Street and Morgan but they are so much a part of the same financial system that they can be expected to whitewash but never to expose the rulers of America and their activities. The historical fact is that the Government, despite pressures and politics, does take legal actions, but no one arouses public opinion any more, no one mobilizes it, nothing much happens.

This is especially true when the House of Morgan and the financial and industrial giants of Wall Street are under fire.

Throughout a large part of 1946 and 1947 a Federal Grand Jury sat in New York City listening to the Department of Justice present the evidence on which it requested an indictment of the Big Six banks: the six most powerful private banking houses remaining in the nation: Morgan, Stanley & Company, First Boston Corporation, Dillon Read & Company, Kuhn, Loeb & Company, Barney & Company, and Blythe & Company. Also involved were the smaller firms: Mellon Securities Corporation, Lazard Frères, Lehman Bros., Kidder, Peabody & Company, Halsey, Stuart & Company, Goldman, Sachs & Company, Stone & Webster Securities Corporation, and many others.

There are 730 members of the Investment Bankers Association, but 38 of them manage 91% of the nation's business, and of these 38 the Big Six of Wall Street did 57% of the total. Fourteen additional New York bankers did 21% of the total, and 18 outsiders—with Wall Street connections, of course —did another 12%. This left 692 firms with only 9% of the nation's financing.

The Big Six divided the job in this way:

Morgan, Stanley & Co., $2,142,000,000, or 23.2% of total;
First Boston Corporation, $986,000,000, or 10%;
Dillon, Read & Co., $680,000,000, or 7.4%;
Kuhn, Loeb & Co., $618,000,000, or 6.7%;
Smith, Barney & Co., $472,000,000, or 5.1%;
Blythe & Co., $388,000,000, or 4.2%.

In the five-year period 1934-1939, according to TNEC Monograph 24, the investment banks handled a total of $36,100,000,000 and in the first six months of 1946, according to a Department of Justice representative who said the figures were not complete, the business done was $4,465,800,000.

It is obvious from these colossal figures that any manipulation, any monopolization or any action not for the public benefit taken by a few men and a few firms controlling so many billions of dollars must seriously affect the economics of the nation.

To the Federal Grand Jury the Department of Justice stated that these bankers did in fact have a monopoly, and that they used their power for certain purposes, so that they maintained a stranglehold on the nation's commerce.

The Department charged the bankers with actually deciding upon which industries were to be helped to expand, and which were to be retarded. It accused the bankers of regulating areas for competition and for monopoly; of fixing prices; of deciding on which technological improvements and patents should be made available to the public, and which were to be retarded or completely suppressed.

It accused the bankers of initiating stocks and bonds issues, rather than waiting for an industry to come to them for help.

It maintained that the anti-trust laws were being violated to the detriment of the public.

It concluded that here, at the pinnacle of all financial and industrial power, there was complete monopoly, the very antithesis of "free enterprise," which, according to the National Association of Manufacturers and the press, is "the American way of life."

The charges, evidence and conclusions were of utmost importance to the people of the United States. An informed electorate frequently is able through the pressure of public opinion and the use of the ballot box to restore Democratic procedure which the founders of the Republic wrote into the Constitution, and notably into the Bill of Rights. But it must be informed. And since most of the press does not inform the public—whenever there is danger of making an enemy among the thousand most powerful Americans and inviting a financial loss as a result—it stands to reason that most of the public will not know the facts and will not be able to act intelligently.

In this instance there was almost complete silence.

Not a word appeared in the most powerful newspaper of the country, the *New York Times,* although it was the *Times* itself, long before the investigation began—on September 7, 1944, to be exact—which first mentioned its probability. "Monopoly Attack On Wall Street Looms" was its heading at the time, but when the investigation—not at all an "attack"—was under way, the *Times* forgot all about it. In its 1944 news item it did not, of course, mention the House of Morgan and since Morgan was under investigation the silence of the *Times* —and the rest of the press—is understandable.

The news appeared in the August 5, 1946, issue of *In Fact.* It was picked up and headlined in *Labor,* the official organ of the Railroad Brotherhoods, on August 17, and reprinted in a few papers from then on, notably the *New York Post* (August 14—but no names mentioned) and *PM* on October 25. The tremendous importance of the investigation was recognized by Senator Murray of Montana who inserted the entire *In Fact* article into the *Congressional Record,* and since the *Record* is privileged, all excuses which newspapers might have been able to make in the past became useless. It was news, and all names were named, and no one could get into trouble for reprinting the *Record.* But no one did.

It would be useless to question Heart's International News Service or Howard's United Press on this matter. But the Associated Press is a "cooperative" of more than a thousand dailies and it is dedicated to presenting all the news without the bias of any one owner and it is loud in defense of the code of ethics of journalism. A note to Kent Cooper was rewarded with a carbon copy of its report. It was dated August 9 and consisted of less than one typewritten page, say 250 words. Its first paragraph read:

> "New York, Aug. 9 (AP)—Executives of some of the nation's largest investment banking houses, who declined the use of their names, said today that agents of the Justice Department's anti-trust division have undertaken an intensive investigation into past and present investment banking practices."

Paragraph 2 said the Justice Department declined comment, and the rest of the page was a little speculation.

No names were named. None of the charges of the Department, sensational as they were, was mentioned. Newspapers receiving the Associated Press service did not print the few words they received. And so, while technically no charge can now be brought against the Associated Press of joining in a "conspiracy of silence" with Hearst and Howard and certain newspapers which have their own news services, the end result, silence, was achieved without conspiracy. Just as "a lie which is half a truth is ever the blackest of lies," "a lie which is part a truth is a harder matter to fight," so a news item which is part of a fact is worse than one which is totally a lie, or one which is totally suppressed.

Total suppression was the fate of the 359-page official government report, "Economic Concentration and World War II," issued by the Smaller War Plants Corporation through the Senate Small Business Committee.

The reason for press silence is obvious: no other document ever issued by the government comes so close to naming the men who own and control America.

Specifically, it lists the "eight interest groups" with Wall Street roots which dominate the country, controlling 90 of the 200 biggest corporations, and themselves bound together with interlocking directorates, and united in the two most powerful civilian organizations of the country, the National Association of Manufacturers and the United States Chamber of Commerce. In the words of the document:

> "The relatively few giant corporations of the country which have come to dominate our entire economy are themselves largely owned by only a few thousand stockholders, and are controlled by a mere handful of huge financial interests."

In industry after industry, food, whisky, grocery chains, soap, rayon, two or three or at most four companies supply from half to 80% of all the products sold in the country, and these firms are united through their banking affiliates and their politico-economic associations; they grow bigger and more monopolistic with the years, and every man, woman and child who spends money or for whom money is spent aids them financially and pays them an extra tribute for monopoly.

Looking ahead, the report foresees the same situation in the use of atomic power. The government spent $1,300,000,000 for atomic bomb plants which three firms, Union Carbide & Carbon Company, Eastman Kodak, and duPont operated. Almost all the equipment was built by two firms, Westinghouse and General Electric. Continues the report:

> "The concerns which made the equipment for the manufacture of atomic materials, and the firms which operated the plants, will inevitably have a tremendous headstart over all other firms in scientific knowledge and production 'know-how' in the adaptation of atomic power for peacetime uses."

The concentration of wealth and power in the hands of a few is obviously one of the greatest threats to American democracy. Senator Murray said so in introducing the report:

> "If we believe that our system of free enterprise should be preserved, if we believe that the American economy should be the

expression of a free society, then we cannot stand idly by and watch the march of monopoly to power. We cannot risk the consequences —for in this struggle, if we are too little and too late, there will be no second chance."

If the date of this document and Murray's address to the Senate had been in the Bryan era, or even in the 1920's, there would undoubtedly have followed a press and political campaign of great intensity. The front pages would have told the story, and editorials in the Scripps and Hearst newspaper chains might have repeated them in a demagogic manner, the magazines would have explained the significance and the danger—and been accused of muckraking.

"What has destroyed liberty and the rights of man in every government which has existed under the sun? The generalizing and concentration of all powers into one body," Jefferson wrote, warning of governmental power, whereas here was the documentary proof of a concentration which threatened government itself.

The reason for silence in the 1940's was the mention of the very ogres of the early days of the century. The ogres had become the sacred golden bulls of the press.

First, and far ahead, the report placed the House of Morgan. With one of its banks, the First National, it controlled 41 of the 200 largest non-financial corporations, ten of which had two or more directors in common with J. P. Morgan & Company. Its financial control was listed as exceeding thirty billion dollars.

The Kuhn-Loeb control was second largest, eleven billions, but it was not diversified; it included thirteen major railroads, about 22% of the first class mileage of the country.

The Rockefellers controlled more than six billions, the Mellons a little more than half as much, the duPonts two and a half billions. Here is the full table as it appeared in the *Congressional Record* and as it did not appear in the commercial press of America:

MORGAN-FIRST NATIONAL—$30-BILLION PLUS

Industrials:

U. S. Steel
Gen. Electric
Kennecott Copper
Pullman Inc.
Phelps Dodge Corp.
Montgomery Ward & Co.
Amer. Radiator & Standard Sanitary Corp.
Glen Alden Coal Co.
Natl. Biscuit Co.
Phila. & Reading Coal & Iron Corp.
Continental Oil Co.
St. Regis Paper Co.
Baldwin Locomotive Works

Public Utilities:

Amer. Telephone & Telegraph Co.
Consolidated Edison of N.Y.
Commonwealth & Southern Corp.
United Gas Improvement Co.
Amer. Power & Light Co.
Public Service Corp. of N.J.
Electric Power & Light Corp.
Niagara Hudson Power Corp.
Columbia Gas & Electric Corp.
Natl. Power & Light Co.
Intl. Tel. & Tel.
Amer. Gas & Electric Co.

Railroads:

N.Y. Central R.R.
Alleghany Corp.
Great Northern Ry. Co.
Northern Pacific Ry. Co.
Atchison, Topeka & Santa Fe
Southern Pacific
Delaware, Lackawanna & Western

Banks:

Guaranty Trust Co.
Bankers Trust Co.
N.Y. Trust Co.

ROCKEFELLER—$6½-BILLION PLUS

Industrials:

Standard Oil of N.J.
Socony-Vacuum Oil Co.
Standard Oil of Indiana
Standard Oil of Cal.
Atlantic Refining Co.
Ohio Oil Co.

Banks:

Chase National

KUHN-LOEB—$11-BILLION

Public Utilities:

Western Union Telegraph

Railroads:

Pennsylvania R.R.
Union Pacific
Chicago, Milwaukee, St. Paul & Pacific
Chicago & Northwestern
N.Y., New Haven & Hartford
Wabash
Boston & Maine
Missouri-Kansas-Texas
Delaware & Hudson
Lehigh Valley

Banks:

Bank of Manhattan

Mellon—$3-billion plus

Industrials:
Gulf Oil
Koppers Coke
Aluminum Co. of Amer.
Westinghouse
Jones & Laughlin Steel Corp.
Pittsburgh Coal Co.
Amer. Rolling Mills
Pittsburgh Plate Glass
Crucible Steel Co. of Amer.

Public Utilities:
United Light & Power Co.
Bklyn. Union Gas Co.

Banks:
Mellon Natl. Bank
Union Trust Co.

Railroads:
Virginia Ry. Co.

Chicago Group—$4-billion plus

Industrials:
Intl. Harvester
Armour & Co.
Marshall Field & Co.
Wilson & Co.

Public Utilities:
Commonwealth Edison Co.
Public Service Corp. of No. Illinois
Peoples Gas Light & Coke Co.

Banks:
Continental Illinois Natl. Bank & Trust Co.
First Natl. Bank of Chicago
Northern Trust Co.
Harris Trust & Savings Bank

DuPont—$2½-billion plus

Industrials:
Gen. Motors
E. I. duPont de Nemours
U.S. Rubber Co.

Banks:
Natl. Bank of Detroit

Cleveland Group—$1½-billion

Industrials:
Republic Steel Corp.
Youngstown Sheet & Tube Co.
Goodyear Tire & Rubber
Inland Steel
Wheeling Steel
Cleveland Cliffs Iron Co.
Interlake Iron Corp.

Banks:
Cleveland Trust Co.

Boston Group—$1½-billion plus

Industrials:
United Fruit Co.
United Shoe Machinery Corp.
U.S. Smelting, Refining & Mining

Public Utilities:
Stone & Webster
Edison Electric Illuminating Co. of Boston

Banks:
First Natl. (incldg. Colony Trust)

Today, as a generation ago, it is still Wall Street, still Morgan and still Rockefeller who own and control. Today, however, the few who still protest—in the name of democracy and the general welfare—cannot make themselves heard.

CHAPTER 14

WHO BUYS THE ELECTIONS?

> "He (Nelson W. Aldrich, majority leader of the U. S. Senate, father of Winthrop W. Aldrich of the Chase National Bank, father-in-law of John D. Rockefeller, Jr.) was working now for a definite end—to merge business and politics in the interest of business; to seize, through politics, the instrumentalities of government and use them for the profit of the favored few." (Claude Bower's biography of Senator Beveridge.)

IF IT IS TRUE that money prevails in national and state elections, then it must also be true that the men who put up the money, the handful including the duPonts, Pews, Mellons, Rockefellers and others frequently named in this volume, also control our political life, our Congress, and the Presidency itself.

A conspiracy of silence has always existed on this subject. But in its Sunday edition of January 13, 1924, the *New York World* (and its affiliate, the *St. Louis Post-Dispatch,* which is still one of the few newspapers worthy of being on an honor roll) did publish the first great and sensational exposé of the purchase of the presidency.

The evidence was supplied by Major J. J. Dickinson, a former official of the Department of State, and corroborated by Judge Alton Brooks Parker, who had been defeated by Theodore Roosevelt, who still remains one of the great mythical heroes of the American people.

The Roosevelt campaign against Parker was underwritten "just as they would underwrite building a railroad from here to San Francisco," according to Dickinson, by the following millionaires:

James Stillman (the elder).
E. H. Gary, president of United States Steel, a J. P. Morgan corporation.
E. H. Harriman, railroad king and banker.
Daniel G. Reid, railroad manipulator, and founder of American Can Company.

George B. Perkins, partner in the House of Morgan.
Charles F. Brooker, head of the brass trust.
Robert L. Bacon, another partner in the House of Morgan.

This list was made known to Parker by Colonel Dan Lamont, vice-president of the James J. Hill railroads, about two weeks before the election. On the night before that event Parker made a speech in which he stated that although Theodore Roosevelt was running on a trust-busting program it was all a piece of colossal hypocrisy inasmuch as the trusts themselves secretly were financing his campaign. But Parker did not name names and he never disclosed the Lamont list, although the rumors were that he would do so on election day. Theodore Roosevelt fiercely denied all friendship for the Rockefellers, the Morgans and the other big powers.

Later, the investigation into the insurance corporation scandals, conducted by Charles Evans Hughes, revealed that the New York Life, Equitable and Mutual Life, each had given $50,000 to the Roosevelt campaign; in 1912 the Clapp Committee discovered that Standard Oil had contributed $124,000.

Actually, revelations in a few honest papers, and official investigations years after the fact, could not inform or arouse a large number of citizens. To this day few know of this scandal.

One who was aroused was the great iconoclast of American letters, Mark Twain. He wrote in his journal that "the *World* newspaper convicted Mr. Roosevelt beyond redemption of having bought his election to the Presidency with money. That he committed this stupendous crime has long been suspected." Of the Roosevelt denial, Mark Twain contended Theodore Roosevelt added "falsehood to his burden of misconduct."

Mark Twain adds new facts: A week before election day Roosevelt became frightened and sent for Harriman, who came to Washington, and agreed to raise an additional $200,000, and actually raised $260,000, of which $200,000 was spent in the City of New York to buy the votes of 50,000 floaters, thus making a change of 100,000 votes and carrying the Empire State, and insuring the Republican victory.

Mark Twain remarks that "the rich corporations have furnished vast sums of money" upon the understanding that "their monopolies were to be shielded and protected in return," but he calls it "treachery" for Theodore Roosevelt to follow the popular demand by openly attacking the corporations while secretly taking their money to buy the presidency. "Mr. Harriman and those others had bought him and paid for him," concludes the noted author.

Following the 1912 Clapp Committee investigation, the first of a new series of laws was passed aimed at ending the purchase of elections. But only "ostensibly." The law resulting from the Clapp investigation stopped corporations from contributing to political campaigns but did not stop corporation presidents, directors or whatnots, including the duPont two-year-old children, from putting up five or ten or a hundred thousand dollars.

In the long history of election money, noted only briefly in two books and an occasional chapter in a few others, some diverse motives can be seen, some apparent contradictions—as, for example, the support of Alfred E. Smith, noted Catholic layman, by John J. Raskob, of the DuPont empire, another noted Catholic layman. He actually handed out $249,500, admitted it in a document which appeared on page 2271 of the 9th volume of the Munitions Industry hearings. The duPonts and the House of Morgan frequently supported both the Republican and Democratic candidates, insuring themselves against loss no matter which contestant won.

In 1932 it was obvious that there would be an upset. But it was pointed out at that time by leading liberal writers, such as J. Fred Essaray and Paul Ward, that some of the biggest industrialists of the land were on friendly terms with Franklin Delano Roosevelt, and perhaps, after all, he would remain loyal to what suddenly became known even in the ordinary newspapers as his "class."

But in 1936 the outlook was different. Apparently Mr. Roosevelt meant it when he said he would drive the money-changers out of the temple, that he would finally conquer the reactionaries.

The Republican National Committee called a meeting. Chairman Henry P. Fletcher named sixteen leaders to collect the money to defeat Roosevelt. He said:

"Most of them have never before participated actively in politics. . . . Realizing that the American system is threatened and that the future of the country is menaced, they have agreed to put their shoulders to the wheel."

At that time the term "American system" was still preferred to the National Association of Manufacturers' substitute for the word "capitalism," namely: "free enterprise." Among the sixteen collectors named were:

Sewell Lee Avery, president of Montgomery Ward, onetime part owner of the *Chicago Daily News,* ardent labor-fighter and violator of the new labor laws;

Joseph Newton Pew, Jr., vice-president of Sun Oil Company;

Ernest Tener Weir, chairman of National Steel, whose plant at Weirton was notorious for the use of company "goons" who used force and violence to prevent unionization;

Herbert Lee Pratt, onetime chairman of Standard Oil of New York;

Edward Larned Ryerson, Jr., president of Ryerson & Son, steel and iron company of Chicago.

Chairman of the money-gathering group was William Brown Bell, president of American Cyanamid.

In 1936 there was announced the first of a series of organizations which appealed to the public for support. It called itself the "American Liberty League." It raised a huge fund which was spent in the effort to destroy the New Deal by keeping Franklin Delano Roosevelt out of the White House for a second term and to destroy the Wagner Act.

The financial tie-up of the Republican Party, the corporations, the Liberty League and the super-patriotic organizations is apparent. The list of contributors to the Republican National Committee and the Liberty League is almost identical.

The former reported the following large contributions for January and February, 1936:

Junius S. Morgan, son of J. P. Morgan	$5,000
H. P. Davison, J. P. Morgan & Co. partner	5,000
George F. Baker, First National Bank of New York (Morgan)	5,000
Lammot duPont, chairman General Motors; president duPont de Nemours	5,000
Alfred P. Sloan, Jr., president of General Motors	5,000
W. L. Mellon, director of 32 companies and chairman of Gulf Oil Corp.	2,500
H. E. Manville, Johns-Manville Co.	5,000
W. G. Mather, chairman of Cleveland-Cliffs Iron Co.	2,000
Lester Armour, director of Armour & Co.	4,000
Philip A. Armour, director of Armour & Co.	4,000
Earl F. Reed, counsel to Weirton Steel Co.	5,000
Silas Strawn, lawyer, former head of the U. S. Chamber of Commerce	2,000
Harold S. Vanderbilt, director of over 30 railway companies	3,333
William H. Crocker, Crocker National Bank of San Francisco	5,000

The Republican committee's report of June, 1936, showed contributions of almost half a million dollars, of which the Rockefellers gave $16,000, the Mellons of Pittsburgh (Andrew W., Paul, Richard K., Mrs. Sarah Mellon Scaife and Mrs. Jennie K. Mellon) contributed $25,000 in equal shares, the Union League Club of New York $15,000, and the following notables $5,000 each:

William Woodward of New York
J. F. Lincoln of Cleveland
Lorenz Iverson of West Homestead, Pa.
H. G. Dalton of Cleveland
E. R. Crawford of McKeesport, Pa.
Joseph Wilshire of New York
George Whitney of New York
Edward J. Bermingham of Chicago
Mrs. Laura Corrigan of New York
James A. McDonough of New York
Harry Payne Bingham of New York
Mrs. John T. Pratt of New York
Henry B. duPont of Wilmington, Del.

John M. Schiff of New York
H. H. Timken of Canton, Ohio
B. H. Kroger of Cincinnati

Among the contributors of one to five thousand dollars were Finley J. Shepard, Mrs. David Bruce, Henry S. Morgan, Silas H. Strawn, Hallock duPont, John Francis Neylan, Mr. Hearst's attorney in the San Francisco strike in 1934, Edward L. Ryerson, Jr., of Chicago, Seward Prosser, Philip G. Rust of Wilmington, Delaware.

In the 1936 campaign, political expenditures, including donations to the Liberty League and its subsidiaries, one of which, the Sentinels of the Republic, was anti-Semitic, included:

Irénée, Henry and Pierre S. duPont	$144,000
John D. Rockefeller, Jr., and family	103,000
George F. Baker, the banker	55,000
J. Howard Pew (oil and shipbuilding)	61,000
J. P. Morgan	50,000
Alfred P. Sloan, Jr.	50,000
Ernest T. Weir	47,300
William Randolph Hearst	40,000
Andrew and Richard Mellon	40,000
Donaldson Brown, duPonts, General Motors	31,000

(Senator Black's Lobbying Investigation published the correspondence of Sentinels' officials calling for a Hitler in America, denouncing the Jews, especially those who aided the New Deal.)

Among the largest contributors to the Roosevelt fund in the same election were: Mrs. Doris Duke Cromwell, $50,000; Walter A. Jones of Pittsburgh, $40,000; Clifton H. Scott of Little Rock, $32,500; Curtis Bok, of the publishing family, $25,000; James W. Gerard, ex-ambassador to Germany, $15,000.

One of history's strangest ironies will be the two facts that the largest campaign slush fund to date was raised in 1940 by the same people who in 1944 prevented the same party standard bearer (Willkie) from even attending the convention.

Senator Gillette was howled down in the Senate when he said that the funds for both sides in 1940 might go to twenty million, but he himself announced an official figure of $16,476,039 for Willkie. It was actually eighteen million. The main individual money backers were the duPonts ($68,350), the Pews ($91,025) and the Rockefellers ($30,500). These are the official figures which do not include gifts to other organizations, state organizations, or loans. The Democrats officially received $6,284,463.

But experts for the Campaign Expenditures Committee "estimated that a total of $35,000,000 to $40,000,000 was spent." Said Senator Gillette, head of the investigation:

> "While there have probably been irregularities, frauds, violations, and abuses in all elections of the past, I believe that I do not exaggerate when I say that never before in American history have we seen a more patent, potent and potential attempt to influence the American electorate through the expenditure of huge sums of money than in the campaign that has just closed." (Source: National Radio Forum, NBC, December 2, 1940.)

In the 1940 campaign, as in previous and more recent campaigns, the money which caused this "debauchery" was between 3 to 1 and 5 to 1 Republican Party money. In the past it was sometimes overwhelming enough to corrupt enough people to elect candidates, sometimes it failed because there were sufficient votes which could not be influenced by the expenditure of money.

The law which prohibited corporations from making contributions was proved a failure. Congressman Chet Holifield of California told Congress about it years later. The corporate interests evaded and circumvented the law "in two principal ways":

> "First, by the formation of an independent unincorporated association to 'front' for the corporation interests; and
>
> "Second, by personal contributions from corporation executives and members of their families."

Holifield then gave these 1940 figures:

The duPont family, grand total	$186,780.00
The Pitcairn family, grand total	29,114.71
The Alfred P. Sloan family, grand total	36,000.00
The Queeny family, grand total	42,375.00

The Pew family, grand total 108,525.00
The Rockefeller family, grand total 59,000.00
—(*Congressional Record,* June 21, 1944, page 6480)

In 1944 the National Citizens' Political Action Committee estimated that in ten years the Pew family alone had poured thirteen million dollars into political funds. It stated:

"The Pews of Pennsylvania stand high among the people who would form Dewey's 'kitchen cabinet' if he were elected. Listen to Joe Pew, only two months before Pearl Harbor:

" 'When democracy goes on the march it marches on a road that leads through chaos and revolution and totalitarianism. If we follow that road to its bitter end, we will find ourselves defeated, no matter how brilliant have been our victories on the battlefield.'

"To stop the march of democracy, Joe and the rest of the Pew clan have poured an estimated $13,000,000 into Republican coffers since 1934. They have never fully cashed in on this colossal investment in the cause of reaction, but they are pinning their hopes on Tom Dewey. The Pews have contributed heavily to (1) Frank Gannett's Committee to Uphold Constitutional Government, branded as an extremely isolationist and anti-Roosevelt outfit; (2) The Sentinels of the Republic, anti-Semitic enemy of child labor laws, maternity benefits and unemployment insurance; (3) the Crusaders, whose roster included Sewell Avery and R. Douglas Stewart, father of the founder of America First.

"We wind up with a quotation from Lammot duPont of Delaware, a great pillar of the Dewey cause in the East. Speaking before the NAM in 1942 duPont said:

" 'We will win the war by reducing taxes on corporations, high income brackets and increasing taxes on lower incomes, by removing unions from any power to tell industry how to produce . . . by destroying any and all government agencies that stand in the way of free enterprise.' " (NCPAC News-letter, October 4, 1944.)

The very same corporation heads who put up the major portion of the national campaign funds have of late also intervened in state affairs.

In June, 1942, *In Fact* received a letter from the Democratic State Committee of South Dakota saying that it had obtained from the State capital the list of donations for the Republican organization, indicating that "eastern capitalists" had contributed practically all of the $51,700 fund, an enormous and overwhelming amount of money for a state with so few electors. The amazing and even amusing part of the letter was a request for information about the donors. It was evident that South Dakota did not know who these men and women are. *In Fact* sent on the information, published the list of contributors, supplied the information later used by Senator Guffey, the columnists Lowell Mellett and Drew Pearson, and many others.

The facts are significant because the fund was so large that money remained for the 1944 and 1946 elections. Thus it can be stated that all of South Dakota's men in Congress were elected with the aid of a huge fund raised almost exclusively from leading members and directors of the National Association of Manufacturers, and their friends. South Dakota's men in Congress* are:

Senator Chan Gurney, Republican, Yankton, term to 1951.
Senator Harlan J. Bushfield, Republican, Miller, S.D., 1949.
Representative Karl E. Mundt, Republican, of Madison.
Representative Francis Case, Republican, of Custer.

Bushfield got a direct contribution of $2,000 from the Pew family, making the South Dakota fund $53,700. The Democrats raised a total of $12,838 from 800 contributors, wound up with a deficit of $183. The Republicans in 1944 still had $17,000 for their campaign.

The few powerful men who supplied the money which helped elect South Dakota's men in Congress, and the sums each contributed, follow:

Lammot duPont, $4,000; Irénée duPont, $2,500; Donaldson Brown, vice-President of General Motors, $2,000.

The DuPont Empire is worth more than two billion dollars. The duPont family itself owns $573,690,000 worth of stock in its own corporations, and in United States Rubber. (TNEC Monograph 29, page 116.) Members of the duPont family, their trusts, estates, and corporations, own 20.31% of General Motors, one of the billionaire corporations, 2.18% of Phillips Petroleum Company, 11.51% of United States Rubber and fractions of one per cent in American Sugar Refining, Mid-Continent Pete, and United Fruit (Monograph 29, page 119). The control of General Motors is absolute.

Alfred P. Sloan, Jr., $2,500.

Mr. Sloan is a director of General Motors, also a director of the National Association of Manufacturers. His chief activity at the NAM is chairman of the National Industrial Information Committee, the propaganda agency which has been spending between three and five million dollars a year, influencing the press, radio, schools, movies, churches, agricultural organizations and others in favor of the big business system. Mr. Sloan's name appeared as a donor of sums to reactionary affiliates of the Liberty League when Senator Black conducted his investigation.

Sarah Mellon Scaife, $4,000; Ailsa Mellon Bruce, $5,000; L. W. Mesta, $1,000.

The Mellon family is the fourth richest in the country, according to Monograph 29, owning $390,943,000 worth of stock in its Gulf Oil, Aluminum Company, and Koppers United. Mrs. Scaife is the daughter of Richard Mellon, noted for his remark, "You can't run a coal mine without machine-guns." Mesta Machine Company, a Mellon firm, was a great profiteer in the First World War.

Mary Ethel Pew, $1,000; Earle Haliburton of Duncan, Oklahoma, $5,000; Joseph Pew, Jr., $1,000; Mabel Pew Myrin, $1,000.

The Pews, ninth richest family, own $75,628,000 in Sun Oil stock. They also own the news magazine *Pathfinder* and the *Farm Journal.* The Pews are among the dozen most active heads of the National Association of Manufacturers, they boss Pennsylvania politics, and they contribute to the Sentinels of the Republic, anti-Semitic branch of the old Liberty League.

Colonel R. R. McCormick of the *Chicago Tribune,* $5,000; Colonel Ira C. Copley, Aurora, Illinois, $5,000.

When Colonel Copley bought the *San Diego Evening*

Tribune he announced on page one: "I have no connection with any public utility anywhere and no connections with any other business than the newspaper business anywhere." At the hearings into the corrupt practices of the light and power corporations, Judge Healy of the Federal Trade Commission obtained the following confession from Copley's attorney, B. P. Alschuler: "In January 1928 . . . Copley exchanged preferred and common stock previously held by him for preferred stock of Western United Gas & Electric Corporation. . . . Copley is owner also of $1,000,000 in bonds of WUGE." Evidence was presented that Copley owned $2,400,000 in utility stocks. He also owned or owns: *Aurora Beacon, Elgin Courier, Joliet Herald-News, Illinois State Journal, San Diego Independent, Glendale Press, Pasadena Evening Post, Hollywood News, Santa Monica Outlook, Venice Vanguard, Culver City Star News, Redondo Daily Breeze, San Pedro Daily News.* This exposé by the Federal Trade Commission was one of its most sensational, proving to the American public that public utility men own numerous newspapers, all of which print anti-public ownership propaganda.

Other large contributors were: Catherine Barker Hicox, Chicago, $1,000; Ralph D. Mershon of New York, $1,000; Earl LaGrave of Chicago, $2,700.

A total of $31,000, or the major portion of the $53,700 South Dakota fund, came from the leading families in control of the National Association of Manufacturers. All the rest of it came from persons whose financial, economic and social interests were that of the National Association of Manufacturers. It would be an excellent idea, therefore, for one of our great institutions of learning not in any way indebted to any member, living or dead, of the very same organization, to make a scientific study of the policy line as laid down by the peak association of big business, and the voting record of the four men from South Dakota. Perhaps some bright young man or woman will make this the subject for his or her thesis for a master's degree.

Meanwhile, let us look at the record.

This is not an easy thing to do. The press is deep in the game of politics, it is partisan, and therefore not honest enough to present to its readers, come election time, a truthful diagram of a candidate's past two or four years of voting, the issues involved, and whether or not the vote was for the voter's benefit or for the benefit of the few gentlemen who put up the money. The *New York Times* and the *New York Herald Tribune,* for example, do not publish these charts, whereas almost every liberal and labor publication in America does so.

In 1944 the Labor Institute of America issued a huge lithographed four-colored sheet entitled "The Black Record of Congress." It chose, quite rightly, ten controversial issues, each one affecting the general welfare, since these and only these issues can be made the test of a candidate's honesty and integrity. There was, for example, the Smith-Connally Bill, allegedly designed to avoid strikes, but actually one of the most important measures proposed to destroy the labor movement. Additionally, it prohibited the contribution to political campaigns by labor unions, thus preventing campaign funds from the masses of people to counteract the millions contributed by members of the NAM and other employer groups.

The President proposed a salary limit of $67,200. The press, almost without exception, referred to it as the $25,000 limitation bill, inasmuch as this sum was the net after paying taxes. There was also the usual inadequate income tax bill placing the burden disproportionately on those with moderate income and ignoring, as usual, ability to pay. There was also one of the several Fair Employment Practices Committee bills aimed to establish a government agency to prevent discrimination because of race, color or creed, and one of the many anti-poll tax bills.

There was never any doubt in all these bills as to where the Wall Street corporations, the native Fascist organizations, the brasscheck journalists and radio commentators, and all the forces of reaction stood; nor was there ever any doubt as to where Liberals and Democrats and all who have the welfare of America at heart stood on most of these measures.

The four men from South Dakota voted on all but one or two of the ten bills in accordance with positions first taken by the National Association of Manufacturers' *News,* the *Wall Street Journal,* the *Chicago Tribune* and like-minded groups.

Gurney and Bushfield voted for the Smith-Connally Bill, against the $25,000 limitation, for the National Association of Manufacturers' income tax bill; they were also absent when votes were taken on other important measures.

Case and Mundt voted for the "labor-shackling" Hobbs Bill; Case voted for the Smith-Connally Bill and Mundt was absent; both voted for two NAM sponsored income tax bills which passed the House and both voted against the bill which would have rolled back prices and stopped the rise in the cost of living at a time labor kept its promise not to strike for higher wages. The record of these two men was listed by the *New Republic* and other liberal publications as among the "worst" made in Congress. Only two votes stand to their credit: They voted for the salary limitation and for the abolition of the poll tax, the latter requiring no bravery or integrity for representatives of a state which has no poll tax problem.

In all the charts from 1942 to 1946 the same percentage exists: one or two plus signs against a dozen minus signs. The *New Republic* chart for 1946, for example, has only one plus sign for each senator. Both get minus signs (or a zero for being absent) on the full employment bill (which the National Association of Manufacturers opposed), the confirmation of Aubrey Williams, the price control Bill, the Wallace confirmation, the reciprocal trade agreements, the return of USES to the states, the extension of presidential war powers for another six months.

Both Representatives Mundt and Case get a credit for voting against the poll tax again, and on one minor matter, farm labor deferment, Case got a plus and Mundt a minus, but otherwise this pair voted the NAM line on all other measures, notably: reciprocal trade, Hobbs Bill, Wallace and Full Employment, and the two price control measures.

Mundt, the *New Republic* reported in its voting chart

supplement of May 18, 1942, "has been extremely active as an America First speaker, appearing on eastern platforms with Ham Fish and others, as well as in his native Middle West. He was used especially as a speaker for rallies in German-American communities; his pro-fascist tendencies have been quite clearly indicated in these public addresses." Congressman Fish was one of the fifteen Americans who signed the main Hitler propaganda book which the Nazi agent, George Sylvester Viereck, circulated in the United States. Mundt was endorsed by the Nazi Bund throughout America. Later he became a member of the Thomas-Rankin Un-American Committee.

Case, author of the vicious anti-labor bill which bore his name and which was pushed by the NAM and other big business groups, is one of the most hated members of Congress. President Truman's veto of this bill paved the way for the even more vicious Taft-Hartley Slave Labor Bill.

If Fascism ever comes to America as it came to Italy and Germany (after years of reactionary anti-labor legislation enacted by legislators who favored corporate and property rights over human rights), the verdict of history might well be that these four were, in the words of Mussolini "among Fascists of the first hour."

The record of the four men from South Dakota is one of the blackest in the history of American reaction. The fact that they sponsored and voted for the proposals for legislation appearing in the propaganda output of the National Association of Manufacturers is unchallengeable. The fact that the campaign fund which got them into Congress was raised largely by National Association of Manufacturers' members may be put down as a coincidence by those who believe that the world of politics and big business still runs in a coincidental free enterprise manner. Others may believe that coincidences like those arise out of community of interest and not by mere accident.

(Documentation on South Dakota election money: *Congressional Record,* address by Senator Guffey, March 8, 1945; Lowell Mellett's syndicated column, March 15, 1945; Drew

Pearson's syndicated "Washington-Merry-Go-Round," March 2, 1945; *In Fact,* December 28, 1942, and February 18, 1946; *St. Louis Post-Dispatch,* June 12, 1943.)

The whole subject of money in elections requires an honest congressional investigation. The pamphlet publication, "Economic Affairs," of the Institute of Economic Affairs, New York University, suspended at the end of its fourth volume for some unstated reason. In its time it published factual data of great value. Its August-September, 1946, issue was devoted almost entirely to answering its own front-page question: "Does Money Win Elections?" Part of the answer is given by a chart.

"The chart covers the Presidential elections from 1896 to 1936, the last election before the Hatch Act limited the spending by individual committees to $3,000,000 in any one calendar year," the text explains, noting also the Democratic Party claim that ten or fifteen millions was raised by Mark Hanna, used to elect McKinley, and not officially listed. The report by Dr. Harold W. Davey continues:

> "Since 1900, there has been far less difference in the amounts of election money spent by the two parties.* Yet with only two exceptions, the party whose national committee spent the most money won every time. The first exception was the 1912 election of Wilson when Theodore Roosevelt split the Republican vote. The other was the landslide defeat of Landon by Franklin D. Roosevelt in 1936."

The only study of the power of campaign funds is Professor Louise Overacker's "Money in Elections" and her more recent little volume "Presidential Campaign Funds." "In the major parties," she concludes, "the size of the campaign funds is less significant than the sources from which they draw their support.

"The pattern of financial support in presidential elections

* The "big money" in the Democratic Party grows less with each election. Woodrow Wilson had among his supporters such multi-millionaires as William C. Whitney, Thomas Fortune Ryan, and Bernard M. Baruch. In 1924 "J. P. Morgan had to choose between Calvin Coolidge and his firm's lawyer, John W. Davis. He chose Coolidge," reported the New York *Daily News,* November 8, 1936. Notable contributors to the FDR campaigns included S. Parker Gilbert, a Morgan partner, A. P. Giannini, Basil Harris, Walter P. Chrysler, Fred Fisher of Fisher Bodies, and some officers of the National City Bank.

is a highly significant index of who pulls the strings within the parties, and reflects the pattern of the economic structure and the pyramiding power within the structure.

"In a democracy it is highly important that the voters be fully informed on all these points."

They are not.

PART FOUR

BIG REACTION

CHAPTER 15

BIG MONEY MEN

THE FEW, certainly less than a thousand, who boast they can buy the presidency and who actually put up a large proportion of the campaign funds raised for state and national elections, are big industrialists, big bankers, big newspaper owners, big magazine men, big powers in Wall Street—in short they are the Big Money. Whether or not they buy the presidency, or for a majority of terms control the White House, may be open to question; but no one can question the fact that these same few and their organizations share political, social and economic viewpoints which range between two terms, reaction and Fascism.

As for the use of these words, it is significant that on the very day in which they were written here, Mr. Henry A. Wallace in a public speech declared that "the United States has become the center of world reaction," and Mr. Philip Murray, continuing his campaign against the Taft-Hartley ("slave labor") bill, declared that it was "the first step towards Fascism in America." The terms are being used by American leaders of men—and still being attacked by frightened semanticists.

In this and the following chapter it will be seen that although many names change, and organizations disappear and are replaced, the individuals and the associations which subsidize or which are subsidized by reaction represent the same group, or family, or social stratum. *Plus ca change, plus c'est la meme chose.* It is always reaction which acts, which hands out money, which organizes, which propagandizes on a vast scale, and which commands the attention and favor of the means of communication. The forces of reaction in America are similar to those which acted in exactly the same way before they took the final step, and by arming themselves introduced fascism to the world.

It so happens that the most prominent of the corporation-inspired reactionary organizations which sprang up immediately after the end of the second World War called themselves Tool Owners Union and American Action Inc., but they resembled the old old Liberty League and the National Security League of the days of the first World War just as three generations of a family resemble each other.

The National Association of Manufacturers, which recently celebrated its fiftieth birthday, has a continuous history of opposition to the labor movement. It is the symbol of reaction, the spokesman of reaction, the spearhead of reaction.

This is a legitimate function.

But many ask: what is the relationship between reaction and Fascism?

Recent history supplies the answer. In Italy, for example, the Associazione fra Industriale Generale dell' Industria functioned for many years in much the same way the NAM functions in the United States today. So did the Associazione fra Industriali Metallurgici Meccanici ed Affini, the equivalent of the Iron and Steel Institute. Italy also had its equivalent of the United States Chamber of Commerce, and all these organizations, antedating Mussolini, used their powers and their pressures for their own profit and collaborated with the parties whose unwritten but most important campaign promise was the perpetuation of reaction.

In Germany the Stahlverein, or union of steel makers, the association of Ruhr industrialists, and other organizations similar to the NAM and United States Chamber of Commerce functioned as reactionary forces long before Hitler was known as anybody but a labor spy and stoolpigeon.

In Italy, in Germany and in the United States for half a century or more, the leaders of business, industry and banking have formed associations or subsidized organizations devoted to the maintenance of the status quo, the protection of their wealth and power, the policy of reaction. All this has been within the law.

When reaction resorts to bayonets the result is Fascism.

This is what happened in Germany and Italy, in Spain and in other countries. So far, it has not happened in the United States. The reactionary forces of America are the most powerful in the land, but they have not yet attempted to buy bayonets, to take over private armed forces, to seize and run the government for their own benefit.

So it may be said that throughout the century the same big money and big business forces in America have subsidized a score, perhaps a hundred, more or less powerful organizations, they have been subsidizing reaction, but not Fascism; and that if a day arrives when the reactionary forces resort to arms, then it can be said that the pattern of Italy and Germany has been followed, and reaction has been turned into Fascism.

If history repeats itself here, reaction will choose for its spearhead an organization of veterans, just as the Italian association of manufacturers and chamber of commerce chose the Fascio di Combattimento, of which, incidentally, Mussolini was not a founding member, and the German industrialists chose the Nazis, of which Hitler himself was not a founder.

The American Legion, of course, is a "natural" for Fascist action, and its true history—which is never mentioned in the newspapers or popular magazines—shows that more than one attempt has already been made in that direction. When Alvin Owsley was Legion commander he was prepared to seize Washington. "The Fascisti are to Italy what the American Legion is to the United States," he said in 1922 and confirmed his statements in a letter to the present writer many years later. Several Legion conventions invited Mussolini, honored him, sent him medals. And high ranking Legion officials, including one of its founders, actually plotted to seize the government and prevent

Franklin D. Roosevelt from exercising his duties as President. (See Appendix 21.)

I do not intend in this volume to do more than mention organizations such as The Columbians and the Khaki Shirts of America, which actually wore uniforms, or the scores of small and perhaps totally unimportant outfits, some of them run by crackpots, to which John Roy Carlson has devoted two books.

If history is a guide, it is clear that Fascist organizations of this type become nationally dangerous only when the most powerful and the richest forces of the nation subsidize them.

If ever the day arrives when the same men and organizations now functioning legitimately in the United States for the spread of reaction, invest their millions in a self-admitted demagogue such as Gerald L. K. Smith, or one of the Senators he has endorsed; if ever the great Hearst-Howard-McCormick-Patterson-Gannett axis unites behind one of these leaders, thus forming an alliance of money, press, public opinion, demagoguery and bayonets, then we can expect Fascism to replace reaction in the United States.

It is for this reason that the danger today is not in the so-called "vermin Fascism" which has been attacked and exposed in many books, notably Carlson's, and by many members of Congress, and by a score of liberal organizations, but in the respectable potential Fascism of the most powerful reactionary interests which may at some future time, when even the New Deal is surpassed, decide to place their millions on the bayonets of black or brown shirts, rather than accept the decisions of the ballot boxes.

Respectable Fascism, respectable because of name, power and money, is protected by almost everyone, and particularly by the press and radio. Something like a conspiracy of silence actually exists.

Let me illustrate: On April 16, 1945, I sent several liberals in both Houses of Congress copies of my issue of *In Fact* of that date, publishing the text of the War Department's Army Talk, Orientation Fact Sheet 64, entitled "Fascism." The dean of the House of Representatives, Adolph Sabath, placed it in the *Congressional Record* of the 19th, appending to the text the following statement:

"Mr. Speaker, I only regret that the rules and regulations of the War Department precluded the naming of outstanding American Fascists, such as the duPonts, the Pews, the Girdlers, the Weirs, Van Horn Moseley, H. W. Prentis, Jr., Merwin K. Hart and others, including the 30 Fascists charged with conspiracy and seditious activities and tried, but due to the untimely death of the trial judge, still at large." (Only the Pews protested; they wrote the Congressman it was "a detestable lie" and "scandalous and libelous." It would indeed be a detestable lie, scandalous and libelous, if the record of the Lobbying Investigation, conducted by Senator (now Supreme Court Justice) Black, did not show that the Pews helped finance the Sentinels of the Republic whose anti-Semitic correspondence was made public, and the Crusaders, both affiliates of the respectable Liberty League, denounced in the Senate as run by "leeches, rascals, crooks."

The American press (with notable exceptions of the *Christian Science Monitor, St. Louis Post-Dispatch* and a few other honest newspapers) suppressed all mention of Army Talk 64 and suppressed the list of names which Sabath appended, and which incidentally were privileged, or libel-proof, whether or not they were correct and truthful.

Later, a tragic footnote to the story was supplied by Henry Hoke in his book "It's A Secret." As a result of my sending the official statement on Fascism to Congressmen, and the use made of it by Mr. Sabath, two Congressmen in the service of reaction, John Rankin of Mississippi and Clare Hoffman of Michigan, demanded that the Army drop its work of teaching the soldiers who and what the enemy was. Investigators got busy, members of the Intelligence Section of the Army were transferred or dismissed, personnel was frightened, and the word went out to tone down on Fascism because "Burton" would make trouble for them.

Hoke discloses the fact that H. Ralph Burton, counsel of

the House Military Affairs Committee, took up the request of Rankin and Hoffman, and wrecked the entire Army orientation course. He describes Burton as a thorough reactionary, a one-time attorney for William Ludecke, who had boasted he was No. 2 Nazi in America; an intimate of Walter S. Steele, who was permitted to use the Dies Committee as a forum; and general counsel in Maryland for Father Coughlin's National Union of Social Justice. Rankin, Hoffman and Burton were opposed to knowledge of the truth about Fascism being spread in the United States despite the fact 15,000,000 men and women had been called to arms to fight the world's greatest menace. These three changed the whole policy of the Army.

Not a word on this subject appeared in the public prints.

Nor did the press (with the notable exception of the *New York Times,* which, however, ran the item on its real estate page) pay any attention whatever to the convention of the National Maritime Union on July 7, 1943, at a time the mass of the American Army was not engaged in either the East or the West, and the maritime workers had a list of 4,000 dead and 12,000 torpedoed, a record of casualties proportionately higher than in any branch of the regular forces. The fact that the *Times* gave a column to the news of the NMU passing a resolution naming the leading home-grown fascists as America's greatest enemies, makes the silence on the part of its colleagues all the more impressive; after all the *Times* knows what is news and what isn't—both when it publishes and when it fails to do so. Said the resolution in part:

"Hitler's agents have found their way into high places in our national life—Big Business, Congress, press, radio. They are working frantically to confuse and divide the people, throw the nation into chaos and halt production. Anti-Semitism, red-baiting, union-busting and anti-Negro provocations are the methods through which they attempt to pit labor against capital, the farmer against labor, one national group against the other. . . .

"We reaffirm our wholehearted and unreserved support of our Commander-in-Chief and his victory policies. . . .

"We call upon our Commander-in-Chief to . . . investigate and prosecute those enemies of our national welfare represented by the National Association of Manufacturers in big business: (Senators)

Wheeler, Nye, Connally; (Representatives) Dies, Fish, (Howard) Smith in Congress; Hearst, Patterson, McCormick and Howard in the press; Gerald L. K. Smith, Father Coughlin and all elements in the Christian Front and Ku Klux Klan."

It might have been the mention of the four press lords which persuaded their more liberal, less powerful colleagues to suppress the news entirely, or it might have been the mention of the NAM, the still most sacred, most golden of all calves. At any rate, except for the *Times,* it was not news.

A third illustration was furnished by Attorney General Robert H. Jackson on the occasion of his address to the Massachusetts Law Society, when again an exposé of powerful native fascists was suppressed.

In 1927, five years after Mussolini was in office, and the very year Thyssen called on all German Big Business to subsidize Hitler, some of the protofascist American organizations were exposed by Norman Hapgood in the book "Professional Patriots" (published by A. & C. Boni). "A few," he said of them, "are honest in the sense they are composed of persons who are now trying to make the world safe for money under the pretense of making it safe from disorder." That very neatly summed them up, and sums up their successors—but not all of them have disappeared. Some of the worst remain, and Hapgood's book is a fine reference work today.

"Most of the organizations, especially the smaller ones," he continues, "are backed . . . by promoters who play on the fears of the property class in general, or the fears of some single wealthy old gentleman who is kept awake at night by Bolshevism, or on the fears of army officers that the world they are brought up to believe in is threatened by radical meetings, especially if those meetings are held in parlors. . . .

"They seek to instil the idea that what is meant by patriotism is devotion to business privilege and to the open shop; that law, private violence and officials should put down what under this definition is unpatriotic; that the only approach to our large new industrial questions, being thrashed out between capital and labor, is suppression of one side of the argument."

The list of two decades ago is very interesting. It includes: Allied Patriotic Societies, American Constitutional Association, American Citizenship Foundation, American Defense Society, Better America Federation, Civil Legion, Military Intelligence Association, Military Order of the World War, National Security League, National Civic Federation, National Patriotic Council, National Association for Constitutional Government, National Clay Products Association, Constitutional Anniversary Association, Sentinels of the Republic, United States Patriotic Society, United States Flag Association, the Women Builders of America, and several minor organizations.

Summing them up, Mr. Hapgood said:

> "From the most excusable to the most mercenary they vary in the shade of their morals and their intelligence. What puts them all into the same discussion is that they all participate in the attempt to make of a noble word and emotion the handmaid of greed and cowardice. . . .
>
> "The outstanding fact is that this persistent propaganda to degrade the name of patriotism to the service of the dollar has its most important support among those who make money out of war and of holding down standards of labor."

Today those societies which are alive have not changed their policy, and those which have sprung to life have offered little or no change, except that in the interval more people have grown more enlightened, and see through patriotic hypocrisy of false Americanism and recognize both the subsidizers and their purposes.

One of the first to be exposed was the National Security League, direct ancestor of the American Liberty League, of a decade ago and the present American Action, Inc., of today. The NSL wanted to save America's soul. Its prospectus read: "Help save America! America is in danger of losing her soul. The National Security League offers you the means of putting forth your individual force to help save it. Will you do this by giving us. . ." (and here a sum was suggested.)

This was not part of the crackpottery of the preachers of the lunatic fringe of the present-day Fascist movement, nor was it the demagoguery of the kind Huey Long and Gerald L. K. Smith and the Rev. Dr. Frank Buchman and the Rev.

Father Coughlin and the Rev. James W. Fifield and many other reverend spokesmen of reaction now offer. This was big business selling itself via a religious appeal.

Fortunately, however, the National Security League made a faux pas one day in 1919, after years of successful big armaments propaganda and big war propaganda; it sneered at certain members of Congress and the latter ordered an investigation, which soon disclosed that the real backers, the patriots of the National Security League, were certain persons later to be known as "merchants of death," who mingled patriotism with profit. Notable were:

Nicholas F. Brady, representing the power and light interests; T. Coleman duPont, whose relatives today subsidize a dozen similar organizations; Henry Clay Frick, errand boy for the Mellon interests, lawyer for armament makers; George W. Perkins of the House of Morgan; Simon and Daniel Guggenheim, of the American Smelting Company, the copper kings; J. Pierpont Morgan himself, the leader of the Wall Street bankers who, according to the findings of the Nye-Vandenberg Committee, directed the drift of the United States into the First World War; and the senior John D. Rockefeller.

The Congressional committee decided that these were patriots for war profits; it stated that "if the curtain were only pulled back, in addition to the interests heretofore enumerated, the hands of Rockefeller, of Vanderbilt, of Morgan, of Remington, of duPont, and of Guggenheim, would be seen, suggesting steel, oil, moneybags, Russian bonds (Tsarist bonds, which were defaulted, causing years of plotting against Russia), rifles, powder and railroads." (House of Representatives, Report No. 1173; Investigation of National Security League.)

That was in 1919. Immediately after this exposé the National Security League sought to regain confidence—and new funds—by directing its propaganda against liberals, radicals, pacifists, and communists.

In 1936, when the Spanish Republic was fighting for its life, Hearst paid National Security League President, Lt. General Robert Lee Bullard, former commander of Pershing's

Second Army, for a red-baiting attack on the Loyalists. In 1938 (see "You Can't Do That") the NCL, Bullard and Hearst were still engaged in their red-baiting campaigns.

The American Liberty League, which reached its apogee at about the time the National Security League was in its nadir, actually had among its affiliates two which were openly fascistic, one of them anti-Semitic, and all of them valiantly and patriotically striving to destroy the labor union movement and safeguard the profit of the men who organized and directed the parent society. The anti-Semitic feature may have been incidental, but it was a warning of a wave of the future. The Lobbying Investigation brought to light letters exchanged by the Boston investment banker, Alexander Lincoln, and one W. Cleveland Runyon of Plainfield, N. J., which accused Roosevelt of bringing "the Jewish brigade" to Washington, declared the "New Deal is communist," and suggested that "the old line Americans of $1200 a year want a Hitler."

These Sentinels of the Republic, according to the Lobby Investigation, were financed chiefly by the Pitcairn family of Pittsburgh and Philadelphia, J. Howard Pew, A. Atwater Kent and Nicholas Roosevelt of the *New York Herald Tribune*. The Sentinels supplied editorials to more than 1300 papers urging "a return to American principles."

More overtly fascist was the Liberty League affiliate known as the Southern Committee to Uphold the Constitution, of which even the conservative *Baltimore Sun* said: "This is a hybrid organization financed by northern money, but playing on the Ku Klux Klan prejudices of the South. When Raskob, a Roman Catholic, contributed $5000, he was told that his money would be used to stir up the KKK and also to finance a venomous attack upon Mrs. Roosevelt." Part of the Raskob donation was used to print a paper showing Mrs. Roosevelt with two Negroes.

Vance Muse was manager of the Southern Committee. Its sponsor was John H. Kirby. Its purpose was to back Talmadge. Kirby was also one of the chief sponsors for America's first Hitlerite or Nuernberg-style convention of anti-Semites secretly organized by Major A. Cloyd Gill of the Hearst newspaper editorial staff, and held in Asheville, N. C., in 1936. Under oath, Muse admitted to Senator Black that "the guiding spirits" of the Macon "grass roots" convention to enlist southerners against the New Deal were Governor Talmadge, Mr. Kirby, and the Rev. Gerald L. K. Smith, one of the most notorious spreaders of anti-Semitism in the nation.

Said the *New York Post* (April 18, 1936): "The brood of anti-New Deal organizations spawned by the Liberty League are in turn spawning Fascism." It was one of the few newspapers which recognized, even before the Spanish uprising, what Fascism really meant. But in May, 1937, Pierre S. duPont, challenged on the subject, declared that he would withdraw his support if he found "one trace" of race-hate propaganda. "I have never entertained any prejudices that would mark me with disfavor to any race or people," declared Mr. duPont; "I have one-eighth Jewish blood in my veins that I am not ashamed of." But Mr. duPont did not withdraw.

If there was any doubt about what reaction or native Fascism means by "American principles," a spokesman for the Sentinels has cleared it up brilliantly. W. A. Wilson, member of the faculty of Yale University, proposed that the Constitution be amended. By striking out one phrase, he said, the American ideal would be achieved. Wilson wrote: "My own proposal would be to strike out the general-welfare clause in Article L, Section 8." Editor and economist George Soule of the *New Republic* pointed out that although the Sentinel amendment would prevent the government from serving the best interests of all the people, "it would hardly be necessary, since a majority of the Supreme Court has already narrowly restricted the meaning of the existing welfare clause."

The Wilson proposal had at least the virtue of honesty. The sincerity of the parent organization, the American Liberty League, was challenged when its offer to defend the civil liberties of any victim was accepted by the American Civil Liberties Union. It offered six immediate cases, involving the rights of Negroes, unions, a religious minority, the right of free speech and of assembly. The Liberty League's National Lawyers' Committee referred the matter to its chairman, Raoul E. Desvernine, who refused to help. Mr. Desvernine later became president of the Crucible Steel Company. This leading light of liberty shone again in 1947 when his name appeared as one of the big money men among the "Board of Founders" of the Tool Owners Union which was denied a charter of incorporation by New York State on the ground that it was Fascist.

In its own bulletin to members (September 15, 1936), the Liberty League denounced the New Deal and President Roosevelt for stating that "for many years a free people were being gradually regimented into the service of the privileged few." It denounced the President for using the term "unscrupulous money changers" and was especially bitter over the famous phrases "the privileged princes of these new economic dynasties" and the "economic royalists." Over all its protests the League wrote the headline: "Fomenting Class Hatred."

But the Liberty League propaganda failed because of its timing. Although the New Deal was being attacked, and frequently lied about, by the business interests and by the majority of the press, times were hard and the benefits of the Roosevelt program were visible to millions of people. In those days the most powerful of all newspaper chains, Roy Howard's, and his wire service the United Press, and several other of his suppliers of news, were still on the liberal side; they had not licked the shoepolish of the moneyed interests as Hearst had before them; and their exposé of the dollar motive behind the Liberty League did much to destroy it. One of the United Press' headlines read "Liberty League Controlled by Owners of $37,000,000,000." It listed notably United States Steel, General Motors, Standard Oil, Chase National Bank, Goodyear Tire, and Mutual Life Insurance Company directors as directors of the League. Significantly enough the sum mentioned was only a little less than the billions controlled by the members of the NAM. (In TNEC monographs, NAM-controlled wealth is listed at 60 billions.)

Another coincidence was the testimony of Heber Blankenhorn before the National Labor Relations Board. He stated that big business was spending at least $80,000,000 a year for industrial espionage, for machine guns and gas, for stool-pigeons and goons, for anti-labor racketeering. Chief among the spenders was General Motors. Almost all the spenders were directors of the Liberty League.

Early in the League's history the Senate committee released a report on the first million dollars it had received, showing that 90% came from a few contributors. It named the League and its affiliates, including the Crusaders, Sentinels, New York State Economic Council (later known as National Economic Council), Women Investors in America, and lesser branches. The official list of contributors:

duPont Family	$204,045
duPont Associates	152,622
Pitcairn Family	100,250
J. P. Morgan Associates	68,266
Mellon Associates	60,752
Rockefeller Associates	49,852
E. F. Hutton Associates	40,671
Sun Oil (Pew) Associates	37,260
Banks, brokers	184,224
Utilities	27,069

Total: $929,974 out of $1,084,604 contributed

As usual, the duPont name led all the rest. Irénée gave $5000 and lent the League—the word loan is a euphemism in such matters—$79,750 between August 15, 1934, the day of founding, and December 31, 1935, the day of accounting, and four more duPonts gave $5000 each and lent $10,000 each.

Among other well-known contributors were:

Sewell Avery of Montgomery Ward, $5,000.

Donaldson Brown, of duPont and General Motors, $5,000.

W. L. Clayton, leading cotton broker, banker, and Under Secretary of State for Economic Affairs in the Truman Administration, $5,000.

A. Hamilton Rice, a supporter of the Franco regime in Spain, $2,000.

Alfred P. Sloan, Jr., of General Motors, $5,000 and $10,000 loan.

E. T. Weir, chairman of National Steel, $5,000.

John J. Raskob, loan, $10,000.

William S. Knudsen of General Motors, $5,000.

Perhaps more significant than the money contributions, was the support by the following persons:

John W. Davis, attorney for J. P. Morgan, and onetime candidate for president of the United States, member of National Executive Committee.

Grayson Mallet-Prevost Murphy, of the Morgan Guaranty Trust Co., treasurer.

Joseph M. Proskauer, leading Jewish layman, national executive committee.

Alfred E. Smith, leading Catholic layman, national executive committee.

Dr. Neil Carothers, director, College of Business, Lehigh University, exposed as a contributor to the NAM's "Six Star Service" (college professors paid to disseminate propaganda), national advisory council.

Frederic R. Coudert, Jr., head of a law firm which has represented Tsarist Russia, Hitler's puppet Vichy; now a Congressman; national advisory council.

Dr. Edwin W. Kemmerer, national advisory council.

Demarest Lloyd, national advisory council.

Robert L. Lund ("Listerine Lund"), one of the reorganizers of the NAM, national advisory council.

Channing Pollock, writer, endorser of Spiritual Mobilization, national advisory council.

Hal E. Roach, Hollywood movie producer who collaborated with the Mussolini family, national advisory council.

Dr. Walter E. Spahr, another NAM "Six Star Service" writer, national advisory council.

Mrs. Chase Going Woodhouse.

In the Senate a "freshman" member who had become the "hatchet man" of the administration, Schwellenbach, picked three Liberty League men for a scathing attack. He cautioned Governor Alfred E. Smith not to "give way to the temptation of following the advice of J. Pierpont Morgan and John J. Raskob, and Pierre duPont and all the rest of these rascals and crooks who control the American Liberty League." (*Congressional Record,* January 23, 1936.)

Senator Robert M. La Follette, Jr., noting that the biggest contributions to the League came from the duPonts, A. P. Sloan, the Pews, E. T. Weir, Sewell Avery and Raskob, concluded: "It is not an organization that can be expected to defend the liberty of the masses of the American people. It speaks for the vested interests."

And the *New York Post* (April 18, 1936), then a crusading anti-Fascist paper, reporting in its news columns on the Sentinels, Crusaders, and other Liberty League affiliates, said that "the brood of anti-New Deal organizations, spawned by the Liberty League, are in turn spawning Fascism."

CHAPTER 16

BIG MONEY ORGANIZATIONS

AMERICA REFUSED to listen to the few newspaper correspondents and the still fewer experts, such as Professor Robert Brady ("The Spirit and Structure of German Fascism"), who before the Second World War tried to warn the nation that reaction and Fascism were the real dangers because there was money in them, and because there was big money back of them.

During and after the war the cartel investigators, Thurman Arnold, Wendell Berge, a score of leading liberal Senators, writers of a dozen books on the subject, and finally Mr. O. John Rogge, who really got to the roots of Naziism, united in stating the common finding: that Fascism in all countries is a form of government originated by great industrial empires and cartels, subsidized, placed in power and kept in power for the benefit of the few—and against the general welfare of the many.

This is an established truth. The logical conclusions from the facts of history, therefore, would be that the little crackpot Fascism of the American demagogues is not a danger unless the big money takes it over. Therefore, the first of the several attempts of big American money to put over Fascism in our country is worth recounting, since the episode itself was thrown down rather than played up by the newspapers.

General Smedley D. Butler testified under oath before the McCormack-Dickstein Committee, the first of the Un-American Committees, that he had been offered the leadership of a Fascist coup d'état in America not once but forty-two times. Of these the only important one was that backed by leaders of the American Liberty League, Wall Street bankers and brokers, and the ruling clique of the American Legion.

Despite the effort of all the newspapers (except the three or four which had had a scoop) to destroy the effect of the testimony, and despite newsweekly *Time*'s trying to tell the public it was just a joke, the Committee eventually issued its report confirming General Butler's charge that there had been a Fascist plot to seize Washington. (See Appendix 21.)

Most newspapers again suppressed or buried or belittled the official verdict. The McCormack-Dickstein Committee itself suppressed all those paragraphs of its report which named names, especially those of Morgan bankers, and that of the Liberty League, the equivalent of several of the super-patriotic but secretly corporation-directed organizations which supported Fascism in other lands.

The Committee suppressed the name of John W. Davis, attorney for the House of Morgan. It suppressed the testimony of witnesses that the arming of no less than 500,000 men for General Butler to lead had been discussed, and that it was planned to obtain rifles and bullets from Remington Arms "On credit through the duPonts" . . . "one of the duPonts is on the board of directors of the American Liberty League and they own a controlling interest in the Remington Arms Co. . . ." The Committee suppressed the testimony of General Butler in which the agent plotting the Fascist coup promised him that a new organization would be announced in two or three weeks, and, stated Butler, "in about two weeks the American Liberty League appeared, which was just about what he described it to me."

The reader is urged to turn to the appendix for the most important parts of the documentary evidence, especially the parts which the Un-American Committee suppressed—because this Un-American Committee, like its successors, the Dies Committee, the Wood-Rankin Committee and the Thomas-Rankin Committee, have all been un-American, inasmuch as they have refused to take any action against Fascism and have, in fact, given Fascists the use of their organization as a forum to spread their ideas.

All these un-American Committees have the support of the major portion of the press. In the case of the Liberty League-Legion-Wall Street conspiracy to overthrow the United

States Government, there was one of the most reprehensible conspiracies of silence in the long (and disgraceful) history of American journalism. The sensational value of the news—the main test in our country—can be judged even by the layman from the headlines and opening paragraphs which appeared in the Stern papers (*Philadelphia Record, New York Post,* and two Camden papers) at the time:

$3,000,000 BID FOR FASCIST ARMY BARED
by Paul Comly French
(Copyright [Nov. 20] 1934)

Major General Smedley D. Butler revealed today he has been asked by a group of wealthy New York brokers to lead a Fascist movement to set up a dictatorship in the United States.

General Butler, ranking major general of the Marine Corps up to his retirement three years ago, told his story today at a secret session of the Congressional Committee on un-American Activities.

Before he appeared before the committee, General Butler gave the (correspondent) a detailed account of the offer made to him.

"Of course I told the leaders of this Fascist movement that I wasn't interested in Fascism or in any other Ism," Butler said with characteristic vigor, "and that I wouldn't consider any such proposition.

"The whole affair smacked of treason to me."

He said he was approached by Gerald G. MacGuire, who is connected with the firm of Grayson M.-P. Murphy & Co., 52 Broadway, and asked to organize 500,000 veterans into a Fascist army.

"Shortly after MacGuire first came to see me," General Butler continued, "he arranged for Robert Sterling Clark, a New York broker, to come to my home at Newtown Square, Pa., to see me."

Clark, who maintains offices at 11 Wall Street, is reported to be worth more than $50,000,000.

General Butler outlined the details of the plan. He said MacGuire assured him "they have $3,000,000 'on the line' to start the organization. . . .

"The upshot of his proposition was that I was to head a soldier organization . . . in Washington (to) take over the functions of government. . . . MacGuire explained to me that they had two other candidates for the position of 'man on the white horse.' He said that if I did not accept, an offer would be made to General Douglas MacArthur, chief of staff of the United States Army, whose term of office expires November 22, and that the third choice would be Hanford MacNider, former commander of the American Legion. So far as I know, neither General MacArthur nor Mac-

Nider has been approached. Their names were merely mentioned as 'alternates.'"

If the Un-American Committee wanted to get the whole truth, Butler testified, it should call Banker Murphy (Morgan banker, and treasurer of the Liberty League) Alfred E. Smith (of the Liberty League), General MacArthur, Legion Commander MacNider, and Giannini banker Frank N. Belgrano, and William Doyle, former Department Commander of the Legion in Massachusetts and one of the "Royal Family" or "king makers" of that organization. Apparently the Committee did not want to get the truth.

There was only one means by which General Butler could reach the public with the warning of what the Wall Street men, Liberty Leaguers and American Legion chiefs were planning. The General took to the air. He said:

> Do you think it could be hard to buy the American Legion for un-American activities? You know, the average veteran thinks the Legion is a patriotic organization to perpetuate the memories of the last war, an organization to promote peace, to take care of the wounded and to keep green the graves of those who gave their lives.
>
> But is the American Legion that? No sir, not while it is controlled by the bankers. For years the bankers, by buying big club houses for various posts, by financing its beginning, and otherwise, have tried to make a strikebreaking organization of the Legion. The groups—the so-called Royal Family of the Legion—which have picked its officers for years, aren't interested in patriotism, in peace, in wounded veterans, in those who gave their lives. . . . No, they are interested only in using the veterans, through their officers.
>
> Why, even now, the commander of the American Legion is a banker—a banker who must have known what MacGuire's money was going to be used for. His name was mentioned in the testimony. Why didn't they call Belgrano and ask him why he contributed?

On another occasion General Butler concluded his exposé with the remark that: "I've never known one leader of the American Legion who has never sold them out." (*New York Times,* December 9, 1933.)

Smedley Butler was a great man. He was a Quaker. He had a conscience. He did his duty as a soldier in the Marines. He also wrote some years later:

"I spent 33 years (in the Marines) and during that period I spent most of my time being a high-class muscle man for Big Business, for Wall Street and the bankers. In short, I was a racketeer for capitalism. . . . I helped purify Nicaragua for the international banking house of Brown Brothers in 1909-12. I brought light to the Dominican Republic for American sugar interests in 1916. In China in 1927 I helped see to it that Standard Oil went its way unmolested."

And Fascist ideas, in 1934, "smacked of treason" to this grim and fighting Quaker.

A little more than a decade later the Liberty League was revived under another patriotic name—American Action. But in the years between, scores, perhaps hundreds of large and small organizations, all of them devoted to special interests while pretending to function for the general good, tried to enlist a popular following—they already had the financial support of the old Liberty Leaguers. A few of the most important are worth noting.

The Committee for Constitutional Government

The chief object of this organization's propaganda is to destroy the union labor movement. In this the Committee for Constitutional Government is merely following the National Association of Manufacturers' line. A secondary objective is the destruction of the Sixteenth Amendment and the passage of their proposed Twenty-Second Amendment, which would limit taxation of the rich, ease inheritance and gift duties.

The whole policy of the Committee for Constitutional Government is to safeguard the wealth of the 38,000 American millionaires. If the amendment became law, Henry Ford (in 1944) would have paid only $250,000 on his million dollar income, instead of $800,000. Whereas Joe Smith, making $2,000 a year and paying, say, $175 in taxes, would have had to pay $500. Moreover, according to Congressman Wright Patman, small business would have been wrecked, and also the entire program of aid to veterans, due to a lack of tax money.

The Committee for Constitutional Government lists numerous persons with a Fascist record among its endorsers, officials, advisory board members. The Senate Committee on

Elections and Privileges reported that the organization received the following sums from the following persons in 1940:

J. P. Morgan, 23 Wall St., New York, $1,000; Thomas W. Lamont, same address, $1,000; Howard J. Pew of Philadelphia, $4,000; Joseph N. Pew, Mary Ethel Pew and Mrs. Pew Myrin, $4,000 each.

The Committee for Constitutional Government was founded by Frank E. Gannett, the chain publisher. Its operations have always been in the hands of Dr. Edward A. Rumely, whose name was taken off the door when anti-Fascists kept reminding the public that Rumely was sentenced to one year and a day in the federal penitentiary after his conviction as a German agent in the First World War. Rumely had secretly bought a newspaper, the *New York Mail,* with money supplied by the German government, and used it for German propaganda purposes.

Another notable member is Samuel S. McClure, founder of newspaper syndication, and in the 1930's a propagandist for Mussolini and Italian fascism.

Most active labor-fighter of the organization is ex-Congressman Samuel Pettengill, who also supplies a syndicated column to many newspapers.

On the advisory board is ex-Senator Edward Burke, of Nebraska, former member of the Khaki Shirts of America, first uniformed frankly Fascist organization which wanted to seize the Government.

Nominal head of the Committee for Constitutional Government was the Reverend Dr. Norman Vincent Peale of Marble Collegiate Church, New York. Thanks to exposés by *In Fact,* Dr. Peale resigned. His place was taken by New York University economics professor, Willford I. King.

In a series of exposés during May and June, 1944 (see *Congressional Record*), Congressman Patman called the Committee for Constitutional Government "the most sinister lobby in Washington," the "No. 1 Fascist organization in the United States"; and again on November 8, 1945, challenged by Representative Carl T. Curtis of Nebraska to name Fascists, he replied:

"The Committee for Constitutional Government represents a lot of them. There is this fellow Gannett, a big chain newspaper publisher . . . this fellow Pettengill, a renegade Democrat, and this fellow McClure who spent 2 years over in Italy studying Fascism under Mussolini . . . and Edward Rumely, their wheel-horse, an ex-convict who was convicted for dealing with the enemy —Germany—in World War I. . . . Pettengill, who used to be a member of this house . . . the No. 1 fascist in America. . . ."

This indictment was privileged because made on the floor of the House. But Patman repeated it on a radio broadcast, saying: "Gannett is one of the most dangerous Fascists at large in America. Samuel Pettengill . . . I consider the No. 1 most active Fascist in America." (*Labor,* October 12, 1946.) The charges have not been answered.

Knights of the Ku Klux Klan

The past history of the Klan, known to everyone, tells of hate and murder. All its members are the racist type of Fascists, hardly different from the Hitlerite racists. The Klan apparently financed itself by the sale of bedsheets at three or four times their value.

The most important change in Klan policy came with the arrival of the CIO in the middle 1930's, and the first southern drive of both the CIO and AFL in the middle 1940's. The Klan today makes its largest appeal to big and little business which wants the South to remain un-unionized, underpaid, underfed, and underprivileged.

A report on the meeting of Klan Chapter No. 1, Atlanta, Georgia, held at Redmen's Wigwam, Central and Hunter Streets, May 13, 1946, with Grand Dragon Dr. Samuel Green presiding, says in part:

"Dr. Green was visibly upset by attacks made against him and the Klan. . . . He cursed Walter Winchell. . . . Green rehashed the charges . . . to the effect that the CIO is communist-dominated and said: 'This is an open declaration of war between the Klan and the CIO.'

"Green said: 'The CIO is for the Negroes and Jews.' He also attacked the Political Action Committee."

Reporting from Atlanta, *PM's* correspondent, Karl Pretschold, added:

"Green seems to realize that if the Klan is to grow its growth must be based on opposition to the CIO. . . .

"In fighting the CIO the Klan will expect approval and help from important groups in the South: reactionary employers, politicians who fear unionism and will welcome an ally who'll fight dirty."

There is a long record of the flogging and tarring of union organizers by Klansmen. Neither the Dies Committee nor its two successors, both directed largely by Representative Rankin, have ever taken action against the Klan. Members have stated publicly that they never will. The Klan today is a part of the terroristic branch of business and industry, hardly different from either Hitler's or Mussolini's Brownshirts and Blackshirts. The true color of Fascism became visible when the Klan made union labor its chief target. There is big money in union busting.

National Association of Manufacturers and Churches

The Big Money is also invading the religious field. The National Association of Manufacturers has a special and very active propaganda department, the NAM Committee on Cooperation with Churches, whose purpose is to bring business and religion together. Where an honest preacher has suggested that perhaps the representatives of the democratic majority of Americans, union labor leaders, participate in the conferences, the NAM has withdrawn.

The 1944 annual officers' directory of the NAM frankly tells the purpose of its church work: "Clergymen and businessmen generally have the same broad concepts of a better America" but "difference in their perspectives often clouds this basic agreement and sometimes leads to misunderstandings of motives on both sides." The NAM, through its propaganda branch, NIIC, "has initiated the formation of hundreds of local community businessmen's committees on cooperation with churches, and sponsors a continuous series of regional conferences between the clergy and management."

But who directs this big propaganda movement?

Chairman of the committee is none other than Jasper E. Crane, vice president of E. I. duPont de Nemours & Company.

Spiritual Mobilization

The same business interests aid or subsidize scores of reactionary religious organizations. Spiritual Mobilization was organized by the Reverend Dr. James W. Fifield, Jr., pastor of the Congregational Church of Los Angeles, after a similar organization, Moral Re-Armament, was pretty well discredited when its founder, Reverend Dr. Frank N. D. Buchman, was publicly quoted as thanking God for Hitler. Fifield claimed 2,000,000 followers. He also attempted to mobilize all the preachers in the United States into a reactionary movement whose "basic freedoms pledge" was a thin veil for the fifth freedom advocated by the NAM, namely, "free enterprise." A protest was issued by the Western Unitarian Conference signed by 116 ministers and laymen, which accused the Fifield outfit of thrusting "aside the Federal Council of Churches" in order to champion the National Association of Manufacturers' "American Way of Life." The protest concluded with this paragraph:

"Finally we raise these questions: 1, Why does this organization advertise in Gerald B. Winrod's *The Defender;* 2, Since this is a program of appeal to churches, why does it 'not solicit funds from the clergymen or churches which participate in its program'? 3, From whom does its money come?"

The last question was answered by the Unitarian Reverend E. T. Buehrer, editor of the *Journal of Liberal Religion* (Spring issue, 1945):

"The 'crusade to preserve free enterprise' in America in the face of growing popular demand for social responsibility in government, was destined from the beginning to be a divisive factor in organized religion as it has long been in organized politics. The National Association of Manufacturers, the Committee for Constitutional Government and lesser organizations—the potentially Fascist forces of the nation—have always had their individual spokesmen in the various religious bodies. Now, as active, working groups they have their counterpart in Spiritual Mobilization. . . .

"The National Association of Manufacturers had its attention attracted to the minister. . . . James W. Fifield, Jr., and invited him to be its guest speaker at a meeting in New York. He won the confidence of those present, and their vigorous applause, with his glorification of 'free enterprise,' and he emerged from the meeting with $50,000 which they enthusiastically contributed to the crusade which he was about to organize. Under such auspices was Spiritual Mobilization launched."

Buchmanism

The Episcopalian publication, *The Witness,* did something no commercial publication has ever dared do: it exposed Buchmanism's main purpose: "a trap for labor." Behind all the claptrap of moral regeneration, "sharing of sins," confessing, and religious buncombe, *Witness* editor William Spofford saw clearly that Buchmanism, because it is subsidized by the biggest corporation heads in the world, was one of the many movements designed to fool working people into accepting the viewpoint, whatever it may be, of the corporate interests.

A spokesman for the Catholics, the late Cardinal Hinsley, primate of Great Britain, threatened with excommunication all members of his church who embraced Buchmanism.

A noted Protestant editor, Dr. Guy Emery Shipler of *The Churchman,* reported a Wall Street dinner for Buchmanites almost entirely devoted to Jew-baiting.

The newspapers of America suppressed the news that the nationally known organization, the Jewish War Veterans of the United States, unanimously passed the following resolution:

Whereas, Dr. Frank N. D. Buchman, founder of Moral Re-Armament, also known as the Oxford Group Movement and Buchmanism, is also the author of the expression, "Thank God for Hitler . . . ";

Whereas, Buchmanism has been exposed in the British Parliament;

Whereas, Dr. Guy Emery Shipler, leading Protestant editor, has exposed the Buchmanites, as largely anti-Semitic;

Whereas, Dr. Buchman has cooporated with leading Buchmanites in all enemy nations, notably Himmler, the arch-murderer in Nazi Germany, and the leading Japanese war makers;

Whereas, when the call to fight Naziism came in both Britain and America the Buchmanites claimed exemption from the draft saying they were a religious movement;

Whereas, both in Britain and America public officials have denounced Buchmanites as draft dodgers, and forced them to register;

Whereas, in general, the Moral Re-Armament movement may be described as Fascist, subsidized by native Fascists, and with a long record of collaboration with Fascists the world over;

Therefore, be it resolved by the Jewish War Veterans of the United States, that they join in denouncing Buchmanism, the Oxford Group Movement and Moral Re-Armament as Fascist in its viewpoint, as un-American, and as a menace to the world's war against the common enemy of mankind.

The most noted endorsers and financial subsidizers of Buchmanism:

Heinrich Himmler, the world's greatest mass murderer, and Rudolf Hess, who made a trip to England in the beginning of the war in an effort to align fellow Buchmanites to switch the war—to turn the Allies against Russia instead of Germany.

Henry Ford, who sent his own physician in his private plane to aid Dr. Buchman.

William Randolph Hearst, who in the 1930's published signed propaganda articles by Hitler, Mussolini, Goering and Goebbels.

Harvey Firestone, a rubber baron.

The late Harry Chandler of the *Los Angeles Times,* one of the most violent enemies of labor in the American press.

George Eastman, Paul Shoup, Elmer Howlett and scores of other California industrialists and enemies of labor.

(The Buchmanites use hundreds of noted names as endorsers, Herbert Hoover's, for example, but a friend of the former president informed the writer that Mr. Hoover had never endorsed Buchmanism. In most cases the persons named as followers have been induced to endorse a playlet presented by the Buchmanites. Some of America's greatest labor leaders have been listed through this device, but unions everywhere, especially in the Cramps' Shipyards and in Detroit, have protested Buchmanite infiltration and propaganda.)

Tool Owners' Union

In the 1940's the successors to the Liberty League dropped a lot of the old hypocrisy, declared themselves more and more openly the agencies for the preservation of profits, special privilege, the free enterprise system; and naturally opponents of liberal ideas (such as embodied in the New Deal) and of the chief beneficiaries of those ideas and program, the labor movement.

The Tool Owners' Union was an attempt to enlist a large percentage of the 50,000,000 Americans said to have an interest in the tools of production by holding stocks and bonds, owning life insurance, having bank deposits and operating small businesses or engaging in farming or professional activities. The National Association of Manufacturers and the Liberty League had been content, in the past, with the Hitler-Pareto-James Burnham-Henry Luce-Lawrence Dennis theory of a ruling elite; this was the first appeal for a mass following for reaction.

In 1945 one Hector Lazo, public relations director for the Loose-Wiles Biscuit Company, approached the National Association of Manufacturers and the United States Chamber of Commerce with the idea. "I am completely and thoroughly convinced that this job cannot be done by either the United States Chamber of Commerce or the National Association of Manufacturers, or by either of these two organizations working with their individual identities. It must be done through a new organization, of course, backed by business. . . . We must boldly step into the picture or we will be responsible for the failure of private enterprise . . . a religion with us." Mr. Lazo proposed the name "American Educational Committee," later stated that the Tool Owners' Union "is doing the job I suggested."

Another notable citizen approached by Lazo was Fuller of the SEP. The magazine (September 21, 1946) endorsed Tool Owners' Union as a "middle class movement for the millions."

Among the members and endorsers of Tool Owners Union are:

Raoul Desvernine, director and attorney, formerly of the Liberty League and former president of Crucible Steel.

Dr. Alfred P. Haake, who served with the NIIC or propaganda branch of the National Association of Manufacturers; spoke at meetings of the Citizens USA Committee, which has sponsored speeches by Gerald L. K. Smith and Lawrence Dennis; helped organize the American Economic Foundation with Fred G. Clark of the Crusaders. Haake appears on forums as an "economist," is never described as a paid employee of General Motors.

Whiting Williams, industrial relations consultant, whose name appears (along with that of George E. Sokolsky, the syndicated columnist, and two or three others) in the La Follette Committee's exposé of National Association of Manufacturers' secretly hired writers and speakers.

James G. Stahlman, union-hating publisher of the *Nashville Banner* and onetime chairman of the strikebreaking department of the American Newspaper Publishers Association, lyrically announced (in a two-column poem, no less) that he had "joined a union"—the Tool Owners' Union, of course.

The big newspapers, many of them the very ones which had refused the advertising of Consumers' Union, accepted the advertising of Tool Owners' Union without question.

However, when the T.O.U. sought permission to operate in New York, real union men appeared at the hearings. CIO counsellor Mortimer Wolf and AFL counsellor Emil Schlesinger asked the incorporator and apparent owner, Allen W. Rucker, about the relations of Dr. Haake and "the Fascist Gerald L. K. Smith." "What is a Fascist?" Rucker replied, adding that so far as he knew Smith was "an evangelical preacher with some extreme ideas on economics."

Regional Director William Collins of the AFL declared before the Board: "Its (the T.O.U.'s) real purpose is to acquire gifts of money from corporate sources; to propagandize and pressure a campaign of anti-unionism." Several labor witnesses called Tool Owners' Union a racket. (The labor-baiting columnists and radio commentators, including Pegler, Fulton Lewis, Jr., Kaltenborn, Mark Sullivan, Henry J. Taylor, and the rest, did not take up this type of alleged racketeering.)

In giving its decision, the Board of Standards and Appeals made history. It actually used the word fascist. Denying Tool Owners' Union the right to do business in New York, it stated:

"No more fascistic organization with all the potentiality for undemocratic action and danger to our way of life has yet come before the official attention of this board. The incorporators believe that there is something wrong with our country, and that they want to do something about it. But they reserve for themselves—and in the final analysis the power of determining is in one man—the means by which the dangers they see . . . are to be vanquished. . . . We have just finished a great war started by a man who had his own ideas as to what was wrong in the country in which he was not born."

National Economic Council.
Merwin K. Hart.
American Union of Nationalist Spain.

Hart was the leading voluntary Franco propagandist in America. His New York State Economic Council, now the National Economic Council, had among its first financial backers: Lammot duPont of the DuPont empire; John H. Rand, Jr., leader in the National Association of Manufacturers, and the author of the Mohawk Valley Formula, a widely adopted plan for breaking strikes and smashing unions—largely with the aid of the newspaper press; A. W. Erickson, a big advertising agent; Alfred P. Sloan, Jr., of General Motors, head of the NAM's National Industrial Information Committee; and J. H. Alstyne, president of Otis Elevator Company.

Associated with Hart in propaganda work: John Eoghan Kelly, Reverend Edward Lodge Curran, Coughlin's eastern representative of the Christian Front; John B. Snow, H. W. Prentis, Jr., of Armstrong Cork Company and NAM; Mrs. Dilling, and Congressman Martin Dies.

General Franco and James True, inventor of the "kike-killer," a club he patented for killing Jews, both endorsed the propaganda book "America Looks at Spain." Hart stated as facts in this book certain historic falsehoods, which even Franco admits. For example, Franco's massacre of the workingmen at Badajoz. Franco admits he shot those he terms "enemies"; Hart whitewashes and denies everything. Hart states the Phalange is not Fascist, Franco calls it his Fascist "falange." (These and other falsehoods were exposed in *The Nation,* June 10, 1939, page 678.)

Hart's American Union of Nationalist Spain was largely a Coughlinite Christian Front outfit. Hart wrote for Social Justice before it suspended—under threat of being stopped for sedition. Hart had on his executive committee Lester M. Gray of the New York Christian Front, J. E. Kelly, Reverend Curran, Patrick F. Scanlon, publisher of the *Brooklyn Tablet,* one of the largest reactionary propaganda papers in America, Joseph P. Kamp, publisher of pamphlets containing falsehoods against the CIO; and numerous anti-Semites. (Hart's fascism was defended by Sokolsky, the columnist, and inserted in the *Congressional Record* by Senator Nye—*Congressional Record,* May 23, 1941.) Hart's complete record is given in "Under Cover."

The Hart-Economic Council record includes: opposition to bills ending child labor—this was branded "youth control" and attacked as Russian communist in inspiration; opposition to all health and sickness insurance—this would cost corporations money; disenfranchisement of all on relief (at one time 10,000,000 American citizens). Hart's big work has been fighting the Wagner Act. He and the *New York Times* both engage in this activity. It is no coincidence that a file of the *Times* shows that among the favored few whose letters appear often in its columns is the Franco propagandist Hart. Hart also is reprinted by G. L. K. Smith in his magazine, which was named in the sedition indictments as used by alleged seditionists. It is Hart's Economic Council which later sponsored Upton Close's radio program—not heard in either New York City or Chicago as Mutual's key stations, WOR and WGN, were aware that anti-fascists were prepared to protest to the Federal Communications Commission if this propaganda got into the big cities. (Eventually Close and Hart were refused the air, owing to enlightened protest.)

American Action, Inc.

"Big business here (in America)," said the noted prosecutor of the small-fry Fascists, special assistant to the Attorney General, O. John Rogge, "is not now threatened. It still controls virtually every phase of our economic and political life. Its representatives in legislatures comply with the wishes of the men with money. If a threat to their control should ever really arise, I am convinced that large sections of top business in America would follow the Thyssen pattern—[Thyssen first subsidized Hitler, then got all industry to take over Naziism, use it as an army to seize the nation]. At that time, the Fascists will receive whatever sums they need."

In American Action, the United States has its most important and powerful successor to the Liberty League, subsidized by the biggest money in America, embracing for the first time in one organization demagogues, crackpots, anti-Semites, "Nationalists," the National Association of Manufacturers' biggest leaders, the most powerful newspaper chain in the country, and Big Money.

Some time in January, 1946, *In Fact* and *Federated Press* (which serves hundreds of labor weeklies) obtained the evidence that a great number of men and forces ranging from Reactionary to Fascist, were organizing a movement to fight the Political Action Committee.

Letters from Upton Close to Robert Lund and Joseph Pew, two of the real pillars of the National Association of Manufacturers, revealed the fact the name chosen by the enemies of the PAC would be AAC—American Action Committee. Later, it became American Action, Inc. A board of strategy mentioned by Close included Samuel Pettengill, General Robert E. Wood, John T. Flynn, Merwin K. Hart, and a R. E. Minnis of Wichita, Kansas.

When William A. Larner, Jr., resigned as executive director of the Wichita Town Hall Committee, he signed an affidavit first mentioning American Action Committee (of which his society was a subsidiary) and linking it to the Republican Party. He swore that Herbert A. Brownell, Republican national committee chairman, and its radio director, got Cecil B. DeMille to make an anti-labor speech sponsored by the Wichita committee.

Contributors to the Wichita Town Hall Committee, stated Larner, included Sewell L. Avery of Montgomery Ward, Colonel McCormick, and members of the Pew family.

In March, 1946, Eugene Segal of the Scripps-Howard press, publishing a series of exposés of native American Fascism, disclosed the fact that American Action Committee, in addition to having corporation backers such as Wood and Avery, also was keeping "under cover" "some better known Nationalists" lending their support to it, notably Gerald L. K. Smith and Carl Mote, the Indiana telephone company operator and notorious anti-Semite. In February Smith had sent a mimeographed letter to his backers saying, "I challenge you to join with such men as John T. Flynn, Upton Close, Colonel Robert R. McCormick, General Robert Wood, Merwin K. Hart and Sam Pettengill in the formation of a new dynamic, crusading Nationalist political committee. If you accept this challenge such a committee will sweep the nation."

On October 7, 1946, Carroll Kilpatrick of the *Chicago Sun* reported that American Action, Inc., had raised a million dollars for an election "purge" of PAC-endorsed Congressional candidates. Among the new names of persons helping finance the organization were Ernest T. Weir and Lammot duPont.

The *New York Times* and other newspapers took the advertising of American Action. But when Friends of Democracy offered an advertisement in reply, the *Times* refused it. Friends of Democracy had as its headline the following sentence: "A smoke screen organization for nationalist, pro-Fascists, anti-Semitic and anti-Catholic hate-mongers, pre-war isolationists and present-day defeatists." It also declared that the public deserved to know who was behind American Action, and listed eight persons, as follows:

> "Robert E. Wood, head of America First Committee, who wrote in July, 1941, 'I have not rejected (Father Charles Coughlin's) Christian Social Justice Movement. I welcome their support. . . '
>
> "Merwin K. Hart . . . U. S. Supreme Court Justice Robert Jackson said: 'Merwin K. Hart . . . is well known for his pro-fascist leanings. . . .'
>
> "Upton Close, radio commentator . . . twice dropped from network broadcasts because of unreliability. . . . (Close has since been dropped a third time.)
>
> "Robert M. Harriss . . . . who worked with the hate-mongering Christian Front. . . .
>
> "Samuel B. Pettengill . . . . whose activities Patman labelled 'sinister and sordid.'
>
> "John T. Flynn, former New York head of America First who is now decrying present attempts at world cooperation.
>
> "Col. Robert R. McCormick . . . whose newspaper, the *Chicago Tribune,* is the darling of every anti-Semitic group in the country."

When the national executive council of American Action was announced, a new importance clearly attached itself to the organization: Chairman was Edward A. Hayes, veteran of the two world wars, "actively engaged in fighting against subversives since 1916," and commander of the American Legion, 1933-1934; noted members included Ray Kelly, lawyer, and past national commander of the Legion; Lou Kessler of Seattle, a veteran; Colonel Robert E. Condon, another "active in American Legion." The announcement also said: "American Action will extend its full cooperation and assistance in the broad field of Americanism as set out in the programs of the American Legion, Veterans of Foreign Wars, Disabled American Veterans, Amvets, and all other truly representative American Veterans patriotic and fraternal organizations." Notably absent in the listing was the American Veterans Committee, the only important veteran group which has a truly liberal and democratic program. (Union Labor Legionnaires are part of the Legion, hope to liberalize it.)

Prominent on the national committee was Robert M.

Harriss, listed as a "cotton broker," but not identified as the financial adviser to Father Coughlin during the days of the subversive Social Justice, the speculations in silver, and the years of preaching of anti-Semitic falsehood, along the Hitler line, in America.

A "substantial amount of money" was contributed for the work of American Action by General Wood, according to a confidential money-raising letter which Friends of Democracy obtained. Other financial angels were Joseph Pew, Lammot duPont, Ernest Weir, John J. Raskob of the DuPont empire and General Motors, and William H. Regnery.

These men were described as "wealthy industrialists seeking the defeat of Congressmen they can't control" and "American Fascists seeking to preserve property rights and ignoring human rights," by Congressman Patman (over Ed Hart's forum, station WINX, Washington, October 13, 1946).

As election day neared, the Scripps-Howard newspapers, which had exposed American Action, made a complete about-face, and published an editorial endorsement.

"To fight Communism, defeat Communist-backed candidates for Congress and rally to this job anti-Communist voters all over the country is the announced excellent purpose of the newly formed organization, American Action, Inc.," wrote Roy Howard's editorial hacks, forgetting that an honest reporter employed by the same Lord Howard had exposed red-baiting by this organization as a smokescreen. That was October 19. On October 28, Gerald L. K. Smith wrote to "all people associated with the America First Crusade" "to cooperate" with American Action. *Gentile News,* which still peddles the notorious forgeries known as "The Protocols of Zion," urged the formation of local units of American Action by its readers. Mrs. Elizabeth Dilling, alleged seditionist, wholeheartedly endorsed American Action.

The first indication that American reactionaries and American Fascists might unite their forces, was noted by Friends of Democracy in its November 30, 1946, issue of *Battle,* under the title "Hatriots Coalesce." It found that "reactionary financiers and rabblerousing bigots moved quickly this month toward a united front.

"Moving in from one side to join Lammot duPont, John J. Raskob and Joseph Pew were Edward F. Hutton, Long Island millionaire (and Wall Street broker); Robert Wason of the National Association of Manufacturers; and Frank Gannett, owner of a New York newspaper chain.

"Moving in from the other was the 'Hitler-like' Gerald L. K. Smith, . . . Elizabeth Dilling . . . and the anti-Semitic Eugene Flitcraft whose *Gentile News* called the united front 'a worthy cause'. . . .

"Cementing the extremes were 'borderline' groups such as the National Economic Council, the Committee for Constitutional Government, America's Future, American Action, Inc. 'Big-Shots' move freely from one of these groups to the other; key figures in each alternately cooperate with the financiers and the anti-Semitic rabble."

An occasion which may have historic importance was the National Economic Council's dinner (in the Waldorf-Astoria, November 12, 1946) to celebrate the victory of reaction in the Congressional election and to honor Upton Close, the radio commentator who had been driven off the air three times by popular protests. Hart presided, and had at the main table the following notables: Messrs. duPont, Raskob, Pettengill. Other prominent persons were Lambert Fairchild; Colonel Edward D. Gray, one of the new leaders of American Action; Harriss, the cotton broker; Joseph Kamp, "labor-baiter whose work was recommended by the Nazis" and whose publications were named in the sedition indictment; Edward A. Rumely; and John A. Zellers, "who once spoke before Nazi agent Frederick Auhagen's American Fellowship Forum," and more recently for a *New York Times* forum—against labor, of course.

"The interlocking directorates of the various unity groups," reported *Battle,* "further is exemplified by America's Future. Active in this group are Hutton; General Wood who also is a big-shot in American Action; Frank Gannett, a leader in the Committee for Constitutional Government; and Robert Wason of the National Association of Manufacturers. Also fitting into the unity picture is Joseph Pew" whose *Pathfinder* "praised the united front" and endorsed American Action as fighting all alien Isms.

This was the first time in five years that a sort of unity existed between the top ranking reactionaries and the so-called "vermin Fascists," several of whom had been named in the sedition indictments, and all of whom had been on the approved list of Welt-Dienst, the chief Hitler foreign propaganda agency. Concluded *Battle:* "During the war period big shots could scarcely risk associating with anti-Semites and Axis sympathizers. The Gerald Smiths, the Eugene Flitcrafts and even the Merwin K. Harts, as leaders of isolated movements, can exercise only limited influence on American life. United, and hiding behind the duPonts, the Raskobs, the Huttons, and the Woods, they can shape America's future."

Significantly, Kenneth Ellis (Federation to Fight Fascism) noted that "American Action, Inc., has a great deal of money. It has a great deal of power. Its members own the financial resources of the Republican Party. Some of its members own a large part of the financial resources of the Democratic Party. Its chief organizers and promoters have had the endorsement of the Nazi Party, the Falange, and the Sinarquistas; therefore its ramifications are not 'American,' but international, and furnish the political student with evidence of the transition of Fascism from a 'national' to an 'international' type of organization."

Following the celebration of its 1946 election victory, American Action and its sponsors received support from various significant sources: the $65,000-a-year Hearst columnist Westbrook Pegler wrote enthusiastically of founder Merwin Hart as one who works "openly for American principles"; the South Carolina chapter of Columbians, an organization whose heads were being jailed in Georgia, changed its allegiance to American Action; the coalition of hatemongers, fascists, Christian Fronters and the heads of the National Association of Manufacturers and approved by the *New York Enquirer's* editor, William Griffin, who had been named in the first two sedition indictments dismissed by the District Court and now in appeal by the Government; Senator O'Daniel of Texas stated that American Action would "offset the Moscow left wing CIO-PAC"; Federated Press named among new sponsors and endorsers Ogden H. Hammond, propagandist for Franco, Edgar Queeny of the Monsanto Chemical Company, Thomas Creigh, counsel for the Cudahy Packing Company, and Maurice B. Franks of the National Association of Yardmasters, who is a union official but who fights the regular unions.

If General Smedley Butler were alive today he would note history repeating itself, but in more alarming tones. The old American Liberty League and America First have been resurrected, past commanders of the American Legion are directing the new organization, and although there is no repetition of the plot to march 500,000 men on Washington and establish a Fascist dictatorship, there is the appearance for the first time in American history of a coalition of demagogues, hatemongers, "vermin fascists" and the most respectable and most powerful heads of corporate business. It was out of a similar mixture of the three main ingredients, corporation financing, war veterans, and Fascist demagoguery, that the Fascist movement grew and conquered in all the lands in which it has a bloody history.

CHAPTER 17

THE GENERAL WELFARE IN THE ATOMIC AGE

IT MUST by now be as obvious to the reader as it is to the writer that it is not a coincidence that the same names of men and corporations appear in most chapters: they oppose the TVA, the MVA, the St. Lawrence development; they control or influence magazines and the newspaper press; some belong to the National Association of Manufacturers, others to reactionary organizations; some deal in patent medicines, most of them contribute money to the presidential and other political campaigns, some are the American endorsers of Hitler and Mussolini; almost all of them are defenders and spokesmen for "the American Way of Life," the "free enterprise" system which—they say—has made America what it is.

The foregoing chapters, and the documents which follow, cite but a few samples of the thousands of available documents, the millions of words of evidence which the writer has collected in thirty-eight years of journalism, and more especially in the period 1940-1947, when he has had the assistance of many among his 175,000 newsletter subscribers in every state of the Union.

The purpose of the writer has been to follow the Euripidean principle, to "let the facts speak for themselves." There are facts and facts, and one must choose. The philosopher undoubtedly meant an honest selection, an honest presentation, made perhaps by some olympian mind inhabiting a region where prejudice is unknown.

The facts in this volume, and the documentation, were chosen for several reasons, the most important of which is their general suppression, or at best, their "burial," by those whose first duty it is to publish them—the newspapers, magazines, radio, and lesser means of communication.

The facts here presented speak for themselves, and require little explanation, almost no editorial comment. But, since it is not only a convention that the concluding section, or at least the concluding chapter of a volume of this nature should contain certain "constructive criticism," and because there is actually a great public demand for editorial opinion, the present writer must yield to the extent of enlarging on the following statements:

1. The American public is misinformed. The press has failed in its duty.

2. The report of the Commission on Freedom of the Press confirms the charge that the newspapers do not serve the people, do not serve Democracy, can vulgarize mankind, and can endanger the peace of the world. A free (honest) press is therefore of more importance than anything else in America.

3. Under the present system, the rulers of the nation are able to deceive the people; they can even destroy what is best for the majority, not only the New Deal, but any Square Deal.

4. They can also lead the nation into the Third World War, using the atomic bomb, which will destroy civilization.

5. Atomic fission, and the harnessing of water power throughout the world, can assure plenty for its two billion inhabitants. But the few oppose such development today as they have throughout the hundred years of the industrial revolution.

6. The American Way is not the free enterprise of the National Association of Manufacturers but the greatest good of the greatest number.

1. Misinformed America

The great, startling, and tragic impression of many years of journalism can be summed up in one little phrase: the people do not know.

Every fact stated in this book, every document in the appendix, should have been common knowledge. Given a really free press, by which is meant an honest press in the service of freedom, not merely a press free to do almost everything to gain profits (or power) for its owners, the American people would be the best informed in the world, and an informed electorate would be able to produce a governing body which would devote itself to the most important phrase in the preamble of the Constitution of the United States: to "promote the general welfare."

The fact is the public does not know but is very anxious to know. The thousands of professors, school teachers, lawyers, doctors, labor union leaders, rank and file workers, members of Congress, and others who have written the author every year for the past seven years—and only 3,000 letters a year could be answered—prove beyond question that even the better-informed are ill-informed. There is a great hunger, a real need for information in our country, which the agencies of mass information wilfully refuse to fill.

On many subjects which concern the health, wealth and happiness of the American people, we cannot say today, "we hold these truths to be self-evident." Many of the most vital truths about our political and business system, our social and economic system, are not common knowledge, as they should be.

The chief reason for this state of affairs is the failure of the press (and lesser means of mass communication) to serve the people. The critics of the press began saying so at the turn of the century, but since the press itself would not give their views to the public, only a small minority of the American people has known the cause of this blockade.

In 1947 the Commission on Freedom of the Press in its report confirmed everything the critics said, went even further in a general indictment which damns the newspapers as an enemy of the progress of the United States. (I shall refer to this report immediately; its importance lies more in its authoritative sponsorship than in any new findings.)

If only a good minority of the American press—and not 1% or less—really served the interests of its readers, the most intelligent stratum everywhere would know, as a small minority in New York, St. Louis, Chicago and York, Pennsylvania, does know, a major portion of the facts as given in this book, and similar documentary evidence, which the vast majority of our newspapers have suppressed.

If we had an honest press, every citizen in South Dakota would know about the $53,700 fund raised by a dozen Eastern industrialists to support two Senators (Bushfield and Gurney) and two Representatives (Case and Mundt) who voted for the National Association of Manufacturers' sponsored anti-labor laws and for every reactionary measure introduced in Congress which would directly and financially benefit members of the National Association of Manufacturers.

If we had an honest press in Montana the people of that state would know how much MVA could improve their living conditions.

If we had an honest press the St. Lawrence development would have been completed years ago.

If we had an honest press both sides of every controversial question would be known to the public, and it would no longer be possible to lead a nation into war for the benefit of a few bankers and munitions makers.

Or oil interests.

As for atomic energy. . . .

The fight against David Lilienthal as chairman of the Atomic Energy Commission continued for days as a sort of individual filibuster by one of the discredited Bourbon Senators, Boss Crump's McKellar, enemy of the Tennessee Valley Authority and the people of the South. Few paid any attention to it. McKellar stood for "pork and patronage"; McKellar lied and lied about Lilienthal being a Communist, and even tried out the old anti-Semitic Hitler line of asking him about his parents, and where they were born. It was, as the Republican *New York Herald Tribune* said, a "sordid scene."

Its significance, however, became apparent when from both sides of the Senate chamber the elder "statesmen" arose to take their stand on the side of McKellar.

Who were these gentlemen among Senators? And why were they joining their despicable colleague?

"The answer, which is very simple, comes in two parts,"

wrote the *Herald Tribune* Washington correspondent Joseph Alsop (February 14, 1947). "It is significant first of all that the first voice raised against Lilienthal after that of McKellar should have been the voice of Senator Styles Bridges of New Hampshire. Bridges' burning conviction that the views of the power lobby were the charter of American liberties has long been known to most people in Washington. It is also significant that one of the two or three atomic committee members probably opposed to Lilienthal should be Senator Richard Russell of Georgia, which is about the only remaining state where the power people have a real grip on local politics.

"These are straws in the wind. . . . The majority of the American power industry has gained wisdom in the past 14 years. But there is still a strong minority. . . . These men are putting the heat on. They are putting it on, furthermore, because they are well aware of the probable revolutionary effect of energy production of atomic fission, and wish to get this incalculable national asset into the kind of mediocre, fumbling hands they regard as 'safe.' "

2. *One Solution: A Free Press*

Under these circumstances, the present writer reverts again to a theory based on almost four decades of experience. It is a theory originally propounded by a man who began public life as the first and greatest advocate of freedom of the press in the history of America, the author of the First Amendment to the Constitution—which ennobles one and only one private enterprise—the newspaper business.

Jefferson declared: "The basis of our government being the opinion of the people, the very first object should be to keep that right; and were it left to me to decide whether we should have government without newspapers, or newspapers without a government, I should not hesitate a moment to prefer the latter." (To Carrington, 1787.)

It is generaly conceded that given a free press, all other freedoms are safe.

A free press is a fulcrum and lever by which the whole world can be moved.

But, unfortunately . . . these instruments more than any other are now controlled by a few, perverted for wealth and power rather than used for the general welfare.

For twenty years the present writer has published the irrefutable proof that the force Jefferson believed higher than government is actually a commercial, prostituted, irresponsible, falsifying agency, actually an enemy of the American people. In these years only two or three notable voices joined in this warning.

In March, 1947, however, the most important report on the press in our history was made by the Commission on Freedom of the Press, headed by Chancellor Robert Hutchins of the University of Chicago. The Commission refused to name names of publishers and papers, thus discounting its findings considerably. Perhaps so large a majority of the newspapers came in for censure that a short honor roll of honest exceptions—say, six or seven, or less than 1% of the nation's 1750 dailies—would have been better.

The Commission, however, dignified and made authoritative the indictment of the American press first written by Will Irwin in 1910 (in *Collier's;* 24 publishers refused to use the articles as a book); by Upton Sinclair in 1920 (he had to publish "The Brass Check" himself); by Harold L. Ickes and the present writer.

In addition to Chancellor Hutchins the following persons participated in the investigation, in the writing of the report, and several books on related subjects:

Zechariah Chafee, Jr., vice chairman, professor of law at Harvard.
John M. Clark, professor of Economics, Columbia.
John Dickinson, professor of law, University of Pennsylvania; general counsel, Pennsylvania Railroad.
William E. Hocking, professor of philosophy, emeritus, Harvard.
Harold D. Laswell, professor of law, Yale.
Archibald MacLeish, poet, former Assistant Secretary of State.

Charles E. Merriam, professor of political science, emeritus, University of Chicago.
Reinhold Niebuhr, professor of ethics and philosophy of religion, Union Theological Seminary.
Robert Redfield, professor of anthropology, University of Chicago.
Beardsley Ruml, chairman, Federal Reserve Bank of New York.
Arthur M. Schlesinger, professor of history, Harvard.
George N. Shuster, president, Hunter College.

The Commission not only confirmed every charge ever made against the press, but went beyond anything stated by previous critics. The Commission used such phrases as the following:

"These instruments can spread lies faster and farther than our forefathers dreamed when they enshrined the freedom of the press in the First Amendment of the Constitution."

"The press can be inflammatory, sensational and irresponsible."

"Many a lying, venal and scoundrelly public expression must continue to find shelter under a 'freedom of the press' built for widely different purposes. . . ."

"One of the most effective ways of improving the press is blocked by the press itself. By a kind of unwritten law the press ignores the errors and misrepresentations, the lies and scandals of which its members are guilty."

"The news is twisted."

"Too often the result is meaninglessness, flatness, distortion, and the perpetuation of misunderstanding among widely scattered groups."

"Instances of press lying."

"Deliberate falsifications and reckless misstatements of fact."

"The time has come for the press to assume a new public responsibility."

The Commission's report begins by saying that the answer to the question if the free press is in danger is Yes. The report continues:

"The few who are able to use the machinery of the press as an instrument of mass communications have not provided a service adequate to the needs of the society. . . .

"Those who direct the machinery of the press have engaged from time to time in practices which the society condemns. . . .

"These agencies (of mass communication) can advance the

progress of civilization or they can thwart it. They can debase and vulgarize mankind. They can endanger the peace of the world."

"When the man who claims the moral right of free expression is a liar, a prostitute whose political judgments can be bought, a dishonest inflamer of hatreds and suspicion, his claim is unwarranted and groundless. From a moral point of view, at least, freedom of expression does not include the right to lie as a deliberate instrument of policy."

"The press must also be accountable. It must be accountable to society for meeting the public need and for maintaining the rights of citizens and the almost forgotten rights of speakers who have no press. It must know that its faults and errors have ceased to be private vagaries and have become public dangers."

"The agencies of mass communications are big business, and their owners are big businessmen."

"The published charges of distortion in the press resulting from the bias of its owners fall into the categories that might be expected. . . . Bias is claimed against consumer cooperatives, against food and drug regulations, against Federal Trade Commission orders designed to suppress fraudulent advertising, and against FCC regulations affecting newspaper-owned broadcasting stations."

"One of the criticisms repeatedly made is that the press is dominated by its advertisers. . . . A recent illustration indicates the kind of pressure that may be exerted."

"The press ignores the errors and misrepresentations, the lies and scandals of which its members are guilty."

"The news is twisted by the emphasis on firstness, on the novel and sensational; by the personal interests of the owners; and by pressure groups. . . .

"When we look at the press as a whole, however, we must conclude that it is not meeting the needs of our society. The Commission believes that the failure of the press is the greatest danger to its freedom."

The Commission courageously used the words "lie" and "liars" in referring to the press and the press lords. It even used the old-fashioned term "prostitute" for certain owners of newspapers, a term which is more applicable today for editors and publishers than it was a generation ago for poor underpaid newspaper workers.

The Commission noted the importance of Federal Trade Commission orders "designed to suppress fraudulent advertising." There is only one writer and one publication which has for many years made this one of the tests of the integrity or corruption of 99% of the press, and the reader will have no difficulty in guessing both names.

The Commission, without crediting the copyright source, the newsletter *In Fact,* takes up its February 25, 1946, exposé of the attempt by United States Steel during the strike that year to corrupt some 2500 newspapers by sending them editorials (against labor) and news items (against labor) along with paid advertising (against labor). It notes that *Editor & Publisher* claims that only 15% of these newspapers were so corrupted, at that time, but that is not the whole truth. Months later, when CIO organizers came to certain towns, the corrupt dailies and weeklies there began publishing the old Steel Company's editorials—and obtaining new advertising as a result.

However, none of these items is of much importance compared to the two main facts of the Commission's indictment: the press is not serving society; the press and the other agencies of mass communication "can vulgarize mankind. They can endanger the peace of the world."

Thousands of plans and suggestions have been received by the present writer for establishing an honest press. Most of them are unworkable. The only solution would be more newspapers endowed by someone like Marshall Field (founder of *PM* in New York and *The Sun* in Chicago) or the establishment of a chain of standard daily newspapers by a powerful organization possessing the required number of millions of dollars—at least $5,000,000 for each venture—enough to hold on until successful.

The Cooperatives, the Farmers Union, the AFL, the CIO, the Railroad Brotherhoods, could establish honest newspapers.

If a decent number succeeded they would at least serve as a yardstick for the press in the big cities, they would either draw away readers or they would, indirectly, force the rivals to stop suppressing and mishandling the news. But these must be "straight" newspapers, they must not be the political organs of their owners, even if the latter numbered millions and represented, perhaps, a majority of the people. All they would have to do is print the news.

We would then at last have a free press, the insurance for all our freedoms. The great Joseph Pulitzer said that "Our Republic and its press will rise or fall together." We must, therefore, have a "rising" press, otherwise our present irresponsible newspapers will drag the nation down with them.

3. They Destroy the New Deal

It was not only the "New Deal" in the early 1930's that captured the imagination of the majority, it was also the new view of democracy which animated the spirit of millions of people. Anyone who spent some time in Washington between 1933 and 1939, when war preparations began to dominate the capital, could not help being impressed, and frequently involved, in something which was not Mr. and Mrs. Lindbergh's Fascist "wave of the future," but the Democratic wave of the living present. For once it seemed to many persons that campaign promises were not merely campaign promises, that the ideals of Jefferson and Lincoln were not just paper words but guides to laws, that the phrase "the common people" would be rescued from the joke makers and political fakirs, that Government was about to serve the general welfare.

It did so.

For years the thousand money-seeking Americans through their National Association of Manufacturers, the United States and many local chambers of commerce, their hired Congressmen and hired columnists, and especially through their control of at least 95% of the American press, were unable to stop democracy in action.

In the summer of 1944 Aubrey Williams noted the desperate efforts of our real public enemies—not the few gangsters but the few who control wealth and power—to check the New Deal. He mentioned especially the fight against the Security and Exchange Commission which required them to "tell the truth about what they were selling"; the Wages and Hours Act which provided a living wage; and the Labor Standards

Act which prevented them from throwing a man into jail "for asking his fellow worker to join a union."

"They don't like it," he wrote. "To destroy these and other laws enacted in behalf of people, they have undertaken to poison the people against the people's government. They have marked for destruction:

The Wages and Hours Act
The Fair Labor Standards Act
The Fair Securities Exchange Act
The Fair Employment Practices Commission
The Federal Communications Commission
The unemployment feature of the Social Security Act
The Farm Security Administration
The Production Credit Administration
The National Housing Administration
The Bank for Co-operatives
The Tennessee Valley Authority
The HOLC

"They are fighting the Wagner-Dingell-Murray Bill which would lay the foundation of the public health program in the nation.

"What we have here is a head-on collision between those who hold that government is the agent of the people to help them meet situations that are beyond their individual and group power; and those who hold that government should be limited to a police function, to a State Department to deal with foreign nations, and to a Tax Collecting Department." If the enemies of the public welfare program succeeded, it would mean "low taxes for the rich, high taxes for the poor," the cutting of wages, lengthening of the work week, unemployment. "In a coldblooded statement, a member of the board of the NAM declared that 'it is socially undesirable to have full employment.' "

The elections of 1946, returning a majority of reactionary Republicans and Democrats, resulted almost immediately in the announcement of their program to destroy most of the gains and reforms Mr. Williams enumerated.

The National Association of Manufacturers first of all destroyed the Office of Price Administration, using advertising and the support of the press in its claims that an immediate flow of goods at lower prices—in accordance with their so-called law of supply and demand—would soon right the exasperating situation. The result was a continuous rise in prices (unaccompanied by a parallel rise in wages) which in 1947 resulted in predictions of a new panic, or at least a "recession," and a call by the President for a reduction of prices to prevent economic disaster.

Thanks to the aid it got from the press, the NAM also was able to put over the most vicious anti-labor bill in the century's history—the Taft-Hartley measure which was aimed to destroy the Wages and Hours Act (the Fair Labor Standards Act), the Norris-LaGuardia anti-Injunction law, and the Wagner Act, and gains the unions had fought for and given blood and treasure for during many bitter years.

The press suppressed the news when not one but eighteen members of the House (and, later, five Senators) accused the National Association of Manufacturers of writing the bill, named the NAM lobbyists.*

We see in this episode the continuation, in even more vicious circumstances, of the situation described in the Fourth Chapter. The American people are the victims of the unholy alliance of Big Business, the National Association of Manufacturers, the members of Congress elected with funds supplied by business, and the press owned or controlled or enslaved to business and the perpetuation of the policy of suppressing the news inimical to business interests.

The magazine press, to which the largest section of this book is devoted, did nothing in the 1947 episode to enlighten the public, to make up for the corruption of the newspaper press.

The American public was fooled, as usual.

* Documentation: *Congressional Record,* April 14-16; statements by Congressmen Lesinski, Sabath, O'Toole, Holifield, Buchanan, Klein, Mrs. Norton, and Blatnik; *In Fact,* issues of April 28 and May 5, 1947.

4. Endangering World Peace

The existing press cannot serve the people of America. It cannot serve two masters. Therefore, most of the "constructive" recommendations made by the Commission (and thousands of others who have ideas and plans for a free press) are naïve and useless. On the contrary, the press can vulgarize mankind, and to a great extent it does. It can also, as the Commission reported, "endanger the peace of the world."

A similar charge has been made and proved not once but a dozen times during, before and after the wars of Europe of the past half century. In addition to the three Ms, Money, Men and Munitions, it was discovered at a time wars became more and more the affairs of people rather than that of hired soldiers or even professional or standing armies, that Morale played a great part in deciding defeat or victory, and that the press pretty well accounted for good or bad morale.

The press for almost a hundred years has also been the instrument by which such merchants of death as Zaharoff produced international war scares—and thus promoted armament races, which according to the findings of the Nye-Vandenberg Committee contributed greatly to making war. (See Appendix 11.)

During the atomic scare period of the spring of 1947 the Progressive Citizens of America paid $3,500 for a full page advertisement in the *New York Times* which asked in bold type: "If you mean OIL, Mr. Truman, why say GREECE?" A mass meeting in Madison Square Garden had heard noted speakers, including Henry A. Wallace and Dr. Harlow Shapley, the famous Harvard scientist, plead for peace and against the menace of a Third World War which the Truman Doctrine, arming (as well as feeding) Greece and subsidizing the Turkish military clearly indicated.

The Truman Doctrine was directed against the spread of both the Soviet influence and the Soviet philosophy (Marxian communism) in Europe—according to his March 12 address to the Congress, but in the British labor press, a large part of the European press, and even in the newspapers and weeklies and newsletters which serve Wall Street, it was stated openly that it was the American free enterprise system, the plan for doing bigger business, and especially the oil wealth of Arabia, that the Truman Doctrine was aiming at.

"World War III has begun," Henry Luce's most circulated magazine, *Life,* told its 22,000,000 readers (March 31): "it is in the opening skirmish stage already." *Life* reprinted a large section of a book by James Burnham, who had succeeded Lawrence Dennis as the "intellectual" sponsor of American "elite" Fascism. Burnham proposed the establishment of an American Empire "not necessarily worldwide in literal extent but world-dominating in political power, set up at least in part through coercion (probably including war, but certainly the threat of war) and in which one group of people . . . would hold more than its equal share of power."

This plea for war and for the establishment of a worldwide American ruling state—successor to the publisher's own "American Century," which envisaged a smaller totalitarian regime—was indorsed by Luce and many newspapers. Although avoiding typical Hitlerian phrases, the same doctrine of a superior people taking over the world and ruling it, began to appear in the standard press, whereas the organs of Wall Street were much more honest in favoring a doctrine inevitably leading to war if it brought greater commercial markets under the American flag. For example, *Business Week* (March 22, 1947) said in the headline over its main news item: "New Diplomacy, New Business; U. S. Drive to Stop Communism Abroad Means Heavy Financial Outlay for Bases, Relief and Reconstruction. But in Return, American Business is Bound to Get New Markets Abroad."

If we had an honest press the people of America would have been informed during the great debate on military aid to Greece and Turkey—as distinguished from funds for food, shelter and clothing—of the opposition view which feared the new policy would involve the country in war. The newspapers suppressed, distorted or buried a view which, according to the Gallup Poll of April 28, 1947, was, despite the press, the view of the majority of the people of the country. Seventy-three percent feared the Third World War. Again, as with each of the four Roosevelt campaigns, public opinion was the exact opposite of what the newspapers tried to form.

5. A World of Plenty

If we had an honest press the people of America would know both their friends and enemies. They would know that the enemy of all people, from the day of creation to the present, is reaction. They would know what reaction is, what it does, how close it is to Fascism.

More than a hundred years ago, in the early days of the Industrial Revolution, it became known to many men that the earth, the soil and the wealth hidden in the subsoil, were enough to provide for the wants of all its inhabitants. In more recent times scientists, inventors, geologists, and planners produced the means to end poverty everywhere, to bring in the world's great age. Even before atomic fission was used for the first time—to destroy human beings by the hundreds of thousands—it was already possible to feed, clothe and shelter the earth's two billion human beings. The National Survey of Potential Product Capacity in the dark days of 1934, when there were 12,000,000 unemployed in the United States, and even a greater number, perhaps 20,000,000, on relief, reported that there could be plenty for all. In 1945 President Kirtley Mather of the American Association of Scientific Workers presented (in "Enough and to Spare") the scientific evidence that the good earth—and its scientific management—would provide for all the inhabitants thereof a decent living, human dignity, and true freedom. In 1947 the World Federation of Trade Unions reported to the United Nations, meeting at Lake Success, that if it could work out an international policy, exploiting the world's resources, controlling prices and controlling profits, there could be employment for all, and the world's population could absorb the wealth of goods produced, poverty would end, wars would end, and peace and happiness would be universal.

The representatives of the Federal Council of the Churches of Christ in America (Protestant), the National Catholic Welfare Conference, and the Synagogue Council of America (Jewish) issued a "Declaration on Economic Justice" (October 16, 1946) stating that "the material resources of life are entrusted to man by God for the benefit of all" and suggesting that means be found "to distribute God's gifts equitably." (Although the thousand Americans who own or control most of the nation's wealth and resources belong to these three religious denominations, not a word from any one of them greeted the declaration of their spiritual leaders.)

With the possibility of harnessing atomic fission to industrial use, all doubt that science could remake the world—as well as destroy it—disappeared.

"We have the means," Dr. Vannevar Bush, wartime head of American scientific research, told Columbia University alumni, "for removing starvation and disease. We have almost unlimited power in sight, that can make the waste lands bloom.

"We have the possibility of banishing disease. . . .

"We know, or can know, how to learn the truth, and to tell it to one another throughout a healthy world that is secure against the ravages of nature. It is the setting for a world of peace and unity.

"One thing is lacking: good will and understanding." (The curious reader may search the *New York Times* of June 4, 1947, for this statement. He is advised to find the headline: "Patterson Backs 'Military Mind.' " Dr. Bush is mentioned, even quoted, but not the foregoing paragraphs.)

In China and India starvation remained endemic. In the United States people talked of a "recession" instead of a depression.

But there was no longer a question, among scientists, of potential plenty or enough for everyone; it was now a question of abundance. Abundance remained unattainable because it is impossible to have good will and understanding so long as profits take precedence in certain men's minds.

6. The American Way

Is what the American people want un-American?

When the slavery mob killed Lovejoy and wrecked his press, the nation-wide protest was led by Wendell Phillips, one of the great libertarians of our country. Wendell Phillips (for many years head of the Anti-Slavery Society) held no post of authority, and his words are merely the words of a patriot:

"No reform, moral or intellectual, ever came from the upper class of society. Each and all came from the protest of martyr and victim.

"The emancipation of the working people must be achieved by the working people themselves.

"We affirm, as a fundamental principle, that labor, the creator of wealth, is entitled to all it creates.

"Affirming this, we avow ourselves willing to accept the final results of the operation of a principle so radical—such as the overthrow of the whole profit-making system, the extinction of all monopolies, the abolition of privileged classes, universal education and fraternity, perfect freedom of exchange, and, best and grandest of all, the final obliteration of that foul stigma upon our so-called Christian civilization—the poverty of the masses. . . . Therefore,

"Resolved, That we declare war with the wages system, which demoralizes the life of the hirer and the hired, cheats both, and enslaves the workingman; with the present system of finance, which robs labor, and gorges capital, makes the rich richer and the poor poorer, and turns a republic into an aristocracy of capital; with these slavish grants of the public lands to speculating companies, and whenever in power we pledge ourselves to use every just and legal means to resume all such grants heretofore made; with the system of enriching capitalists by the creation and increase of public interest-bearing debts."

The public lands no longer provide a scandal, but much more scandalous is the attack on the use of the public rivers for light, power, and public welfare; against the TVA, the St. Lawrence development and the MVA.

The most important principle in Wendell Phillips' declaration was stated by a man in public office. He said merely:

"It has so happened in all ages of the world, that some have labored and others have without labor enjoyed a large proportion of the fruits. This is wrong and should not continue. To secure each laborer the whole product of his labor, or as nearly as possible, is a worthy object of any good government."

Any government official who made the same statement in the days of the Dies Committee, the Rankin Committee and the Thomas Committee would be hauled up on "loyalty" charges. The idea conflicts with the "free enterprise" principle of the National Association of Manufacturers, it conflicts with the viewpoint of John W. Davis, the chief attorney for the House of Morgan, who wrote the document which serves as a guide for the Un-American Committee in functioning in favor of reaction and big business.

(Of course, the author of the statement that the whole product of labor should belong to the laborer, that no man should be allowed to make a profit on the work of another man, is not Karl Marx, but Abraham Lincoln. Is or is it not good Americanism to take up the fight for the Wendell Phillips and Lincoln doctrines, despite the sure knowledge the reactionaries or the Un-American Committee and the entire near-fascist political and journalistic world will reply with the usual campaign of falsehood and red-baiting and "smears," if not threat of arrest and imprisonment? The present writer still believes that both Phillips and Lincoln were better Americans to follow than the men of the National Association of Manufacturers in Congress.)

The present world is capable of providing security for all through abundance; the coming age will use atomic power either to destroy our civilization or to create a new or ideal civilization. But there are also men and forces which will fight to the death to prevent progress.

No attempt has been made here to draw up a list of the thousand Americans who belong to this minority, nor even to fix the number.

The present writer is aware that these thousand Americans are the men who, as leading spirits of the National Association of Manufacturers, decided just after the first election of Franklin Delano Roosevelt that the "capitalist system" of the United States having again and again and again led to disaster, it was time to change that term into something more palatable, and so the phrase "free enterprise" was decided upon.

From 1933 to the present day every candidate for office, including both Mr. Roosevelt and Mr. Truman, was approached on the subject, and every politician and statesman at one time or another has issued a declaration in favor of free enterprise. No public leader has opposed it.

The propaganda for free enterprise, now being made into the most sacred cow of all the idols created by the press and worshiped by all who profit by it, is accompanied by a witch-hunt against everyone who asks a question or makes a challenge. It attacks the majority which voted for the New Deal, the liberals who follow Wallace, and everyone who strives for Lincoln's ideal. Red-baiting, demagoguery, take the place of reason, of the orderly presentation of the facts.

The world moves into opposing camps, and there is not only talk of the coming war, but vast preparation. Nations are impoverished because of billions of dollars voted in the annual budgets for war supplies, for maintaining armies and navies, for the scientific search for weapons more powerful than the newest untried atomic super-bombs.

Reaction is on the march in many countries; Fascism still exists in some, is being revived in others; Socialism has been adopted by several nations; Communism has spread throughout a large part of Europe and Asia, and in the United States for the first time in its history there is a growing doubt that Capitalism is the best way of all, the well-advertised "American Way of Life." There is not only great doubt, but even greater confusion in America.

At no time in history has there been such a need for information, and at no time in history has there been such an exchange of charge and countercharge of suppression, distortion, iron curtains, and the dissemination of falsehood.

The most powerful newspaper chain in America prints in a score of cities, in a total of millions of copies every day, the motto of its founder: "Give Light and the People Will Find Their Own Way." This was the motto Scripps put on his masthead, and it remains today an ironic reminder that his living partner, Howard, has joined Hearst in becoming the editorial antagonist of the labor unions, the New Deal, the liberal and progressive movements in America which both once sponsored.

The press, the magazines, the radio, the movies, are commercial "free" enterprises; they are not in business to give light so that the people can find their own way. They are out for the money.

Right or wrong, the present writer holds to his belief that in a nation and in a world where the means of mass communication are honest and free, when they function for the general welfare instead of private profits, there will be a resulting general enlightenment, there will be progress, because nothing will stop the march of an informed people.

APPENDIX 1.

THE 13 MOST POWERFUL FAMILIES IN AMERICA

(*Editorial Note:* The following table is from page 116, Monograph 29, Temporary National Economic Committee, Investigation of Concentration of Economic Power, 76th Congress, 3d Session. The monograph can be had from the Superintendent of Documents, Washington, D. C., for $2. It deals entirely with the 200 largest nonfinancial corporations.)

TABLE 6—Identified stockholdings in 200 largest nonfinancial corporations of 13 family-interest groups with holdings over $50,000,000.

(Value of holdings in thousands of dollars)

Family	*Total*	*Corporations in which main holdings are—*
1. Ford	624,975	Ford Motor Co.
2. DuPont	573,690	E. I. duPont de Nemours & Co., United States Rubber Co.
3. Rockefeller	396,583	Standard Oil (N. J.) (Indiana) (California), Socony-Vacuum Oil Co., Inc.
4. Mellon	390,943	Gulf Oil Corp.; Aluminum Co. of America, Koppers United Co.
5. McCormick	111,102	International Harvester Co.
6. Hartford	105,702	A&P Tea Co.
7. Harkness	104,891	(Same as Rockefeller)
8. Duke	89,489	Duke Power Co., Aluminum Co., Liggett & Myers Tobacco Co.
9. Pew	75,628	Sun Oil Co.
10. Pitcairn	65,576	Pittsburgh Plate Glass Co.
11. Clark	57,215	Singer Mfg. Co.
12. Reynolds	54,766	R. J. Reynolds Tobacco Co.
13. Kress	50,044	S. H. Kress & Co.
Total:	$2,700,574,000.	

"Three interest groups, all of the one-family type, stand out—the duPont, Mellon, and Rockefeller groups. . . All three groups represent large fortunes, as measured by the market value of the stock held, as well as huge aggregations of economic power resting upon control of large industrial corporations. . .

"The holdings of the three families—as well as those of any other interested groups covered by the study—of course represented only part of the total wealth of those groups. . . It is quite possible that for some groups these outside investments had a larger aggregate value than their identified stockholdings in the 200 largest corporations.

APPENDIX 2.

THE 12 SUPER RULERS OF AMERICAN INDUSTRY

Twelve billionaire corporations and their representatives in the Special Conference Committee, the super ruling body of American business. Source: Senate Civil Liberties report, part 45, page 16783.

American Telephone & Telegraph Co.: W. S. Gifford, president; E. F. Carter, vice-president, E. S. Bloom, president (Western Electric Co.); W. A. Griffin, assistant vp.

Bethlehem Steel Co.: Eugene G. Grace, president; J. M. Larkin, vice-president.

E. I. DuPont de Nemours: Lammot duPont, president: Willis F. Harrington, vice-president; William B. Foster, director of service dept.

General Electric Co.: Owen D. Young, former chairman; W. S. Burrows, vice-president; G. H. Pfeif, supervisor of personnel.

General Motors Corp.: Alfred P. Sloan jr., president; John L. Pratt, vice-president; Donaldson Brown, vice-president.

Goodyear Tire and Rubber Co.: E. J. Thomas, general superintendent.

International Harvester Co.: A. A. Jones, asst. to vice president; George J. Kelday, manager of industrial relations.

Irving Trust Co.: Harry E. Ward, president; Northrop Holbrook, vice-president.

Standard Oil of N. J.: W. S. Farish, chairman; W. C. Teagle, president.

U. S. Rubber Co.: L. D. Tompkins, vice-president; C. S. Ching, director of industrial and public relations.

United States Steel Corporation.

Westinghouse Electric & Mfg. Co.: A. W. Robertson, chairman; F. A. Merrick, vice chairman; W. G. Marshall, vice-president; E. S. McClelland, director of personnel.

(Editorial Notes: With the exception of the Irving Trust Co., all are members of the NAM.

The La Follette-Thomas report stated that this was a secret organization. It met at the offices of Standard Oil, 30 Rockefeller Plaza, New York City. In 1947 Mr. Edward S. Cowdrick, an industrial relations consultant with offices at that address, stated that the SCC as such was no longer in existence but admitted that virtually all the billionaire companies which had comprised it were now his clients. Meetings were held, "sometimes individually, sometimes as a group, but we are no longer organized, if that distinction means anything," Mr. Cowdrick stated.

The Civil Liberties report stated that the 11 industrial corporations employed more than 1,300,000 workers, paid wages and salaries of $2,400,000,000, and had combined assets of $13,500,000,000. The group met for "the purpose of formulating common labor-relations programs for all American industry, and has led in systematizing the promotion of policies consistently pursued by the NAM since its formation. "Not only are most of the member corporations of the Special Conference Committee at once members of the inner controlling group of the NAM and the leaders among American industrial giants in their respective fields, but also they represent a secret coalition in direct furtherance of the specific forms of company union fathered by the Colorado Fuel & Iron Co.," the Senate report said.

In 1943, Prof. Robert A. Brady of Columbia University, in a book entitled "Business as a System of Power," described the Special Conference Comm. in one of the few printed references ever made to it. He wrote:

"The most important line of policies within the NAM, in short, seems to be traceable directly or indirectly to this inside clique within the inner councils of the organization. . . . Nowhere else is shown so clearly the dominating position in the NAM of concerns such as those which are members of the Special Conference Comm. Public relations techniques were born, nurtured, and brought to flower within these ranks. . . ."

In 1947, speaking against the Taft-Hartley anti-labor bill, Senator Thomas again exposed the Special Conference Committee as a secret general staff for employers whose aim is to destroy the labor movement. Again, as a decade earlier, the entire American press suppressed the news. (See *Congressional Record,* 1947, pages 4401-16.)

APPENDIX 3.

THE POWER OF THE BIG EIGHT BANKS

(*Congressional Record,* November 30, 1944, Senator Norris's speech, as introduced by Senator Langer.)

MR. NORRIS. I desire at this point to give à list of eight leading banks in New York City, as follows:

Bank of America National Association, Bank of Manhattan Trust Co., Bankers' Trust Co., Chase National Bank, Chemical Bank & Trust Co., Guaranty Trust Co., National City Bank Co., New York Trust Co.

Almost any list of the large banks of Wall Street could be taken and the result would be about the same, but I have selected this list, because to take all the banks and gather the facts in regard to them would mean a job that would require months of toil.

The 8 banks on the list I have given have 287 directorships in insurance companies; they have 301 directorships in other banks. That shows how they are interlocked with other banks. They have 521 directorships in public-utility companies. That shows how they reach out over the country and handle the public-utility business of the country. These 8 banks have 585 directorships in railroad, steamship, and airplane transportation companies. So we cannot eliminate or reduce an appropriation for airplanes without treading on the toes of the money power of Wall Street. . . . .

These 8 banks—and they are only a part of the great combination of wealth represented by banks in Wall Street, which are operating through interlocking directorships—have directorships in 846 manufacturing companies. So, there are 846 corporations engaged in all lines of manufacturing that these banks, either directly or indirectly, control, because the man who controls or the men who control the money of the country also control the country, as the Senator from Oklahoma [MR. THOMAS] so well said yesterday. Let a combination of men control the finances of the United States, and they control all the activities of all the people of the United States. These 8 banks have 1,201 directorships in other corporations, making a total of 3,741 directorships held by the 8 banks in various corporations. . . .

MR. NORRIS. Mr. President, what does all this show? It demonstrates very clearly, in my judgment, that the control of all the business of the United States is drifting rapidly toward corporations. Especially when we consider the development and the advance that has been made in this control, as shown by me a short time ago, it demonstrates, it seems to me, that all of us soon will be hired men, working for some corporation.

When we look over the public-utility field and see how the house of Morgan is gradually and rapidly getting control, as shown by the figures and the statistics I put into the RECORD, can we reach any other conclusion than that any of these organizations, any of these operating companies, any of these holding companies, will find it impossible to do anything contrary to the wishes of the men who control the money strings in Wall Street? In that case it has almost reached the point now when it is one man, J. P. Morgan.

J. P. Morgan, with the assistance and cooperation of a few of the interlocking corporations which reach all over the United States in their influence, controls every railroad in the United States. They control practically every public utility, they control literally thousands of corporations, they control all of the large insurance companies.

Mr. President, we are gradually reaching a time, if we have not already reached that period, when the business of the country is controlled by men who can be named on the fingers of one hand, because those men control the money of the Nation, and that control is growing at a rapid rate. There is only a comparatively small part of it left for them to get, and when they control the money, they control the banks, they control the manufacturing institutions, they control the aviation companies, they control the insurance companies, they control the publishing companies; and we have had some remarkable instances of the control of the publishing companies presented before a subcommittee of the Committee on the Judiciary.

These corporations forget nothing. We had illustrations given us where a magazine would start out on a particular line, but would find itself called on the carpet by some one from one of these great institutions. They were told what the policy must be. Absolute failure stared them in the face unless they obeyed. Through the control of advertising, which, incidentally, to a great extent, is handled by corporations which this money trust controls, they control the avenues of publicity.

Mr. President, the tramp on the street who munches a crust of bread somebody has given him is very likely eating something which came from a corporation controlled by this great Money Trust. Bread is manufactured by corporations, and shipped all over the country, and the price is kept up, while the price of wheat goes down. We have to pay practically the same price for a loaf of bread when wheat is 25 cents a bushel in the Western States, as we paid when wheat was $2.50 a bushel. It is all controlled by corporations. The clothing we wear, the food we eat, the automobiles, in the main, that we use, the gasoline and the oil we buy to operate them, to a great extent are controlled by this financial center represented by this spider. . . .

MR. NORRIS. Of course, Mr. President, a beautiful theory can be woven, and it can be said that if we get a big corporation that covers everything we will be able to reduce the prices of products to the consumers. But human nature is just the same now as it was a hundred years ago. Give to a man the power, especially if he has in his heart the greed that comes with great financial power as a rule, and when he gets the power the consumer will not get any benefit—the man will get it. When the power is all in the hands of one or a few men, the consumer will be bled white. That has been the lesson of history.

APPENDIX 4.

45 CORPORATIONS WITH MORE THAN $1,000,000,000 IN ASSETS

Forty-five American business enterprises now are included in the billion-dollar assets class in spite of a sharp decline in resources of the nation's leading banks since the end of World War II, according to the copyrighted annual survey by United Press. Metropolitan Life Insurance Co., leader in assets since 1944, continues to head the list.

The billion-dollar companies and their assets are as follows:

Company	Latest Assets	Dec. 31, 1945
Metropolitan Life	$ 8,045,443,467	$ 7,561,997,270
Bell Telephone	7,380,925,721	6,765,557,026
Prudential Ins.	6,829,542,249	6,359,281,870
Bank of America	5,538,321,000	5,626,063,927
National City Bank	4,873,737,691	5,434,372,600
Chase National	4,860,581,123	6,092,600,648
Equitable Life	4,273,313,396	3,849,438,783
New York Life	4,026,689,280	3,814,176,784
Guaranty Trust	2,841,800,875	3,813,507,042
Standard Oil (N. J.)	2,659,987,889	2,531,808,387
Manufacturers Trust	2,250,225,889	2,693,184,469
Continental Ill. Bank	2,227,056,285	2,826,963,072
Pennsylvania R. R.	2,180,349,028	2,223,731,246
First Natl. Chicago	2,097,755,803	2,474,512,923
General Motors	2,079,607,229	1,813,885,559
Northwestern Mutual	2,052,432,583	2,019,054,746
John Hancock Mutual	2,037,505,696	1,837,622,237
U. S. Steel	2,003,517,407	1,890,768,775

Mutual Life N. Y.	1,845,769,521	1,800,758,756
N. Y. Central	1,698,490,561	1,736,143,217
Security 1st National	1,659,169,327	1,736,143,217
Southern Pacific	1,624,401,763	1,685,942,471
Central Hanover	1,613,528,102	1,972,323,270
Travelers Ins.	1,589,220,051	1,512,224,247
Bankers Trust	1,486,679,439	1,921,945,613
First National Boston	1,444,796,245	1,704,193,331
Consol. Edison	1,356,101,046	1,323,687,070
Northwest Bancorp.	1,265,000,000	1,380,633,781
E. I. duPont de N.	1,263,797,827	1,204,921,184
C. & S. Corp.	1,258,004,793	1,205,243,639
Aetna Life	1,247,466,207	1,152,901,151
Chemical Bank	1,238,076,886	1,637,503,776
Santa Fe Road	1,218,572,341	1,246,835,971
Union Pacific	1,206,682,734	1,287,117,897
Socony-Vacuum	1,135,165,509	1,075,776,859
Baltimore & Ohio	1,158,971,371	1,166,926,644
Natl. Bank Detroit	1,120,474,473	1,326,506,470
Irving Trust	1,105,777,671	1,428,354,898
First Bank Stk. Cp.	1,104,198,507	1,204,564,383
Marine Midland Cp.	1,092,157,661	1,218,727,151
Bank of Manhattan	1,087,398,746	1,359,074,439
Massachusetts Mutual	1,084,443,467	1,014,155,467
Penn Mutual	1,070,105,857	1,016,977,550
Mutual Benefit Life	1,069,057,670	1,006,512,914
Cleveland Trust	1,053,716,069	1,111,814,791
Totals	$103,456,016,995	$107,065,003,625

—(Source: UP annual dispatch, *New York Herald Tribune,* July 2, 1947.)

The forty-five companies composing the "club" today are more than twice the number of billion-dollar institutions in the United States in the so-called boom year of 1929. Newcomers this year are First Bank Stock Corp., Minneapolis, and Massachusetts Mutual Life, Springfield, Mass.

(*Editorial Note:* The *Herald Tribune* omitted in its concluding paragraph of the copyright UP dispatch, the following phrase: "Then [in the so called boom year of 1929] only 20 companies had assets of one billion or more, and in 1939, just prior to World War II, there were but 28 concerns." Seventeen corporations entered the billionaire class during the Second World War.)

APPENDIX 5.

NOTED NAMES ON THE MORGAN "PREFERRED LIST"

Calvin Coolidge.
Charles A. Lindbergh, Jr.
John J. Pershing.
Alfred P. Sloan of General Motors, the DuPont Empire and the NAM.
Richard B. Mellon of Alcoa and the Mellon Bank.
Owen D. Young, chief writer of the Dawes Plan for German reparations.
Walter S. Gifford of American Telephone and Telegraph Co.
Myron C. Taylor of United States Steel; FDR's and Truman's special envoy to the Vatican; endorser of Mussolini and fascism.
Walter C. Teagle, of Standard Oil.
Sosthenes Behn of International Telephone and Telegraph Co.
Marshall Field.
Charles E. Mitchell, banker.
John W. Davis, Morgan attorney and one time candidate for President of the United States; also author of the directive of the Dies Un-American Committee.
William Gibbs McAdoo, later Senator, and member of the committee which investigated the Morgan company.
Newton D. Baker, who tried to write a whitewash of the Morgan firm in relation to the war.
Charles D. Hilles, Republican Party national committeeman from New York.
Robert E. Olds, former Under Secretary of State, the man who planted a fake story with the Associated Press aimed to stir up war with Mexico, in aid of the U. S. oil interests—see *Freedom of the Press*, p. 176.
William H. Woodin, later Roosevelt's Secretary of the Treasury.
Bernard M. Baruch.
Norman H. Davis, spokesman for the Roosevelt administration abroad.
John J. Raskob, former chairman of the Democratic National Committee, official of the DuPont and General Motors corporations.
O. P. Van Sweringen, the railroad man.
F. L. Carlisle, power and light.
P. A. S. Franklin, head of Morgan-controlled ocean shipping.
Silas H. Strawn, Henry Machold, Seward Prosser, Arthur Woods, F. H. Ecker, a life insurance firm official, J. R. Nutt, Charles Francis Adams, later Secretary of the Navy.

APPENDIX 6.

J. P. MORGAN & CO. AND THE ST. LAWRENCE SEAWAY

J. P. Morgan & Co.
Wall Street, corner Broad, New York
Drexel & Co., Philadelphia
Morgan, Grenfell & Co., London
Morgan & Cie, Paris

New York, February 5, 1934

Dear Senator La Follette:

My attention has been called to a speech which you made . . . pending treaty for the St. Lawrence seaway, and specifically to certain erroneous statements with reference to the firm of J. P. Morgan & Co. Ordinarily we do not feel called on to reply to unfounded or incorrect statements regarding this firm. When, however, a statesman of your position makes such statements, even though they may be based upon this information furnished to you, we feel warranted in calling them to your attention.

In the course of your remarks you say: "J. P. Morgan & Co. and their allied interests are seeking to destroy this administration and they are seeking to prevent the ratification of this treaty", etc. Both these statements are absolutely without foundation. . . .

On September 18, 1929 this firm issued a public statement, which had wide currency, declaring its complete aloofness from any position as to the St. Lawrence River project. . . .

Permit us to make clear again with all emphasis that we have not directly or indirectly attempted to influence in one way or the other ratification of the St. Lawrence Treaty or the character and manner of the proposed St. Lawrence power development. . . .

Very truly yours,

Thomas W. Lamont

APPENDIX 7.

J. P. MORGAN & CO. AND PUBLIC POWER

(*Congressional Record,* November 30, 1944. Letter from Senator La Follette to Thomas W. Lamont, inserted in speech by Senator Langer.)

MR. THOMAS W. LAMONT,

J. P. Morgan & Co., New York City.

Dear MR. LAMONT: I shall be pleased to place your letter of February 5 on behalf of J. P. Morgan & Co. in the CONGRESSIONAL RECORD in response to your request. . . .

The entire record supports the conclusion that corporations and agencies in which the influence of J. P. Morgan & Co. is notorious have been using every resource to block public development of St. Lawrence power in the interest of lower electric rates.

If the St. Lawrence Treaty is defeated, it will, in my opinion, be due largely to the false propaganda which has been directed for nearly 2 years against this project, and to the opposition fomented by utility interests affiliated with J. P. Morgan & Co. . . .

To assert that J. P. Morgan & Co., with its vast utility holdings and enormous stake in the maintenance and excessive rates in the greatest market for power and electricity in the world, is indifferent to a public power project larger than Muscle Shoals and Boulder Dam combined is to tax the credulity of the Senate and the public and to belie the public records of both State and Federal Governments.

You state that no member of the firm of J. P. Morgan & Co. has opposed the public power and navigation project covered by the treaty.

Every Member of the United States Senate has received numerous printed statements demanding the defeat of the treaty, mailed at frequent intervals in the last 2 years by the Chamber of Commerce of the State of New York.

J. P. Morgan and 12 of his partners, including yourself, were listed as members of this chamber at the time it initiated the propaganda referred to.

The treasurer of the organization, who collected the funds and disbursed the expenditures for this campaign against the treaty, is Junius S. Morgan, Jr., the son of the head of the firm. Mr. Morgan still holds the office of treasurer today.

I have made an analysis of the published roster of the membership of the chamber for 1932, when the effort to defeat the treaty began. With data derived from standard financial manuals and directories, this analysis shows:

1. The 13 members of the firm of J. P. Morgan & Co. listed as members of the Chamber of Commerce of the State of New York are: J. Pierpont Morgan, Thomas W. Lamont, Henry S. Morgan, Junius S. Morgan, Jr., Thomas S. Lamont, Henry P. Davison, E. T. Stotesbury, Charles Steele, Thomas Cochran, R. C. Leffingwell, Harold Stanley, George Whitney, and Francis D. Bartow.

2. Less than 10 percent of the membership show an address outside of New York City. It includes 510 bankers and 71 railroad and utility directors and officials. Of the 510 bankers, 64 are also directors of railroad or electric-power corporations.

3. Power and public-utility interests are represented in the list by Floyd L. Carlisle, chairman of the boards of the Niagara Hudson Power Corporation, the Consolidated Gas Co. of New York, and the New York Edison Co.; Harold Stanley, a member of the firm of J. P. Morgan & Co. and director of the Niagara Hudson, the United Corporation, and the United Gas Improvement Co.; E. T. Stotesbury, a Morgan partner and director of the United Gas Improvement Co.; and George Whitney, a Morgan partner and director of Consolidated Gas.

4. Junius S. Morgan, Jr., of J. P. Morgan & Co., is listed as treasurer of the chamber.

On November 18, 1932, a representative of the chamber appeared before the Borah subcommittee of the Committee on Foreign Relations and presented an elaborate report, together with a "summary and resolutions," denouncing both the power and navigation projects and demanding the rejection of the St. Lawrence Treaty. . . .

I submit that if the 13 partners of J. P. Morgan & Co. who were members of the chamber on October 6, 1932, have been, as you state, indifferent to the action of the Senate on the treaty, their protest should not be directed to a Senator but to the officers of the chamber who caused such attacks against the treaty to be transmitted to Members of the Senate.

The fact is that the report and resolutions adopted on October 6, 1932, incorporated the misstatements, exaggerations, and half-truths which have since been chiefly relied upon and most widely circulated in the effort to defeat the treaty.

You and I, Mr. Lamont, do not need to quibble over terms. When I say that J. P. Morgan & Co. and its partners have consistently opposed everything that is vital about this great public-power project I do not mean that either Mr. Morgan or you have gone about making speeches against it or that you have gone up to Albany or down to Washington to buttonhole legislators and lobby against bills which you feel jeopardize your strangle hold on the business of distributing electric energy to the people of New York and other States.

It is through your innumerable agents, like this man Machold, that your influence is as effectively exerted as if you were operating in person. You will perhaps recall the recent address at Utica, December 8, 1933, of W. Kingsland Macy, a successor of Machold as chairman of the State Republican Committee. He said:

"It is intolerable that the invisible government set up by Mr. Machold in Albany during the legislative sessions, operating through his control of the clerkship under Mr. Hammond, manipulating chairmanships and directing legislation, should be permitted to continue.

"The trouble is not that Mr. Machold believes in the private ownership of public utilities but that he apparently believes in the private ownership of the State government." . . .

Our flowing streams are peculiarly adaptable to development and use for the public benefit. In his avowed purpose of removing credit, production, and transportation from selfish exploitation, the President has wisely insisted upon the public development of water power under terms which will insure to every home its maximum benefits in cheap and increased use of current and the relief of needless drudgery—in short, a richer life for the average American family.

If American financiers remain hostile to such broad national purposes, then I seriously doubt whether they can service as a useful instrumentality of society when we succeed in eradicating the greed and ignorance that produced the depression.

You will recall the words of President Roosevelt in his inaugural address of March 4, 1933.

"Plenty is at our doorstep, but a generous use of it languishes in the very sight of the supply. Primarily this is because the rulers of the exchange of mankind's goods have failed, through their own stubbornness and their own incompetence, have admitted their failure and abdicated. Practices of the unscrupulous money changers stand indicted in the court of public opinion, rejected by the hearts and minds of men. . . .

"The money changers have fled from their high seats in the temple of our civilization. We may now restore that temple to the ancient truths. The measure of the restoration lies in the extent to which we apply social values more noble than mere monetary profit."

The St. Lawrence Treaty will, in my opinion, be ratified. If the withdrawal of further opposition by members of your firm, even at this belated hour, is made effective, it will unquestionably be welcomed by the American people.

Very truly yours,

"ROBERT M. LA FOLLETTE, JR.

APPENDIX 8.

THE PAGE CABLE

(Ambassador Walter Hines Page's cable to President Wilson suggesting America declare war on Germany, and mentioning the position of the House of Morgan and the Allied loans.)

March 5, 1917.

To the President

"The inquiries which I have made here about financial conditions disclose an international situation which is most alarming to the financial and industrial outlook of the United States. England has not only to pay her own war bills, but is obliged to finance her Allies as well. Up to the present time she has done these tasks out of her own capital. But she cannot continue her present extensive purchases in the United States without shipping gold as payment for them, and there are two reasons why she cannot make large shipments of gold. In the first place, both England and France must keep the larger part of the gold they have to maintain issues of their paper at par; and in the second place, the German U-boat has made the shipping of gold a dangerous procedure even if they had it to ship. There is therefore a pressing danger that the Franco-American exchange will be greatly disturbed; the inevitable consequences will be that orders by all the Allied governments will be reduced to the lowest possible amount and that trans-Atlantic trade will practically come to an end. The result of such a stoppage will be a panic in the United States. The world will be divided into two hemispheres, one of them, our own, will have the gold and the commodities: the other, Great Britain and Europe, will need these commodities, but it will have no money with which to pay for them. Moreover, it will have practically no commodities of its own to exchange for them. The financial and commercial result will be almost as bad for the United States as for Europe. We shall soon reach this condition unless we take quick action to prevent it. Great Britain and France must have a credit in the United States which will be large enough to prevent the collapse of world trade and the whole financial structure of Europe.

"If the United States declare war against Germany, the greatest help we could give Great Britain and the Allies would be such credit. If we should adopt this policy, an excellent plan would be for our government to make a large investment in a Franco-British loan. Another plan would be to guarantee such a loan. A great advantage would be that all the money would be kept in the

United States. We could keep on with our trade and increase it, till the war ends, and after the war Europe would purchase food and enormous supply of materials with which to reequip her peace industries. We should thus reap the profit of an uninterrupted and perhaps an enlarging trade over a number of years and we should hold their securities in payment.

"On the other hand, if we keep nearly all the gold and Europe cannot pay for reestablishing its economic life, there may be a world wide panic for an indefinite period.

"Of course we cannot extend such a credit unless we go to war with Germany. But is there no way in which our government might immediately and indirectly help the establishment in the United States of a large Franco-British credit without violating armed neutrality? I do not know enough about our own reserve bank law to form an opinion. But these banks would avert such a danger if they were to establish such a credit. Danger for us is more real and imminent, I think, than the public on either side of the Atlantic understands. If it be not averted before its manifestations become apparent, it will then be too late to save the day.

"The pressure of this approaching crisis, I am certain, has gone beyond the ability of the Morgan financial agency for the British and French governments. The financial necessities of the Allies are too great and urgent for any private agency to handle, for every such agency has to encounter business rivalries and sectional antagonisms.

"It is not improbable that the only way of maintaining our present preeminent trade position and averting a panic is by declaring war on Germany. The submarine has added the last item to the danger of a financial world crash. There is now an uncertainty about our being drawn into the war; no more considerable credits can be privately placed in the United States. In the meantime a collapse may come."

(Signed) (Walter Hines) PAGE

(U. S. State Department, Foreign Publications, 1917, supplement 2, Vol. 1, pp. 516-8.)

(Report of Lawrence Brown—New Republic)

"The full text of this (the Page) cablegram was released to the public by the Nye Committee on December 14, 1934. The United Press put the text of the cable into its munitions story of that day. So far as we can learn the Associated Press, International News Service and Universal Service did not. We have examined some twenty leading papers of the country, both in New York City and elsewhere, and find the following interesting facts: Only four of these papers carried the text of the cable. The *New York Post,* the

New York World-Telegram, the *Louisville Courier-Journal* and the *Pittsburgh Press* did so. The *Cleveland Plain Dealer* carried the U.P. munitions story, but, in the edition that we examined, cut out all mention of the Page message. The *New York Tribune* printed a denial that the Nye Committee would investigate the cable but did not print the cable itself. A number of other papers printed a denial of an investigation of Morgan's, but were careful, even in the denial, not to mention the existence of the cable. Is this the freedom of the press about which the publishers have lately been so solicitous?"

APPENDIX 9.

PRESIDENT WILSON ON THE CAUSES OF WORLD WAR I

(From a speech delivered in St. Louis, September 5, 1919. Reprinted from the *Congressional Record,* Sept. 8, 1919, page 5006; *St. Louis Globe Democrat,* Sept. 6, 1919.)

Why, my fellow citizens, is there any man here or any woman—let me say is there any child here—who does not know that the seed of war in the modern world is industrial and commercial rivalry? The real reason that the war that we have just finished took place was that Germany was afraid her commercial rivals were going to get the better of her, and the reason why some nations went into the war against Germany was that they thought Germany would get the commercial advantage of them. The seed of the jealousy, the seed of the deep-seated hatred, was hot successful commercial and industrial rivalry.

(The next paragraph describes the German dismantling of the Belgian industrial plant and the destruction of machinery which could not be moved into Germany.)

This war was a commercial and industrial war. It was not a political war.

APPENDIX 10.
AMERICA'S WORST NEWSPAPERS

(Condensed from the table published by Leo C. Rosten in his *The Washington Correspondents,* Harcourt, Brace & Co. Reprinted by permission.)

TEN NEWSPAPERS CONSIDERED "LEAST FAIR AND RELIABLE" BY 93 WASHINGTON CORRESPONDENTS

paper	*1st choice*	*2nd choice*	*3rd choice*	*points*
Hearst Newspapers (*)	59	20	8	714
Chicago Tribune	24	37	10	455
Los Angeles Times	2	7	16	103
Scripps-Howard (**)	4	5	4	77
Denver Post	0	4	6	38
N. Y. Herald Tribune	0	4	4	32
Washington Post	2	1	2	31
Phila. Record	0	3	5	30
Daily Worker (N. Y.)	1	1	2	21
Phila. Inquirer	1	1	2	21

(*) Editorial note: Some replies merely said "Hearst"; others named Hearst papers. Best known Hearst papers, considered the worst in America, are: *New York Journal-American, New York Mirror, Chicago Herald-American, San Francisco Examiner, Los Angeles Examiner, Detroit Times.*

(**) Biggest of the Scripps-Howard papers, which rank fourth on list of America's worst, are: *New York World-Telegram, Cleveland Press, Pittsburgh Press, Denver News, Washington News, San Francisco News, Indianapolis Times.*

APPENDIX 11.
DuPONT INFLUENCE IN THE AMERICAN PRESS

(The following testimony and documents are from the Munitions Hearings; they concern the plan of the DuPonts to plant a propaganda campaign for the use of poison gas in wartime. Gas was held to be more humane than other weapons, but public opinion was against it. The DuPonts, according to testimony, sent their agent, Charles K. Weston, to Paris, to use the press to change public opinion.)

(1) Letter from Weston dated Dec. 10, 1920 to DuPonts:

My mission seems to be going fairly well; I have met a number of our American newspaper correspondents, and have I think succeeded in selling them our ideas. One cannot tell of course until the results begin to appear in American newspapers.

The correspondents in Paris report to the offices here, so it is apparent that if the men in London get the right angle, it will be wonderfully helpful.

In Paris I shall devote my energy very largely to bringing the correspondents in contact more closely with the American sources of news, at the same time trying to give them the proper angle so that they will appreciate the importance of the news.

—(Source: Munitions Hearings, Part 11, Dec. 6, 7, 10, 1934.)

(2) Letter to Weston from F. J. Byrne, of DuPont firm:

Recently there have appeared a number of dispatches in the American papers along the lines that are very desirable to us. These look to me as if they have been cabled to this country as a result of your visit to the other side:

1) The *Boston Transcript* of Dec. 21, 1920, carried a fine story on "Britain Foresees Gas Warfare," dated from London.

2) The *Washington Herald* had a cable dispatch written by Wythe Williams from Paris about German dye plots against the US. This was taken up by the Manufacturers Record and made the subject of a splendid full page editorial.

3) The *Evening Bulletin* of Philadelphia had a dispatch from London talking about the importance of British action passing the dye bill and its relation to American affairs.

4) The *Public Ledger* of Jan. 8, 1921, had a dispatch from Paris about "Germany Sets Dye Trade Trap."

These dispatches are syndicated in many cases to appear in different places throughout the country, so that the publicity on these four items I mentioned must have been very considerable. (Munitions Hearings, Part 11, Exhibit 928, page 2581).

(3) Statement addressed to Senators by Stephen Raushenbush, sec'y of Munitions Investigation:

I call your attention to paragraph 3, as to the matter of control of the press. He (Weston, in another letter, exhibit 926) speaks of having arranged certain articles to come out in France. He goes and talks with some prominent people there and gets news stories which seem to be calculated to have a very definite effect on public opinion here. (Munitions Hearings, page 2416).

(To Weston) You take credit . . . for a story in the *Boston Transcript* . . . "Britain Foresees Gas Warfare," a story by Wythe Williams from Paris about German dye plots against the US; the *Evening Bulletin* of Phila a dispatch . . . and the *Public Ledger,* a dispatch from Paris. . . . (Ex 928).

Raushenbush: You had to send a man . . . to keep the pot boiling . . . with dispatches . . . to make the American people see the importance of favoring your particular industry?

Weston: That is exactly what we were after.

(4) Letter from Weston to Meade, of DuPont firm:

Guy Martin and the articles which he wrote for the Paris editions of the *New York Herald* (*Tribune*) and the *Chicago Tribune* throw an interesting sidelight on my visit. . . . They were written by Ben A. (sic) Raleigh, an old newspaper acquaintance whom I left on guard in Paris. He assumed the name of Guy Martin for publication purposes. . . . He as my agent will carry out any suggestion. (Munitions Hearings, exhibit 929).

(5) Report from Ben K. Raleigh, representative of DuPonts, appointed by Weston, publicity head of the firm, to deal with the newspapers and reporters in Paris. Dated Jan. 25, 1921:

The Associated Press carried a cable on the substance of an interview I had with Prof Blondell. . . . The *Public Ledger* Syndicate and the *Chicago Tribune* Syndicate papers are to be supplied with a story I have arranged which will point out that the French Govt, upon confidential information from its investigators in Germany regarding a coming great German dump of goods, will further increase its coefficient tariff rates on dyestuffs, chemicals, etc. . . . This story should bring out some editorials in the American press, and it might be possible to have it suggested to some of the newspapers that editorial treatment of the cable would be of public service.

Dr. Jacoby . . . showed me yesterday a clipping from one of the *Ledger* Syndicate newspapers . . . the article I supplied.

I sent you a cable yesterday notifying you of the coming appearance of the stories for the *Public Ledger* Syndicate and the *Chicago Tribune* papers. I hope to get some more material over the Associated Press wires shortly. . . . [Ed. note: the AP is the most powerful news service in America, and is supposed to be absolutely free of controls. It has been used by the corporations, banks, special interests, anti-labor outfits, etc., as numerous Congressional investigations have shown. It was recently ordered to stop monopolistic practices.]

By the way, I suppose that an occasional luncheon, etc., in the furtherance of the project would not be objected to, but I should like authorization. In this case Dr. Chapin paid for the lunch, but

I want to be in a position to come back at him and the other people who we want to cultivate, including such men as (Wythe) Williams of the *Public Ledger,* Roberts [then head] of the associated Press . . . Floyd Gibbons of the *(Chicago) Tribune.* . . .

Carl Ackerman [now head of the School of Journalism, Columbia University], who dropped into the *Ledger* Bureau while I was there, over on a visit from London, requested me to remember him to you. . . .

(Munitions Hearings, part II, Ex. 926, pp. 2578-80.)

APPENDIX 12.

THE NEWSPAPER PRESS CONTROLS THE MAJORITY OF RADIO STATIONS

Wattage	NUMBER OF STATIONS OWNED OR CONTROLLED BY NEWSPAPER PUBLISHERS			*Total number of stations in United States*	*Percentage of total owned or controlled by newspapers*
	Directly	*Indirectly*	*Total*		
50,000	11	33	44	53	83.0
5,000 or 20,000	66	89	155	225	68.9
1,000 or 2,500	48	60	108	162	66.7
200 or 500	113	88	201	446	45.1
Total	238	270	508	886	57.3

Figures compiled from unpublished records of the Federal Communications Commission.—*Guild Reporter,* July 26, 1946.

APPENDIX 13.

THE CURTIS PUBLISHING COMPANY AND SUBSIDIARIES

December 31, 1941

SECURITIES

General Investment Account

	Book Value	*Market Value*
Government Bonds	$ 4,127,900.00	$ 4,131,637.73
State and Municipal Bonds	2,050,755.07	2,188,155.00
Canadian Bonds	82,491.25	76,218.75
Industrial Bonds	164,567.50	164,140.00
Railroad and Utility Bonds	146,602.03	139,612.50
Bank and Insurance Stocks	613,498.30	382,681.75
Utility Preferred Stocks	1,338,231.61	1,333,372.00
Utility Common Stocks	180,813.47	147,487.50
Industrial Preferred and Common Stocks	8,270,106.56	8,137,972.29
Guaranteed Railroad Stocks	821,592.63	877,588.25
	$17,796,558.42	$17,578,865.77

APPENDIX 14.

TIME OWNERSHIP

Statement of the Ownership, Management, Circulation, Etc., Required By The Act of Congress of March 3, 1933.

Of *Time, The Weekly Newsmagazine,* published weekly at Chicago, Illinois, for October 1, 1935.

State of New York }
County of New York } ss.

2. That the owner is: (If owned by a corporation, its name and address must be stated and also immediately thereunder the names and addresses of stockholders owning or holding one per cent or more of total amount of stock. If not owned by a corporation, the names and addresses of the individual owners must be given. If owned by a firm, company, or other unincorporated concern, its name and address, as well as those of each individual member, must be given) Time Incorporated, 135 East 42nd St., New York, N. Y.:

Henry P. Davison, 23 Wall St., New York, N. Y.
F. DuSossoit Duke, Greens Farms, Vt.
Mimi B. Durant, 139 East 79th St., New York, N. Y.
General Publishing Corporation (Henry R. Luce) 15 Exchange Place, Jersey City, N. J.
William V. Griffin, 140 Cedar St., New York, N. Y.
Crowell Hadden III, Trustee, Estate of Briton Hadden, 40 Wall St., New York, N. Y.
Edith H. Harkness, 4 East 60th St., New York, N. Y.
William H. Harkness, 654 Madison Ave., New York, N. Y.
Louise H. Ingalls, 1657 Union Trust Bldg., Cleveland, Ohio
Robert L. Johnson, 135 East 42nd St., New York, N. Y.
Margaret Zerbe Larsen, 435 East 42nd St., New York, N. Y.
Wilton Lloyd-Smith, 63 Wall St., New York, N. Y.
Henry R. Luce, 135 East 42nd St., New York, N. Y.
John S. Martin, 135 East 42nd St., New York, N. Y.
Samuel W. Meek Jr., 420 Lexington Ave., New York, N. Y.

3. That the known bondholders, mortgagees, and other security holders owning or holding 1 per cent or more of total amount of bonds, mortgages, or other securities are: (If these are none, so state). None.

Sworn to and subscribed before me this 27th day of September, 1935.

(Seal) Herbert E. Mahoney.

(My commission expires March 30, 1936.)

APPENDIX 15.

THE PRESS IN CHAINS

Five press lords—Hearst, Howard, McCormick, Patterson and Knight—own the most powerful segment of the American Press.

Town	*Paper*	*Owner*	*Circulation**
Akron	Beacon-Journal	Knight	131,246
Albuquerque	Tribune	Scripps-Howard	16,496
Albany	Times-Union	Hearst	50,684
Birmingham	Post	Scripps-Howard	75,680
Boston	Record	Hearst	390,966
Boston	American	Hearst	207,203
Boston	Advertiser	Hearst	660,440
Baltimore	News-Post	Hearst	220,127
Baltimore	American	Hearst	323,859
Chicago	Daily News	Knight	491,046
Chicago	Herald-American	Hearst	531,309

Town	*Paper*	*Owner*	*Circulation**
Chicago	Tribune	McCormick	1,076,045
Cincinnati	Post	Howard	155,188
Cleveland	Press	Howard	264,589
Columbus	Citizen	Howard	83,135
Detroit	Free Press	Knight	417,336
Detroit	Times	Hearst	405,887
Denver	Rocky Mt. News	Howard	80,415
El Paso	Herald-Post	Howard	29,350
Evansville	Press	Howard	41,937
Fort Worth	Press	Howard	45,086
Houston	Press	Howard	82,936
Indianapolis	Times	Howard	94,886
Los Angeles	Examiner	Hearst	379,746
Los Angeles	Herald-Express	Hearst	404,461
Kentucky	Post (Cinn. Post)	Howard	......
Knoxville	News-Sentinel	Howard	101,303
Memphis	Press-Scimitar	Howard	128,343
Memphis	Commercial-Appeal	Howard	167,987
Miami	Herald	Knight	131,353
Milwaukee	Sentinel	Hearst	158,266
New York	Daily News	Patterson	2,354,444
		(Sunday.	4,599,524)
New York	Mirror	Hearst	1,006,279
New York	Journal-American	Hearst	673,708
New York	World-Telegram	Howard	383,454
Oakland	Post-Enquirer	Hearst	73,786
Pittsburgh	Sun-Telegraph	Hearst	198,985
Pittsburgh	Press	Howard	251,572
San Antonio	Light	Hearst	74,086
San Francisco	Call-Bulletin	Hearst	169,987
San Francisco	Examiner	Hearst	233,623
San Francisco	News	Howard	143,489
Seattle	Post-Intelligencer	Hearst	164,199
Washington	Times-Herald	Mrs. E. Patterson	262,216
Washington	News	Howard	109,694

* Editor and Publisher, Yearbook, 1947.

APPENDIX 17.
CONTROL OF THE N.A.M.

76th Congress, 1st session. SENATE Report No. 6, part 6.
Violations of Free Speech and Rights of Labor.
Labor Policies of Employers' Associations.
Part III. The N. A. M.

page 47

Section 2. Control of the N. A. M.

The reorganization described in section 1 above brought a new leadership into the affairs of the N. A. M. . . . Large concerns were more frequently represented on the directorate. Nationally recognized corporations became active in the affairs of the associations.

The available information indicates that Charles R. Hood, president of the American Rolling Mill Co.; Robert B. Henderson, president of the Pacific Portland Cement Co.; Robert L. Lund, president of the Lambert Pharmacal Co., were in the original group which planned and executed the reorganization of the National Association of Manufacturers. This committee is not informed of the members of the "Brass Hats" or the full list of industrial and financial leaders who, in 1933, conceived of a program of "business salvation" and selected the National Association of Manufacturers to carry it out. It is known, however, that a large group of other leading businessmen joined the original sponsors in the practical execution of the plans formulated in 1933. (12) (Footnote 12 follows)

The men who have been active in the association, some since 1933, others since 1934-35, as large contributors, directors, officers, or as members of public relations committee or the National Industrial Information committee, are the following:

Ernest T. Weir, National Steel Corporations;
Colby M. Chester, chairman of board, General Foods Corp.
Harry A. Bullis, vice president, General Mills Co. of Ohio;
Lammot duPont, president, R. I. duPont de Nemours & Co.;
Edgar M. Queeny, president, Mansanto Chemical Co.;
C. L. Bardo of the New York Shipbuilding Corp.;
W. T. Holiday, president, Standard Oil Co. of Ohio;
F. A. Merrici, president, Westinghouse Electric & Manufacturing Co.;
W. B. Bell, president, American Cyanamid Co.;
George H. Houston, president, Baldwin Locomotive Works;
F. N. Bard of the Barco Manufacturing Co.;

C. S. Davis, president, Borg-Warner Corporation; also former president of the United States Chamber of Commerce.
S. Bayard Colgate, president, Colgate Palmolive-Peet Co.;
W. D. Fuller, president, Curtis Publishing Co.;
F. W. Lovejoy, president, Eastman Kodak Co.;
Russell Grinnell, president, General Fire Extinguisher Co.;
O. E. Braitmayer, vice president, International Business Machines Corp.;
Walter J. Kohler of Kohler Co.;
John E. Edgerton of Lebanon Woolen Mills;
William B. Warner, president, McCall Corporation.
George W. Merck, president, Merck & Co.;
George McNeir, chairman, Mohawk Carpet Mills;
C. C. Carlton, secretary, Motor Wheel Corporation;
H. L. Ferguson, president, Newport News Shipbuilding & Dry Dock Corp.
W. H. Taylor, president, Philadelphia Electric Co.

APPENDIX 18.

INDUSTRIAL ESPIONAGE

TABLE 7.—Companies represented on the board of directors of National Association of Manufacturers sometime during 1933-37, which used labor-espionage service and/or industrial munitions.

Name of company (SMALL CAPS *indicate large contributors of National Association of Manufacturers*)	*Detective agencies used*	*Munitions Purchased*
		Amount
AMERICAN CAN CO.	Corporations Auxiliary, Burns, Pinkerton	....
AMERICAN ROLLING MILL CO.	Corporations Auxiliary	$2,817.16
AMERICAN SMELTING & REFINING CO.	Pinkerton	....
REVERE COPPER & BRASS CO.	National Metal Trades	....
Ames Baldwin Wyoming Co.	....	605.60

ANACONDA COPPER MINING CO.	....	4,470.48
Anaconda Wire & Cable	Corporations Auxiliary	....
THE BALDWIN LOCOMOTIVE WORKS	Pinkerton, Corporations Auxiliary	....
BENDIX AVIATION CORPORATION	Railway Audit	4,866.47
Bibb Manufacturing Co.	....	1,365.12
CLARK THREAD CO.	Railway Audit	366.74
CONGOLEUM-NAIRN, INC.	Pinkerton	....
CRANE CO.	Corporations Auxiliary	....
CURTIS PUBLISHING CO.	Pinkerton	....
Detroit Steel Castings Co.	Corporations Auxiliary	....
E. I. DUPONT DE NEMOURS & CO.	....	1,944.49
GENERAL ELECTRIC CO.	Pinkerton	....
B. F. GOODRICH CO.	Corporations Auxiliary, National Corporation Service, Pinkerton	7,740.60
Hazel-Atlas Glass Co.	National Corporation Service	653.38
HOOKER ELECTROCHEMICAL CO.	Pinkerton	....
Hughes Tool Co.	Pinkerton	....
Illinois Tool Works	National Metal Trades	....
LINK-BELT CO.	National Metal Trades	....
JOHN MORRELL & CO.	Pinkerton	1,147.54
MOTOR WHEEL CORPORATION	Corporations Auxiliary	....
NATIONAL STEEL CORPORATION	....	....
Weirton Steel Co.	Central Industrial Service	11,778.17
Great Lakes Steel Corporation	....	307.20
NEW YORK SHIPBUILDING CORPORATION	Pinkerton	484.15
PITTSBURGH PLATE GLASS CO.	Corporations Auxiliary	3,151.40
REMINGTON RAND, INC.	Bergoff, Burns, Railway Audit, Foster's, Cal Crim.	372.50
REPUBLIC STEEL CORPORATION	....	79,712.42
STANDARD OIL CO. OF OHIO	....	809.60
STEWART-WARNER CORPORATION	National Metal Trades	....
SUN OIL CO.	....	2,431.22
UNITED GAS IMPROVEMENT CO.	....	....

PHILADELPHIA ELECTRIC CO.	Pinkerton, Burns, Railway Audit	408.00
WHEELING STEEL CORPORATION	National Corporation, Railway Audit, Corporations Auxiliary	303.75
THE YALE & TOWNE MANUFACTURING CO.	National Metal Trades	....

—(Source: N.A.M. Investigation)

APPENDIX 19.

N.A.M. PRESS RELATIONS

(*Editorial Note:* A large part of the La Follette Committee's exposé of the N.A.M. is devoted to corruption of the press.)

D. Memorandum on Community Public Information Programs to Combat Radical Tendencies and Present the Constructive Story of Industry, April, 1937

Now, more than ever before, strikes are being won or lost in the newspapers and over the radio. The swing of public opinion has always been a major factor in labor disputes, but with the settlement of strikes being thrown more and more into the laps of public officials, the question of public opinion becomes of greater importance. For it is public opinion—what the voters think—that moves those elected to action along one course or another. . . .

V. Possible Activities

A. Newspapers

1. Get one paper to develop its own series of stories on growth of Smithtown industries, how they have developed, their payrolls, their service to the community, their taxes, etc. Your Public Relations man would cooperate in getting proper material.

2. Get another paper to carry a series of stories and pictures of industrial and business men, with the accent on those who have either started at the bottom and become executives of big companies, or who started their own companies on a shoestring and became big.

4. Have Special Committee invite editors to lunch on occasions.

B. Radio

1. Much the same as with newspapers, get one station to carry a series telling about various Smithtown industries. This might be done by speeches, or the station might be propositioned on letting a local amateur dramatic group dramatize a series of playlets presenting the story of Smithtown industries.

C. Speakers Corps

1. Organize group of perhaps 25 speakers drawn from all walks of life as ministers, lawyers, etc.

D. Schools

1. See that school libraries have material available for reading and research presenting our viewpoint. Same for public libraries, all of whom should be contacted to find out what type of material they might need that could be provided.

4. Where the schools have motion picture machines, arrange to have pictures produced by Council shown and keep abreast of other pictures available for this purpose. For instance, picture now out by Iron and Steel Institute.

G. Foreign Language Groups

1. This is important. Industry, or even the government has never bothered to tell these people what America is all about. Yet radicals are always working among them. Few people appreciate the importance of these millions of people, for they vote. And if they are never told both sides of a story, they cannot be blamed for believing the only side they have eternally dinned in their ears.

Much of the effectiveness of this program depends upon the calibre of the Special Committee on Public Information. If they are of a type who will give some time to sitting down with editors, ministers, foreign language groups, heads of women's clubs, etc., and are influential enough to make their weight felt with newspapers, radio stations and other business people within the town, the carrying through of the program will be immeasurably increased. On the other hand, if the Public Relations man is forced to go it alone without a strong committee back of him, his job will be more difficult.

National Association of Manufacturers
Public Relations Department,
James P. Selvage, Director.

—(Source: Same report.)

APPENDIX 19.

THE N.A.M.

76th Congress, 1st Session. SENATE. Report No. 6, part 6.

Violations of Free Speech and Rights of Labor

Report of the Committee on Education and Labor

Labor Policies of Employers' Associations

Part III

The National Association of Manufacturers

The National Association of Manufacturers joined the open-shop movement and adopted at its convention in New Orleans in April 1903, a "Declaration of Labor Principles." The association declared in these principles the unrestricted supremacy of the employers in the establishment of conditions of work, just as the National Metal Trades Association had done 2 years earlier. The National Association of Manufacturers itself said that its labor principles "marked the first declaration by a representative national body for the open shop as a cardinal policy of American manufacturing."

Mr. Van Cleave also had special writers on the pay roll of the association. Senator Thomas J. Walsh, of Montana, brought out in the cross-examination of Mr. Van Cleave's secretary, Mr. Ferdinand C. Schwedtman, that one Charles M. Harvey, of the *St. Louis Globe Democrat,* also a contributor to the *Atlantic Monthly,* had been hired by Mr. Van Cleave to write articles for him.

One of the speakers who did missionary work for the National Association of Manufacturers was Ellis L. Howland, an editor of the *New York Journal of Commerce.*

Lobbying and legislative pressure politics, sometimes approaching dangerously close to a perversion of representative government, were the principal devices used by the representatives of the association in these earlier struggles. This direct approach was implemented by propaganda, secret, and pervasive; a powerful weapon used by the association and its affiliated employer organizations, to sway public opinion against labor and in favor of the position taken by the association. Propaganda, under the euphemistic designation of "education," was a substitute constantly employed by the association to efface the impression or the consciousness of industrial evils, instead of correcting their fundamental causes.

Chapter II. Control of the National Association of Manufacturers

Section 1. Reorganization of the National Association of Manufacturers, 1933

After the national election of 1932, even before the progressive policies of the new administration had been crystallized in legislation, certain industrial leaders took steps to unify business sentiment and to initiate an expensive program of public education in sympathy with the aims of business. A group of wealthy businessmen who styled themselves the "Brass Hats" met occasionally in New York City to discuss problems of "business salvation." Out of this group grew a more formal committee of the National Association of Manufacturers. This committee brought about a reorganization of the association, introduced new leadership, and formulated a program of united action by corporate interests.

The available information indicates that Charles R. Hook, president of the American Rolling Mill Co.; Robert B. Henderson, president of the Pacific Portland Cement Co.; Robert L. Lund, president of the Lambert Pharmacal Co.; were in the original group which planned and executed the reorganization of the National Association of Manufacturers.

TABLE 3—15 largest contributors of the National Association of Manufacturers, Jan. 1, 1933, to Oct. 31, 1937.

	Total
E. I. duPont de Nemours Co.	$118,600.00
General Motors Corporation	66,520.00
National Steel Corporation	42,050.00
United States Steel Corporation	41,450.00
Monsanto Chemical Co.	36,775.00
Westinghouse Electric & Manufacturing Co.	35,912.00
Chrysler Corporation	35,400.00
Bethlehem Steel Corporation	29,250.00
Texas Corporation	27,500.00
Borg-Warner Corporation	27,141.67
Republic Steel Corporation	24,650.00
Socony-Vacuum Oil Co.	22,000.00
Swift & Co.	21,150.00
Standard Oil Co. of New Jersey	20,600.00
Eastman Kodak Co.	20,216.00
Total	$569,214.67

The companies which belong to the group of large contributors which were represented on the board of directors of the National Association of Manufacturers at some time during the years 1933-38, and companies which were continuously represented on the board of directors for 3 or more years are given in table 4. In this group will be found the president, the chairman of the board, the vice presidents, treasurers, and the most active, the most generous supporters of the National Association of Manufacturers, and its public relations and propaganda activities. In this group are found T. M. Girdler, of Republic Steel Corporation; Colby M. Chester, of General Foods Corporation; H. A. Bullis, of General Mills, Inc.; Lammot duPont, of E. I. duPont de Nemours & Co.; Walter J. Kohler, of Kohler Co.; John E. Edgerton, of Lebanon Woolen Mills; S. Bayard Colgate, of Colgate-Palmolive-Peet Co.; Robert L. Lund, of Lambert Pharmacal Co.; William B. Warner, of McCall Corporation; C. L. Bardo of New York Shipbuilding Corporation; H. L. Furgeson, of Newport News Shipbuilding & Dry Dock Co.; W. T. Holliday, of Standard Oil Co., who in 1939 was president of the United States Chamber of Commerce. The control of the association is in the hands of these interests. By giving financial support, by actively participating in the councils of the association, and by stirring other companies to lend their names and help to the work of the association, these men have assumed the leadership and the responsibility for the activities of the association.

Section 4. Attempt at Nullification After Enactment of S. 1958 (Wagner Act)

Immediately after passage of S. 1958 by the Congress (75th), even before the signing of the act by the President on July 5, the National Association of Manufacturers and the National Industrial Council took steps to consider and clarify their future attitude toward the act. On June 29, George F. Kull, chairman of the State association group of the National Industrial Council, and Sidney E. Cornelius, chairman of the employment relations group, sent letters to their respective members inviting them to attend a secret meeting at the Hotel Roosevelt, New York City, on Tuesday, July 9. Mr. Kull advised, "Please avoid giving out any bulletins or public announcements on this meeting." Mr. Cornelius also suggested, "No publicity on this meeting is necessary, *so do not mention it in your bulletins.*" On the same day, June 29, Robert L. Lund, and C. L. Bardo, president of the National Association of Manufacturers, sent out invitations to members of the board of directors and members of the executive committee of the association to attend special all-day conferences on July 10 and 11, the day after the Council meeting, at the Waldorf Astoria Hotel in New York City. Mr. Lund's letter stated, "It seems highly advisable in the light of recent developments to call a meeting of our board of directors." The agenda presented by Mr. Lund included:

1. Consideration of Wagner Labor Disputes Bill as passed; validity; future policy, etc. * * *
2. President's Tax program * * *
3. Reorganization of N.R.A. * * *

4. Future organized effort necessary to protect American industrial system.

5. Social Security—Form of advice to offer our members with respect to this important legislation which is now a law.

Chapter V. The Propaganda Campaign of the National Association of Manufacturers

The National Association of Manufacturers had opposed the principal legislative measures sponsored by the national administration during the congressional session of 1935. It had opposed the National Labor Relations Act, the Social Security Act, the Banking Act, the Utility Holding Company Act, and the President's tax program. In spite of the association's opposition, all these measures became law. This was a great blow to the association; but its officers remained undaunted and they redoubled their propaganda efforts. The program of "education" that was initiated in 1933 and 1934 now became its principal weapon of defense for the status quo, and it was carried forward with mounting intensity.

As time went on the public relations committee of the National Association of Manufacturers perfected its program of community education. A highly developed program was formulated early in 1937, and on April 13, 1937, it was submitted to the members of the committee on public relations of the National Association of Manufacturers. The purpose that this program was designed to accomplish is indicated by the introductory paragraph of this outline:

"Now, more than ever before, strikes are being won or lost in the newspapers and over the radio. The swing of public opinion has always been a major factor in labor disputes, but with the settlement of strikes being thrown more and more into the laps of public officials, the question of public opinion becomes of greater importance. For it is public opinion—what the voters think—that moves those elected to action along one course or another."

The fundamental philosophy of the association's leadership in 1934, based on a conception of automatic operation of the economic system, found itself in conflict with measures then being taken by governmental agencies to cope with a national crisis. And consequently the association, unable to explain the economic readjustments that had taken place after 1929, forthwith blamed "Communists," "impatient reformers," "disturbers," "persecutors," and "teacher propagandists," for the misunderstandings that had arisen.

In writing of the association's "education program" for school children, James P. Selvage, director of the public relations department, did not speak of truth, or facts, or education, but referred to the theory that "pictures have become accepted more and more as the most impressive medium for leaving a lasting impression on children," and that "here is an unlimited field of distribution in which we would be reaching children during their formative years."

Section 5. Purposes of Propaganda

The National Association of Manufacturers in letters, bulletins, and speeches consistently refers to its information program and the various methods of disseminating this program as designed to mold public opinion. Before this committee the program was described as an attempt to educate the public with regard to advantages of private industry. Upon further analysis, the program appears as an attempt, first, to affect the organizational efforts of labor unions, and second, to render public opinion intolerant of the aims of social progress through legislative effort.

The director of public relations of the National Association of Manufacturers, James P. Selvage, was not unmindful of the potential value of its program as a weapon against labor when he wrote, as quoted in the preceding section, "Now more than ever before, strikes are being won or lost in the newspapers and over the radio."

The effectiveness of publicity against labor unions has been compared favorably with the use of labor spies and tear gas. The National Association of Manufacturers deemed it of interest to its members to print in its labor relations bulletin a digest of an article by Don Gridley which had appeared in *Printers' Ink* of March 11, 1937, in which Gridley suggested that advertising, instead of tear gas and labor spies, be used as a weapon against strikers. In this article Gridley stated that, "If manufacturers would invest one-tenth of the money in advertising preparation that they are apparently quite willing to invest in labor spies, tear gas, and other methods, which have proved worse than useless, they will stand a far better chance of winning public support than is possible under present circumstances."

The speaker supplied free by the association was George E. Sokolsky, "ex-radical," ex-China correspondent for the *New York Times,* industrial "consultant" for the Iron and Steel Institute, newspaper columnist and "the outstanding advocate of the open shop in America." Mr. Lloyd explained in a special bulletin dated September 22, 1936, that Mr. R. M. Welch, the manager of personnel of Youngstown Sheet & Tube Co., had recommended Sokolsky. Mr. Lloyd stated that "Mr. Sokolsky's early life was spent as a Communist and a radical. He has now reformed, and has a real message to deliver to those of us who are interested in the welfare of industry. He calls a spade a spade."

In finances, organization, sponsorship, arrangements, publicity, and the selection of speaker, the civic progress meeting in Youngstown is representative of the surreptitious methods of the National Association of Manufacturers. Mr. Lloyd confirmed the secrecy of the proceedings in Youngstown:

"Senator La Follette. Well, the net effect was that the activity of the National Association of Manufacturers and its having prompted the meeting, its contributing 50 'bucks', and furnishing Mr. Sokolsky, was all concealed from the public, wasn't it?

"Mr. Lloyd. Yes; that was not generally known."

John W. Hill testified that George Sokolsky was assigned to carry out the work which the National Association of Manufacturers required. The arrangement was summarized in the following testimony:

"Senator La Follette. * * * I understand the arrangement to be as follows, and if I am incorrect, please indicate so: You arranged with Mr. Sargent of the National Association of Manufacturers that you would pay Mr. George Sokolsky $1,000 a month for certain services that Mr. Sokolsky was to render to the National Association of Manufacturers; and that the National Association of Manufacturers was to pay you $1,000 a month for the services that Mr. Sokolsky rendered to the National Association of Manufacturers; is that correct?

"Mr. Hill. Right."

In return for his services, Hill & Knowlton paid George Sokolsky fees ranging from $1,000 to $2,000. Between June 1936 and February 1938, Mr. Sokolsky was paid by Hill & Knowlton fees amounting to $28,364.50, of which at least $6,000 came from the National Association of Manufacturers.

In addition to these amounts received from Hill & Knowlton, George Sokolsky also received direct payments from the National Association of Manufacturers between May 1936 and March 1938 amounting to $3,409.36. Part of this money was payment to Mr. Sokolsky by the National Association of Manufacturers for radio speeches.

Frank Purnell, president of the Youngstown Sheet & Tube Co. was questioned concerning the special service undertaken by Hill & Knowlton for the six steel companies of which his company was one. . . .

"Senator La Follette. Did you ever get anything from him since then?

"Mr. Purnell. Of course, there were a lot of pamphlets by Sokolsky, or newspaper items; I can't trace it, but I have seen articles by him, and I can't trace them.

"Senator La Follette. You are not implying, are you, that Mr. Sokolsky got any of this money for writing his syndicated column which appears in the *New York Herald Tribune* and other newspapers?

"Mr. Purnell. I don't know anything about that.

"Senator La Follette. Did you get any services out of Mr. Sokolsky aside from this meeting of the Foremen's Club that you know anything about?

"Mr. Purnell. No, sir."

The activities of the National Association of Manufacturers became so bold and sometimes indiscreet that a scandal occurred in 1913, when public charges were made that agents of the association had given "financial rewards" to Congressmen to promote its legislative program. Both Houses of Congress passed resolutions to investigate the lobbying activities of the association. These investigations disclosed that: the association had placed an employee of the House of Representatives on its pay rolls in order to obtain information not available to the public; the association's agents had contributed large sums of money to congressional candidates in their campaigns for reelection and had opposed representatives friendly to labor; the association had carried on a disguised propaganda campaign through newspaper syndicates and through the chautauqua circuits by placing publicists on its pay roll, and by distributing large quantities of propaganda material to schools, colleges, and civic organizations throughout the country; the association's agents had promoted employees' alliances as an aid in opposing candidates friendly to labor. Responsible officials of the National Association of Manufacturers did not renounce any part of their activities revealed before the Senate and House committees in 1913. On the contrary they reasserted the necessity of pursuing the course which they had followed previously in order to counteract the "operations of organized labor."

In order to carry out its program the National Association of Manufacturers, together with other associations, organized in 1916 the Chamber of Commerce of the United States and the National Industrial Conference Board. . . .

In this period while opposing union organization under the cover of "patriotism and freedom" the association's representatives maintained their unyielding attitude on social legislation just as they had done prior to 1913. The continued opposition to modification of the antitrust laws to exempt labor unions from the application of the law, legislation restricting the issuing of injunctions by Federal courts against labor unions in industrial disputes, regulation of child labor, regulation of the hours of work on Government contracts, the establishment of collective bargaining in employment relations among interstate carriers, and many other legislative proposals designed to correct some of the basic dislocations which gave rise to social unrest.

Until 1933 the National Association of Manufacturers had been under the control principally of smaller industrial concerns. After the national election of 1932, a group of industrial leaders who called themselves the "Brass Hats" held informal meetings in

Detroit and New York to determine the proper action they should take for "business salvation." They selected the National Association of Manufacturers because of its organization and experience as their vehicle for a campaign and financed it by contributions from large corporations.

The management of the National Association of Manufacturers was reorganized in 1933, in accordance with the plans of the "Brass Hats." Robert L. Lund, president of the Lambert Pharmacal Co., of St. Louis, became president of the association and Walter B. Weisenburger, formerly an executive of the St. Louis Chamber of Commerce, was selected as executive vice president of the association to carry out this reorganization and to initiate the new program of activities. Charles R. Hook, president of American Rolling Mill Co., started an underwriting campaign by securing contributions from T. M. Girdler of the Republic Steel Corporation, Frank Purnell of the Youngstown Sheet & Tube Co., and others. Participation in this underwriting was conditioned upon the reorganization of the association's management. The American Iron and Steel Institute and the Associated Industries of Cleveland advised their members to support the revised program of the National Association of Manufacturers.

A group of 262 nationally known companies supplied 50 per cent of its income during the period 1933 to 1937. Largest contributor during this period was E. I. Du Pont de Nemours & Co. with $118,600, most of which was donated in 1936 and 1937.

7. The Propaganda Campaign

The association's propaganda campaign projected in 1933 and started in 1934, went into effect in full swing in the summer of 1936, just prior to the national election. Through newspapers, radio, motion pictures, slide films, stockholders' letters, pay-roll stuffers, billboard advertisements, civic-progress meetings and local advertising, the National Association of Manufacturers blanketed the country with a propaganda barrage which surpassed its "Industrial Conservation Movement" of 1916-20 in intensity, scope and variety of technique. With the cooperation of large member corporations and local employers' associations affiliated with the National Industrial Council, the association's "educational" program reached every important industrial community in the United States. Its message was directed against "labor agitators," against governmental measures to alleviate industrial distress, against labor unions, and for the advantages of the status quo in industrial relations, of which company-dominated unions were still a part. Anti-union employers and local employers' association executives used the propaganda material of the National Association of Manufacturers to combat the organizational drive of unions in local industrial areas. This was particularly the case in the steel producing centers of Ohio where a labor organizational drive was under way.

The National Association of Manufacturers has blanketed the country with a propaganda which in technique has relied upon indirection of meaning, and in presentation upon secrecy and deception. Radio speeches, public meetings, news, cartoons, editorials, advertising, motion pictures, and many other artifices of propaganda have not in most instances disclosed to the public their origin with the association. The Mandeville Press Service, the Six Star Service, Uncle Abner cartoons, George Sokolsky's services, the "American Family Robinson" radio broadcasts, "Harmony Ads" by MacDonald-Cook Co., "civic progress meetings" and many other devices of molding public opinion have been used without disclosure of the origin and financial support by the National Association of Manufacturers.

5. With the funds of this group of powerful corporations, the National Association of Manufacturers has flooded the country with biased propaganda directed against organizations of American workingmen and against social legislation adopted by Congress. This propaganda, for the most part unidentified to the public as coming from the National Association of Manufacturers, is reiterated day after day through the means of every channel of public expression, in the press, over the radio, in schools, on billboards, by public speakers, by direct mail, and in pay envelopes. In some cases the National Association of Manufacturers has contrived to arrange for the sponsorship of its propaganda by others, for the purpose of misleading the public into believing that it came from an independent source. Much of this propaganda is intended to influence the public with reference to elections, and, officials of the association have boasted that its propaganda has influenced the political opinions of millions of citizens, and affected their choice of candidates for Federal offices.

7. The committee condemns the deliberate action taken by the National Association of Manufacturers to promote organized disregard for the National Labor Relations Act. Such action by a powerful and responsible organization encourages disrespect for the law and undermines the authority of government.

8. The National Association of Manufacturers' campaign of propaganda stems from the almost limitless resources of corporate treasuries. Not individuals but corporations constitute the membership of the association and supply its funds. It is this fact that makes the political aspects of the association's campaign of propaganda a matter of serious concern. In effect the National Association of Manufacturers is a vehicle for spending corporate funds to influence the opinion of the public in its selection of candidates for office. It may be questioned whether such use of the resources of corporate enterprise does not contravene the well established

public policy forbidding corporations to make contributions in connection with political elections. The National Association of Manufacturers is to be condemned for cloaking its propaganda in anonymity and for failing clearly to disclose to the public whom it is trying to influence that this lavish propaganda campaign has as its source the National Association of Manufacturers.

9. Finally, the committee deplores the failure of the National Association of Manufacturers and the powerful corporations which guide its policies to adapt themselves to changing times and to laws which the majority of the people deem wise and necessary.

APPENDIX 20.

THE FIRST FASCIST PLOT TO SEIZE THE U.S. GOVERNMENT

(*Editorial Note:* General Smedley Butler testified before a Congressional Committee that several Wall Street bankers, one of them connected with J. P. Morgan & Co., several founders of the American Liberty League, and several heads of the American Legion plotted to seize the government of the United States shortly after President Roosevelt established the New Deal. The press, with a few exceptions, suppressed the news. Worse yet, the McCormack-Dickstein Committee suppressed the facts involving the big business interests, although it confirmed the plot which newspapers and magazines had either refused to mention or had tried to kill by ridicule. In the following quotations the suppressed parts are in italics.)

General Butler's Testimony regarding his interview with Gerald G. MacGuire, of the brokerage firm of Grayson M.-P. Murphy:

Then MacGuire said that he was the chairman of the distinguished-guest committee of the American Legion, on Louis Johnson's staff; that Louis Johnson had, at MacGuire's suggestion, put my name down to be invited as a distinguished guest of the Chicago convention; *that Johnson had then taken this list, presented by MacGuire, of distinguished guests, to the White House for approval; that Louis Howe, one of the secretaries to the Presi-*

dent, had crossed my name off and said that I was not to be invited—that the President would not have it.

I thought I smelled a rat, right away—that they were trying to get me mad—to get my goat. I said nothing.

"He (Murphy) is on our side, though. He wants to see the soldiers cared for.

"Is he responsible, too, for making the Legion a strikebreaking outfit?"

"No, no. He does not control anything in the Legion now."

I said: "You know very well that it is nothing but a strikebreaking outfit used by capital for that purpose and that is the reason we have all those big clubhouses and that is the reason I pulled out from it. They have been using these dumb soldiers to break strikes."

He said: "Murphy hasn't anything to do with that. He is a very fine fellow."

I said, "I do not doubt that, but there is some reason for his putting $125,000 into this."

Well, that was the end of that conversation.

* * *

I said, "Is there anything stirring about it yet?"

"Yes," he says; "you watch; in two or three weeks you will see it come out in the papers. There will be big fellows in it" . . . *and in about two weeks the American Liberty League appeared, which was just about what he described it to be.* (The committee report suppresses the italicized words.)

We might have an assistant President, somebody to take the blame; and if things do not work out, he can drop him. *He said, "That is what he was building up Hugh Johnson for. Hugh Johnson talked too damn much and got him into a hole, and he is going to fire him in the next three or four weeks."*

I said, "How do you know all this?"

"Oh," he said, "we are in with him all the time. We know what is going to happen."

* * *

General Butler's Testimony of his interview with Robert Sterling Clark.

He (Clark) laughed and said, "That speech cost a lot of money." Clark told me that it had cost him a lot of money. *Now either from what he said then or from what MacGuire had said, I got the impression that the speech had been written by John W. Davis—one or the other of them told me that*—but he thought it was a big joke that these fellows were claiming the authority of that speech. . . .

He said, "When I was in Paris, my headquarters were Morgan & Hodges (Harjes). We had a meeting over there. I might as well tell you that our group is for you, for the head of this organization. Morgan & Hodges (Harjes) are against you. The Morgan interests say that you cannot be trusted, that you are too radical, and so forth, that you are too much on the side of the little fellow; you cannot be trusted. *They are for Douglas MacArthur as the head of it. Douglas MacArthur's term expires in November, and if he is not reappointed it is to be presumed that he will be disappointed and sore and they are for getting him to head it."*

I said, "I do not think that you will get the soldiers to follow him, Jerry . . . He is in bad odor, because he put on a uniform with medals to march down the street in Washington, I know the soldiers."

"Well, then, we will get Hanford MacNider. They want either MacArthur or MacNider. . . They do not want you. But our group tell us you are the only fellow in America who can get the soldiers together. They say, 'Yes, but he will get them together and go the wrong way.' That is what they say if you take charge of them."

I said, "MacNider won't do either. He will not get the soldiers to follow him, because he has been opposed to the bonus."

"Yes, but we will have him in change." (Charge? ed note.)

And it is interesting to note that three weeks later after this conversation MacNider changed and turned around for the bonus. It is interesting to note that.

He said "There is going to be a big quarrel over the reappointment of MacArthur" and he said, "you watch the President reappoint him. He is going to go right and if he does not reappoint him, he is going to go left."

I have been watching with a great deal of interest this quarrel over his reappointment to see how it comes out. He said "You know as well as I do that MacArthur is Stotesbury's soninlaw in Philadelphia—Morgan's representative in Philadelphia. You just see how it goes and if I am not telling you the truth."

I noticed that MacNider turned around for the bonus, and that there is a row over the reappointment of MacArthur. So he left me saying, "I am going down to Miami. . . ."

* * *

Testimony of Paul Comly French of *Philadelphia Record,* in the Smedley Butler-Legion hearing.

At first he (MacGuire) suggested that the General (Butler) organize this outfit himself and ask a dollar a year dues from everybody. We discussed that, and then he came around to the point of getting outside financial funds, and he said it would not be any trouble to raise a million dollars. *He said he could go to John W. Davis (attorney for J. P. Morgan & Co.) or Perkins of the National City Bank, and any number of persons to get it.*

Of course, that may or may not mean anything. That is, his reference to John W. Davis and Perkins of the National City Bank.

During my conversation with him I did not of course commit the General to anything. I was just feeling him along. Later, we discussed the question of arms and equipment, and he suggested that they could be obtained from the Remington Arms Co., on credit through the DuPonts.

I do not think at that time he mentioned the connections of DuPonts with the American Liberty League, but he skirted all around it. That is, I do not think he mentioned the Liberty League, but he skirted all around the idea that that was the back door; one of the DuPonts is on the board of directors of the American Liberty League and they own a controlling interest in the Remington Arms Co. . . . He said the General would not have any trouble enlisting 500,000 men.

APPENDIX 21.

THE FASCIST PLOT OFFICIALLY CONFIRMED

Union Calender No. 44

74th Congress 1st Session	House of Representatives	Report No. 153

Investigation of Nazi And Other Propaganda

February 15, 1935—Committed to the Committee of the Whole House on the state of the Union and ordered to be printed

Mr. McCormack, from the committee appointed to investigate Nazi and other propaganda, submitted the following

REPORT

(Pursuant to House Resolution No. 198, 73d Congress)

Fascism

There have been isolated cases of activity by organizations which seemed to be guided by the fascist principle, which the committee investigated and found that they had made no progress. . . .

In the last few weeks of the committee's official life it received evidence showing that certain persons had made an attempt to establish a fascist organization in this country.

No evidence was presented and this committee had none to show a connection between this effort and any fascist activity of any European country.

There is no question that these attempts were discussed, were planned, and might have been placed in execution when and if the financial backers deemed it expedient.

This committee received evidence from Maj. Gen. Smedley D. Butler (retired), twice decorated by the Congress of the United States. He testified before the committee as to conversations with one Gerald C. MacGuire in which the latter is alleged to have suggested the formation of a fascist army under the leadership of General Butler (p. 8-114 D.C. 6 II).

MacGuire denied these allegations under oath, but your committee was able to verify all the pertinent statements made by General Butler, with the exception of the direct statement suggesting the creation of the organization. This, however, was corroborated in the correspondence of MacGuire with his principal, Robert Sterling Clark, of New York City, while MacGuire was abroad studying the various forms of veterans' organizations of Fascist character (p. 111 D.C. 6 II).

The following is an excerpt from one of MacGuire's letters:

> I had a very interesting talk last evening with a man who is quite well up on affairs here and he seems to be of the opinion that the Croix de Feu will be very patriotic during this crisis and will take the cuts or be the moving spirit in the veterans to accept the cuts. Therefore they will, in all probability, be in opposition to the Socialists and functionaries. The general spirit among the functionaries seems to be that the correct way to regain recovery is to spend more money and increase wages, rather than to put more people out of work and cut salaries.
>
> The Croix de Feu is getting a great number of new recruits, and I recently attended a meeting of this organization and was quite impressed with the type of men belonging. These fellows are interested only in the salvation of France, and I feel sure that the country could not be in better hands because they are not politicians, they are a cross-section of the best people of the country from all walks of life, people who gave their "all" between 1914 and 1918 that France might be saved, and I feel sure that if a crucial test ever comes to the Republic that these men will be the bulwark upon which France will be served.
>
> There may be more uprisings, there may be more difficulties, but as is evidenced right now when the emergency arises and party difficulties are forgotten as far as France is concerned, and all become united in the one desire and purpose to keep this country as it is, the most democratic, and the country of the greatest freedom on the European Continent (p. III D.C. 6 II).

This committee asserts that any efforts based on lines as suggested in the foregoing and leading off to the extreme right, are just as bad as efforts which would lead to the extreme left.

Armed forces for the purpose of establishing a dictatorship by means of Fascism or a dictatorship through the instrumentality of the proletariat, or a dictatorship predicated in part on racial and religious hatreds, have no place in this country.

APPENDIX 22.

THE BIG SUBSIDIZERS OF AMERICAN REACTION AND FASCISM

(*Editorial Note:* All the names of persons, corporations, organizations subsidized, and amounts given, are taken from the Lobby Investigation, headed by Senator Black, now a member of the Supreme Court. The document is known as: 74th Congress, 2d Session, Digest of Data, Special Committee to Investigate Lobbying Activities, U.S. Senate.

(The Crusaders were originally organized to restore liquor. The Sentinels were the most fascist of all the Liberty League affiliates. In their files Senator Black found letters saying "the old line Americans of $1200 a year want a Hitler," "the New Deal is communist," Roosevelt brought "a Jewish brigade" to Washington, and "the Jewish threat is a real one."

(The Sentinels supplied editorials to 1300 papers "urging a return to American principles.")

Name	*Organization*	*Amount*
Addinsell, H. M. President, Chase Harris Forbes Corp.; director, Cities Service Power & Light Co., Philips Petroleum Co., U. S. Electric Power Co.	Crusaders	$ 100
	American Liberty League	200
Allen, E. M. President, Mathieson Alkali Works; Director, Austro-American Magnesite Corp., etc.	Crusaders	100
	American Liberty League	200
Armour, Lester	Crusaders	2,500

Name	*Organization*	*Amount*
Ames, Theodore Partner, Broody, McLellan & Co.	Crusaders	10
	American Liberty League	120
Avery, Sewell	Crusaders	5,000
Baker, George D. F. First National Bank, A. T. & T., U. S. Steel	National Economy League	1,250
Ball, George A. (Muncie, Indiana).	Crusaders	5,000
Bamberger, Clarence (Salt Lake City) Officer, director, 9 corporations; stockholder in 20	Crusaders	125
Brown, Donaldson Vice-President, General Motors Corp.; Director, E. I. duPont de Nemours & Co.	American Liberty League	20,000
	Crusaders	500
Carpenter, R. R. M. Vice-President, E. I. duPont de Nemours & Co.	American Liberty League	20,000
Carpenter, W. S., Jr. Vice-President, E. I. duPont de Nemours & Co.	American Liberty League	4,834
	Economists National Committee	100
Chadbourne, T. L. Director, 13 corporations, including Zonite Products Co.	American Liberty League	6,250
Chrysler, Walter	Crusaders	876
Clayton, W. L. Partner, Anderson-Clayton Co. (cotton brokers); Chairman, Export Insurance Co., New York	Southern Committee to Uphold the Constitution	100
	American Liberty League	7,750
Copeland, Charles C. Secretary, E. I. duPont de Nemours & Co.	American Liberty League	15,000
DuPont, A. M. L. Trustee, Wilmington Trust Co.	American Liberty League	5,000
DuPont, Henry B. Director, Wilmington Trust Co.	American Liberty League	20,000
	Southern Committee to Uphold the Constitution	500

Name	*Organization*	*Amount*
DuPont, Irénée Vice-chairman, E. I. duPont de Nemours & Co.; director, General Motors Corp.	Crusaders	10,000
	Sentinels of the Republic	100
	American Liberty League	86,750
	Southern Committee to Uphold the Constitution	100
	Minute Men ond Women of Today	1,400
DuPont, Lammot President, E. I. duPont de Nemours & Co.; chairman, General Motors Corp., GM Acceptance Corp., and 3 banks	Crusaders	1,000
	American Liberty League	15,000
	N. Y. State Economic Council	1,000
	Economists National Committee on Monetary Policy	1,000
	Southern Committee to Uphold the Constitution	3,000
	Repeal Associates	
	Farmers Independence Council	5,000
DuPont, Pierre S. Vice-President, Wilmington Trust Co.; director, General Motors Corp.	Southern Committee to Uphold the Constitution	5,000
	American Liberty League	5,300
DuPont, S. Hallock	American Liberty League	20,000
DuPont, William, Jr., President, Delaware Trust Co.	American Liberty League	20,000
Erickson, A. W. Chairman, McCann - Erickson (adv. agency); director, Congoleum, Nairn, Newskin Co., Bon Ami, etc.	Crusaders	100
	Liberty League	875
	N. Y. State Economic Council	350

Name	*Organization*	*Amount*
Echols, A. B. Vice-president of DuPont; director, Wilmington Trust Co., Grasselli Chemical Co., Hotel DuPont, Viscoloid Co.	Crusaders	75
	Sentinels of the Republic	25
	American Liberty League	575
	American Federation of Utility Investors	250
	Farmers Independence Council	110
Emery, Joseph H., Jr. Advisory Board, Chase National Bank	Crusaders	
	American Liberty League	
Farish, W. S. Standard Oil	Crusaders	200
Greef, Bernard Partner, Greef & Co., brokers	Crusaders	5
	American Federation of Utility Investors	100
Hawkes, A. W. Congoleum Nairn, Senator	American Liberty League	250
Heinz, Howard President, H. J. Heinz Co.; director, Mellon National Bank	American Liberty League	2,500
	Crusaders	5,876
Houston, George H. President, Baldwin Locomotive Works; director, Standard Steel Works, etc.	Crusaders	100
	American Liberty League	500
	National Economy League	50
Hutton, Edward F. Former chairman, General Foods, Inc.; chairman, Zonite Corporation; director, Manufacturers Trust Co., Chrysler	Crusaders	5,000
	American Liberty League	20,000
	National Economy League	300
Kemmerer, Prof. E. W. Princeton	Southern Committee	5
	American Liberty League	5
Kent, A. Atwater	Sentinels of the Republic	1,000

Name	Organization	Amount
Knudsen, William S. Vice-President, General Motors Corp.	American Liberty League	10,000
Kroger, Bernard	Sentinels	500
La Boyteaux, W. H. President, Johnson & Higgins; director, Grace National Bank, etc.	Crusaders	100
	American Liberty League	100
	American Taxpayers League	40
Lasker, Albert (Advertising)	Crusaders	5,000
Lloyd, Horatio (Morgan Partner)	Sentinels	1,000
McCall, S. T. Vice-President, American Brake Shoe Co., American Manganese Steel Corp.	Crusaders	50
	American Liberty League	100
Mellon, Andrew W. Head of Mellon interests	American Liberty League	1,000
Merrick, F. A. President and director, Westinghouse Electric, Westinghouse Supply, Laurentide Mico Co.	Crusaders	876
Milbanks, Jeremiah	Crusaders	200
Moffett, George M. President and director, Corn Products, director 6 large corporations	Crusaders	7,500
	American Liberty League	10,000
Montgomery, E. W. Director 2 cotton mills, and 2 cotton corporations	Crusaders	50
	American Liberty League	125
Morris, E. M. President, Associated Investment Co., Morris Finance Co., Motor Indemnity Association, Motor Underwriters	Crusaders	25
	American Liberty League	50
	Economists National Committee	100

Name	*Organization*	*Amount*
Morris, John A. Member, Gude, Winmill & Co.	Crusaders	75
	American Liberty League	400
	Sentinels of the Republic	10
Pepper, Geo. Wharton (ex-Senator)	Sentinels	500
Pew, J. Howard President, Sun Oil Co.; director, Sun Shipbuilding & Drydock Co.; director, Philadelphia National Bank	American Liberty League	20,000
	Sentinels of the Republic	5,000
	Crusaders	4,000
	National Economy League	5,000
Pitcairn, H. F.	Sentinels	5,000
Pitcairn, Rev. Theo	Sentinels	3,500
Pitcairn, Raymond	Sentinels	91,000
Pratt, John L. Vice-President, General Motors Corp.	American Liberty League	20,000
Purnell, Frank President, Youngstown Sheet & Tube	Crusaders	
	American Liberty League	
Raskob, John J. Vice-President, E. I. DuPont; director, General Motors Corp.; director, Bankers Trust Co.	American Liberty League	20,000
	Southern Committee to Uphold the Constitution	5,000
Roosevelt, Nicholas	Sentinels	500
Sanis, E. C. President, J. C. Penney Co.	Crusaders	100
	American Liberty League	100
Schiff, John M. Partner, Kuhn Loeb	N. Y. State Economic Council	200
Sloan, Alfred P. President, General Motors Corp.; director, E. I. DuPont; director, Pullman, Inc.	Farmers Independence Council	1,000
	Crusaders	10,000
	American Liberty League	20,000
	Southern Committee to Uphold the Constitution	1,000

Name	*Organization*	*Amount*
	N. Y. State Economic Council	
	National Economy League	1,000
Stotesbury, E. T. (Morgan Partner)	Sentinels	1,000
Strauss, Lionel F. Director, 11 street railway companies	Crusaders	200
	Sentinels of the Republic	25
Sulzberger, A. H. (N. Y. Times)	National Economy League	100
Teagle, W. C.	Crusaders	2,000
Van Alstyne, J. H. President, Oliver Elevator Co.	Crusaders	25
	American Liberty League	100
	N. Y. State Economic Council	100
Weir, E. T. Chairman, National Steel Corp., Weirton Coal Co.; Weirton Steel Co., etc.	American Liberty League	20,000
	National Economy League	500
	Crusaders	10,126
Widener, Joseph E. Director, Baltimore & Ohio Railroad; director, Reading Co.	American Liberty League	20,000
Woodward, William Honorary Chairman, Central Hanover Bank & Trust Co.; director, 7 other corporations	Crusaders (Sound Money committee)	14,000

APPENDIX 23.

THE SUPPRESSED U.S. WAR DEPARTMENT'S EXPOSÉ OF FASCISM

(*Editorial Note:* It was the purpose of the morale division of the Army to issue a weekly fact sheet for the purpose of informing the troops why they were at war. However, the entire program was sabotaged by a coalition of notable American reactionaries, including Mr. Hearst, Congressman Rankin, and one of Father Coughlin's lawyers. The intrigue against the educational program resulted from my publication of Army Talk 64, which follows. The subheads are mostly mine.)

ARMY TALK Orientation Fact Sheet 64

WAR DEPARTMENT

Washington 25, D. C. 24 March 1945

FASCISM!

NOTE FOR THIS WEEK'S DISCUSSION:

Fascism is not the easiest thing to identify and analyze; nor, once in power, is it easy to destroy. It is important for our future and that of the world that as many of us as possible understand the causes and practices of fascism, in order to combat it. Points to stress are: (1) Fascism is more apt to come to power at a time of economic crisis; (2) fascism inevitably leads to war; (3) it can come in any country; (4) we can best combat it by making our democracy work.

You are away from home, separated from your families, no longer at a civilian job or at school and many of you are risking your very lives because of a thing called fascism. . . .

We Americans have been fighting fascists for more than three years. When Cecil Brown, one of the leading war correspondents, came back from the battle fronts, he went on a trip that took him into big cities and small towns all over America. He talked and listened to all kinds of people. He found that most Americans are vague about just what fascism really means. He found few Americans who were confident they would recognize a fascist if they saw one.

And are we in uniform any more certain what fascism is—where it came from—what made it strong? Do we know how fascism leads men to do the things done to people at Maidanek? Do we know how it leads them to attack helpless nations? Are Maidaneks and war inevitable results of fascism? Do all fascists speak only German, Italian or Japanese—or do some of them speak our language? Will military victory in this war automatically kill fascism? Or could fascism rise in the United States after it's been crushed abroad? What can we do to prevent it?

Perhaps we ought to get to know the answers. If we don't understand fascism and recognize fascism when we see it, it might crop up again—under another label—and cause another war.

Fascism and Business

Fascism is a way to run a country—it's the way Italy was run, and the way Germany and Japan are run. Fascism is the precise opposite of democracy. The people run democratic governments, but fascist governments run the people.

Fascism is government by the few and for the few. The objective is seizure and control of the economic, political, social, and cultural life of the state. Why? The democratic way of life interferes with their methods and desire for: (1) conducting business; (2) living with their fellow-men; (3) having the final say in matters concerning others, as well as themselves. The basic principles of democracy stand in the way of their desires; hence—democracy must go! Anyone who is not a member of their inner gang has to do what he's told. They permit no civil liberties, no equality before the law. . . . They maintain themselves in power by use of force combined with propaganda based on primitive ideas of "blood" and "race," by skillful manipulation of fear and hate, and by false promise of security. The propaganda glorifies war and insists it is smart and "realistic" to be pitiless and violent.

Question: How does fascism get in power? How can a violent program that enslaves the people win any support?

Financial Interests Behind Fascism

Fascism came to power in Germany, Italy and Japan at a time of social and economic unrest. A small group of men, supported in secret by powerful financial and military interests, convinced enough insecure people that fascism would give them the things they wanted. . . .

At the very time that the fascists proclaimed that their party was the party of the "average citizen," they were in the pay of certain big industrialists and financiers who wanted to run the people with an iron hand.

The fascists promised everything to everyone: They would make the poor rich and the rich richer. To the farmers, the fascists promised land through elimination of large estates. To the workers they promised elimination of unemployment—jobs for all at high wages. To the small business men they promised more customers and profits through the elimination of large business enterprises. To big business men and the industrialists they secretly promised greater security and profits through the elimination of small business competitors and trade unions and the crushing of socialists and communists. To the whole nation they promised glory and wealth by conquest. They asserted it was their right, as a "superior people," to rule the world.

As soon as their methods had won them enough of a following to form their Storm Troops, the fascists began using force to stifle and wipe out any opposition. Those who saw through the false front of fascism and opposed them were beaten, tortured and killed.

The fascists knew that all believers in democracy were their enemies. They knew that the fundamental principle of democracy—faith in the common sense of the common people—was the opposite of the fascist principle of rule by the elite few. So they fought democracy in all its phases. . . . They played the political, religious, social and economic groups against each other and seized power while these groups struggled against each other.

Little Business Betrayed

Question: How could the fascists keep their contradictory promises, once they got in power? How did their program actually work out?

It was easy enough for the fascists to promise all things to all people before they were in power. Once they were actually in power, they could not, of course, keep their contradictory promises. They had intended in advance to break some, and they did break those they had made to the middle classes, the workers, and the farmers.

As soon as the fascists were in control of the government, the torturings and killings were no longer the unlawful acts of a political party and its hoodlum gangs. They became official government policy. Among the first victims of this official policy were those farmers, workers, and small business men who had believed the promises that had been made to them and who complained that they had been "sucked in." Some simply vanished. Often they came home to their families by return mail in little jars of ashes. . . .

The fascists "solved" unemployment by converting their nations into giant war machines. The unemployed were either conscripted into the army or organized in labor battalions and put to work in war plants.

Why Fascists Are Anti-Union

Deprived of their unions, the working people could be driven to work longer and harder for less and less money, so that those who subsidized and ran fascism could grow richer. By wiping out all internal competition—especially the small and medium-sized business firms—profits were increased still higher for the handful on top. In some cases, the fascists then gobbled control of the top corporations. The living standards of the masses of the people declined, of course. As they earned less and less, they were able to buy less and less of the goods they produced. . . .

Once the fascists were in control of the government, not even the gang on top was safe from its own members. There would be more loot and power per fascist leader if some fascist leaders were eliminated. Some of the party "big-shots" and some of those who had helped them take over were therefore "purged." Many would-be partners in the dictatorship, including some industrialists, wound up in jail, in exile, or dead.

Can It Happen Here?

Some Americans would give an emphatic "No" to the question "Can fascism come to America after it has been defeated abroad?" They would say that Americans are too smart, that they are sold on the democratic way of life, that they wouldn't permit any group to put fascism over in America. Fascism, some might say, is something peculiar that you find only among people who like swastikas, who like to listen to speeches from balconies in Rome, or who like to think that their emperor is god. Their reaction might be that it is something "foreign" that Americans would recognize in a minute, like the goose-step. They might feel that we'd laugh it out of existence in a hurry.

U. S. Has 100% American Fascists

Question: Do all fascists come from Germany, Japan, or Italy?

In a good many European nations, the people felt the same way some of us do: that fascism was foreign to them and could never become a power in their land. They found, however, that fascist-minded people within their borders, especially with aid from the outside, could seize power. The Germans, of course, made efficient use of fascist-minded traitors whom we have come to know generally as "the fifth column."

In France, which was considered a leading democracy of Europe, the betrayal was spearheaded by a powerful clique of native "100% French" fascists. Norway had its Quisling who was as "pure-blooded" a Norwegian as Laval was a "pure-blooded" Frenchman. The Netherlands' Musserts were "100% Dutch," Belgium's Degrelles "100% Belgian," and Britain's Mosleys "100% British." The United States also has its native fascists who say that they are "100 percent American." There were native fascists in the Philippines, in Thailand (Siam), in China, in Burma, in many other countries—all waiting to become willing puppets of the Axis. Not one of these fascists is a "foreigner" who had to be imported from Germany, or Japan, or Italy.

Question: Have any groups in America used fascist tactics and appeals?

Most of the people in America like to be good neighbors. But, at various times and places in our history, we have had sorry instances of mob sadism, lynchings, vigilantism, terror, and suppression of civil liberties. We have had our hooded gangs, Black Legions, Silver Shirts, and racial and religious bigots. All of them, in the name of Americanism, have used undemocratic methods and doctrines which experience has shown can be properly identified as "fascist."

Crackpots and Alleged Seditionists

Can we afford to brush them off as mere crackpots? We once laughed Hitler off as a harmless little clown with a funny mustache.

In January 1944, 30 Americans, many of them native born, were indicted by a Federal Grand Jury on charges of conspiring with "the Nazi party to accomplish the objectives of said Nazi party in the United States." These objectives, according to the indictment, included undermining and impairing "the loyalty and morale of the military and naval forces of the United States." The case ended in a mistrial caused by the death of the presiding judge. The question of re-indictment is still under consideration.

Whenever free governments anywhere fail to solve their basic economic and social problems, there is always the danger that a native brand of fascism will arise to exploit the situation and the people.

Can We Spot It?

Question: How can we identify native American fascists at work?

An American fascist seeking power would not proclaim that he is a fascist. Fascism always camouflages its plans and purposes. Hitler made demagogic appeals to all groups and swore: "Neither I nor anybody in the National Socialist Party advocates proceeding by anything but constitutional methods."

Any fascist attempt to gain power in America would not use the exact Hitler pattern. It would work under the guise of "super-patriotism" and "super-Americanism." Fascist leaders are neither stupid nor naive. They know that they must hand out a line that "sells." Huey Long is said to have remarked that if fascism came to America, it would be on a program of "Americanism."

Three Ways to Spot U. S. Fascists

Fascists in America may differ slightly from fascists in other countries, but there are a number of attitudes and practices that they have in common. Following are three. Every person who has one of them is not necessarily a fascist. But he is in a mental state that lends itself to the acceptance of fascist aims.

1. Pitting of religious, racial, and economic groups against one another in order to break down national unity is a device of the "divide and conquer" technique used by Hitler to gain power in Germany and in other countries. With slight variations, to suit local conditions, fascists everywhere have used this Hitler method. In many countries, anti-Semitism (hatred of Jews) is a dominant device of fascism. In the United States, native fascists have often been anti-Catholic, anti-Jew, anti-Negro, anti-Labor, anti-foreign-born. In South America, the native fascists use the same scapegoats except that they substitute anti-Protestantism for anti-Catholicism.

Interwoven with the "master-race" theory of fascism is a well-planned "hate campaign" against minority races, religions, and other groups. To suit their particular needs and aims, fascists will use any one or a combination of such groups as a convenient scapegoat.

2. Fascism cannot tolerate such religious and ethical concepts as the "brotherhood of man." Fascists deny the need for international cooperation. These ideas contradict the fascist theory of the "master race." The brotherhood of man implies that all people—regardless of color, race, creed, or nationality—have rights. International cooperation, as expressed in the Dumbarton Oaks proposals, runs counter to the fascist program of war and world domination. . . . Right now our native fascists are spreading anti-British, anti-Soviet, anti-French, and anti-United Nations propaganda. . . .

3. It is accurate to call a member of a communist party a "communist." For short, he is often called a "Red." Indiscriminate pinning of the label "Red" on people and proposals which one opposes is a common political device. It is a favorite trick of native as well as foreign fascists.

Many fascists make the spurious claim that the world has but two choices—either fascism or communism, and they label as "communist" everyone who refuses to support them. By attacking our free enterprise, capitalist democracy and by denying the effectiveness of our way of life they hope to trap many people.

Hitler's Red Bogey

Hitler insisted that only fascism could save Europe and the world from the "communist menace." There were many people inside and outside Germany and Italy who welcomed and supported Hitler and Mussolini because they believed fascism was the only safeguard against communism. The "Red bogey" was a convincing enough argument to help Hitler take and maintain power. The Rome-Berlin-Tokyo Axis, whose aggressions plunged the world into global war, was called the "Anti-Comintern Axis." It was proclaimed by Hitler, Mussolini, and Hirohito as a "bulwark against communism."

Learning to identify native fascists and to detect their techniques is not easy. They plan it that way. But it is vitally important to learn to spot them, even though they adopt names and slogans with popular appeal, drape themselves with the American flag, and attempt to carry out their program in the name of the democracy they are trying to destroy.

How to Stop It

Question: How can we prevent fascism from developing in the United States?

The only way to prevent fascism from getting a hold in America is by making our democracy work and by actively cooperating to preserve world peace and security.

Lots of things can happen inside of people when they are unemployed or hungry. They become frightened, angry, desperate, confused. Many, in their misery, seek to find somebody to blame. They look for a scapegoat as a way out. Fascism is always ready to provide one. In its bid for power, it is ready to drive wedges that will disunite the people and weaken the nation. It supplies the scapegoat—Catholics, Jews, Negroes, labor unions, big business—any group upon which the insecure and unemployed can be brought to pin the blame for their misfortune.

We all know that many serious problems will face us when the war is over. If there is a period of economic stress it will create tensions among our people, including us as returned veterans. The resentment may be directed against minorities—especially if undemocratic organizations with power and money can direct our emotions and thinking along these lines.

Citizen's Job to Fight Fascism

The fascist doctrine of hate fulfills a triple mission. By creating disunity—it weakens democracy. By getting men to hate rather than to think—it prevents men from seeking the real cause and a democratic solution of the problem. By fake promises of jobs and security, fascism then tries to lure men to its program as the way out of insecurity. Only by democratically solving the economic problems of our day can there be any certainty that fascism won't happen here. That is our job as citizens.

Citizenship in a democracy is more than a ballot dropped in a box on Election Day. It's a 365-days-a-year job requiring the active participation and best judgment of every citizen in the affairs of his community, his nation, and his country's relations with the world.

Fascism thrives on indifference and ignorance. It makes headway when people are apathetic or cynical about their government

—when they think of it as something far removed from them and beyond their personal concern. The erection of a traffic light on your block is important to your safety and the safety of your children. The erection of a world organization to safeguard peace and world security is just as important to our personal security. Both must be the concern of every citizen.

Freedom, like peace and security, cannot be maintained in isolation. It involves being alert and on guard against the infringement not only of our own freedom but the freedom of every American. If we permit discrimination, prejudice, or hate to rob anyone of his democratic rights, our own freedom and all democracy is threatened.

What is true of America is true of the world. The germ of fascism cannot be quarantined in a Munich Brown House or a balcony in Rome. If we want to make certain that fascism does not come to America, we must make certain that it does not thrive anywhere in the world.

INDEX

The Book

ames names of those who control institutions through the media and sure groups. 99% of media trum- the agenda of the powerful, cover he suborning of the public interest exploitation of the people. Exam- of Montana and Anaconda: the A as a company town. Genesis of magazine, financed by Harriman Morgan; covering up the Ambas- or Page cable to Wilson that called r war on Germany to serve Morgan nancial interests in 1917. Conflict of interest between magazines and advertisers. The pro-Hitler line of Wall-Street-owned newspapers. Commerce Secretary Hoover helps arms industry circumvent the Geneva weapons control conference. Dupont, ally of IG Farben and campaign funding champion, elects Hoover president.

The white-washing of Wall Street. Each major industry dominated by a handful of corporations controlled by a few families like Rockefeller and Morgan. Suppression of anti-fascism in the armed forces. Financing of the Liberty League, the KKK, et al. Smedley Butler and the 1934 Morgan putsch against FDR. The Commission on Freedom of the Press condemns the press as liars and prostitutes. War profiteers destroy our hopes for a world of peace, prosperity and the American way.

The Author

"'The real inside news, the kind newspapers frequently get but dare not print'— Mr. Seldes delighted in uncovering stories that had been overlooked by others, exposing corruption and challenging the practices of leading newspapers." — *New York Times*.

"George Seldes, the inventor of modern investigative reporting, led the sort of swashbuckling life that Hollywood might have scripted for a foreign correspondent and rebel reporter. He interviewed Lenin, Trotsky, Freud, Einstein, and Hitler. He filed dispatches from behind the lines during World War I and covered the Spanish Civil War with his wife, Helen. He was booted out of the Soviet Union in 1923 and fled Italy two years later fearing for his life, after implicating Benito Mussolini in a murder. Ernest Hemingway, Ezra Pound, and Sinclair Lewis were among his drinking buddies.

"Yet the glamour of journalistic success never blinded him to serious shortcomings in the American press." — Jay Walljasper, *Utne Reader*.

Seldes was Berlin, Rome, Dublin, Moscow and Baghdad correspondent for the *Chicago Tribune* from 1919 to 1929, but quit the mainstream media over censorship of his reports. He became an independent journalist, getting the true story out in his first two books, *You Can't Print That!* and *Can These Things Be!* In 1940 he started *In Fact*, a weekly newsletter of investigative reporting and criticism of the press, with a top circulation of 176,000. He uncovered big stories like major corporations trading with the enemy, and the link between smoking and cancer — to be hushed up for another 20 years, by mainstream media hooked on cigarette ads. *In Fact* was shut down in 1950 by an FBI witch hunt against subscribers.

2008 New Paperbacks from ProgressivePress.com

Obama – The Postmodern Coup: Making of a Manchurian Candidate. Remember compassionate conservatism and a humble foreign policy – and what happened then? Webster G. Tarpley reveals that the Obama puppet's advisors are even more radical reactionaries than the neo-cons. A crash course in political science, it distills decades of political insight and astute analysis, from a unique perspective. 320 pages, $15.95.

Barack H. Obama: the Unauthorized Biography Tarpley at his best: erudite, witty, insightful, activist, iconoclastic. This complete profile of a puppet's progress details of Obama's doings in the trough of graft and corruption of the Chicago Combine. His regime will be one of brutal economic sacrifice and austerity to finance Wall Street bailouts, and for imperialist confrontation with Russia and China. Another blockbuster like Tarpley's Bush Bio. 595 pages, $19.95.

The Nazi Hydra in America: Suppressed History of a Century exposes how US plutocrats launched Hitler, then recouped Nazi assets to lay the postwar foundations of a modern police state. Fascists won WWII because they ran both sides. *"A valuable history of the relationship between big business in the United States and European fascism, before, during, and after the second World War. The story is shocking and sobering and deserves to be widely read."* – Howard Zinn, author of *A People's History of the United States.* Includes a blow-by-blow account of the fascist takeover of US media. 700 pp., $19.95.

Corporatism: the Secret Government of the New World Order by Prof. Jeffrey Grupp of Purdue University. Corporations control all basic resources of the world, all the governments and institutions, and prevent us from solving humanity's problems. Their New World Order plan is the global "prison planet" that Hitler was aiming for. 408 pages, $16.95.

Seeds of Destruction: The Hidden Agend[...] Genetic Manipulation. A tiny corporate e[...] out for complete control over the world by [...] patenting the basis of survival: food. F. Wi[...] Engdahl takes us inside the corridors of po[...] corporate boardrooms and backrooms of sc[...] labs, to reveal a diabolical world of greed, [...] intrigue, corruption and coercion. Reads as [...] crime story because it is. A hugely import[...] and unique – work. By the author of *A Cen[...] War*, published by M. Chossudovsky's Gl[...] Research. 340 pages, $24.95

Skulk! a Post-9/11 Comic Novel by Marc Es[...] A racy parody of political surreality with a stunning ending – and a truth tool for every activist toolbox. 180 pp, 14.95

Cruel Hoax: Feminism and the New World Order. The Attack on Your Human Identity. Contemporary Canadian political philosopher Henry Makow PhD shares unusual insights on social and sexual aspects of the conspiracy to enslave humanity. 232 pages, $19.95.

In ***Illuminati: Cult that Hijacked the World,*** the Canadian Jewish writer Henry Makow tackles more taboos like Zionism and British Imperialism, and even Holocaust denial, as he relates how international bankers stole a monopoly on government credit, and took over the world. They run the wars, schools, media, th[e] works. 249 pages, $19.95.

Classics now available from ProgRESSive

Inside the Gestapo: Hitler's Shadow over the World (1940) by Hansjürgen Koehler. Intimate, fascinating defector's tale of ruthlessness, spy intrigue, geopolitics and bizarre personalities of the 3rd Reich. 287 pp, $24.95.

How the World Really Works by Alan B. Jones. A crash course in the conspiracy field, with digests of 11 works like *A Century of War, Tragedy and Hope, The Creature from Jekyll Island*, and *Dope Inc*. 336 pp., $15.

Coming Soon from ProgressivePress.com

New Titles

ving the Cataclysm**, **Your Guide gh the Greatest Financial Crisis in an History, updated edition, by Webster fin Tarpley. The unwinding of the hedge ls and derivatives bubble, and with them, as we knew it in the USA. Richly detailed tory of the financier oligarchy, how they under this nation, and solutions for the crisis r individuals and the nation. Release May 09, 668 pages, $29.95.

error on the Tube: Behind the Veil of 7/7, an Investigation, by Nick Kollerstrom. First book to compile the clear evidence that all four Muslim scapegoats were completely innocent. 7/7 is Bliar's Big Lie and Reichstag Fire, False Flag Terror as pretext for war and an Orwellian, neo-fascist British police state.

Clown Prince Bush the W. A thoroughly tipsy biography of the late resident anti-hero of the White House, by Kennebunkport reporter Ted Cohen. 215 pp, $14.95.

he Complete Patriot's Guide to Oligarchical Collectivism: its Theory and Practice by Ethan, a nonfictional exploration of Orwell's *1984* for our times. A guide to individual empowerment in the midst of institutional monopolization, and a valuable blueprint for taking ownership of our lives and our world.

Between a Rock and a Hard Face: Tales of the Holy City by Samah Jabr. A thoughtful young psychiatrist's perspectives on the plight of the Palestinians.

Global Predator: US Wars for Empire by Stewart Halsey Ross. A damning account of the atrocities committed by US armed forces, starting with the Cuban/Philippines Wars.

The Telescreen: An Empirical Study of the Destruction of Consciousness, by Prof. Jeff Grupp. How the mass media brainwash us with consumerism, war propaganda, false history, fake news, fake issues, fake reality.

ProgRESSive

Reprints

1,000 Americans Who Rule the USA (1947) and ***Facts and Fascism*** (1943) by the great muckraking journalist George Seldes – whistleblower on the American plutocrats who keep the media in lockstep, and finance fascism. Key source books for *The Nazi Hydra.* You'll be amazed how little has changed in 65 years: this is must reading for all who hope to change the US for the better.

Propaganda for War: How the US was Conditioned to Fight the Great War by Stewart Halsey Ross. How propaganda by Britain and her agents like Teddy Roosevelt sucked the USA into the war to smash the old world order. June 2009, 356 pages, $18.95.

Final Warning: A History of the New World Order by David Allen Rivera, updated, Part One. In-depth research nails down the Great Conspiracy in its various aspects as the Fed, the CFR, Trilateral Commission, Illuminati

Descent into Slavery? The revised 1980 classic by Des Griffin. Indispensable history documents the world bankster conspiracy behind the great wars of the 20th century. New edition due in 2009. 310 pp., $16

The Rape of the Mind: The Psychology of Thought Control, Menticide and Brainwashing (1956) by Joost Meerloo, M.D. The good Dutch doctor escaped from a Nazi death camp, only to discover the subtler mass mind control of McCarthy's America. Pioneering, wide-ranging study of conditioning and totalitarianism in both open and closed societies.

Against Oligarchy by Webster Tarpley. Revised edition of his classic work on the history of the Anglo-American empire. How it was built using the tools of intrigue and divide-and-conquer of the Venetian empire. The ongoing battle between materialism and Renaissance values.

Lightning Source UK Ltd.
Milton Keynes UK
07 April 2011

170529UK00001B/144/P